THE TRUE STORY

OF THE

BILDERBERG GROUP

DANIEL ESTULIN

Published by:
TrineDay LLC
PO Box 577
Walterville, OR 97489
1-800-556-2012
www.TrineDay.com
publisher@TrineDay.net

Library of Congress Control Number: 2007906596

Estulin, Daniel
The True Story of the Bilderberg Group—1st ed.
 p. cm. (acid-free paper)
Includes bibliographical references and index.
(ISBN-13) 978-0-9777953-4-5 (ISBN-10) 0-9777953-4-9
1. Bilderberg Group 2. Council on Foreign Relations 3. Trilateral
Commission 4. Political Corruption—United States. 5. Conspiracy—
New World Order 1. Title

FIRST EDITION
10 9 8 7 6 5 4 3

Printed in the USA
Distribution to the Trade by:
Independent Publishers Group (IPG)
814 North Franklin Street
Chicago, Illinois 60610
312.337.0747
www.ipgbook.com

PUBLISHER'S FOREWORD

Publishing sometimes is more an advocation than vocation. I'll get a call; a hardy-timbred voice at the other end of the line says, "My book is going to change the world and ... be a best-seller" Trying not to burst his bubble, but by giving the short-list of particulars about the book biz, and by relating the war stories of trying to break "inconvenient" truths, I gently try to introduce some reality into the long-shot dream.

Well, here is a book that *has* already changed the world and *is* already a best-seller. Daniel Estulin's dogged pursuit of what the world's political and financial leaders have been talking about at their annual secret conclaves — the Bilderberg Group meetings — has lead to astounding revelations, spot-on predictions of world events and a scrambling feverish attempt to blot out the light that Daniel has shone inside the shroud of secrecy: where world events are playthings, Presidents are chosen, wars formatted, energy markets manipulated, and more ... all with major press attending, *but never reporting.*

Looking into secret matters is never easy, nor is dealing with the bias one must slog through. The mainstream media have, until recently, barely mentioned the Group. Meanwhile, the Bildergerg Group has become a bogeyman of the fringe, where their reputation may, in fact, be well deserved.

We have done our best to be accurate; rosters are fluid, Boards of Directors change, etc. To me, the real questions are: "What are these *wise men* doing that demands such extreme secrecy?" and, "Where are they taking us?"

When the Group's actions are put into historical context, as Daniel has done, one can begin to understand the apparent scope of what "they" intend, and why they need such a high level of hush to implement it. That there are such things as national and personal sovereignty, and the attendant human freedoms and liberties standing in the way of their stated objectives, seems of little consequence to them.

I stand with Daniel and most people of the world for the true democratic ideals of our Republic, not the current cryptocratic rule "of the elite, by the stooges and for the corporations." I am sure that most of the Bilderberg Group feel that their stealthy road to a secret future has been paved with good intentions. But, it just may be that many of us, like myself, don't really want to go to ... *there.*

Kris Millegan,
Publisher
September 22, 2007

ACKNOWLEDGMENTS

This may be the most difficult part of the book to write, because the list of collaborators, independent researchers, in and out of government sources, private investigators, U.S. Army, Navy and Air Force analysts, Spanish Generals, cooks, chefs, bellboys, cleaning persons, waiters and waitresses at Bilderberger hotels, who have wholeheartedly given of their energies and time, overlooking the dangers that such meetings could cause them, is simply too long to mention on the pages of my book, or rather our book, because I am the vehicle of the collective psyche of a society whose natural instinct spells *freedom*.

I extend my sincerest and deeply felt gratitude to numerous members of international secret service agencies in Washington, London, Moscow, Madrid, Paris, Caracas, Rome and Ottawa, whose inside knowledge on intelligence issues and wisdom often kept my spirits up in the darkest of hours. Without their priceless intelligence gathering, this book would have forever remained an unrealisable dream.

Special thanks go out to Canada, my country, who gave our family home and hope for a better future without asking for anything in return. I repaid that debt of gratitude in 1996 when I uncovered the Bilderberger's diabolical plans for Canada's breakup. My love goes out to Canada's wonderful and decent and freedom loving people who that fateful year answered my desperate plea for help by taking to the streets en masse to resoundingly destroy Bilderberger hopes of silently breaking up Canada. When I need uplifting, I think of these people and their faith in the goodness of Men.

A note of gratitude to the good Fortune and infinite Faith, who have never left my side, who kept me ploughing away one centimeter at a time, even when there was no hope and no energy to spare. In the most desperate of moments I made it through because I believed in my two Fs.

Thanks to my friend John Harraghy and his wisdom — a man who belongs to an unrepeatable generation of truly great men — and to Geoffrey Matthews from Amherst Island, Ontario, Canada, the man who for years has been at the helm of the best newspaper in the country, the legendary *Eye Opener*. To all those kind, faceless people who have sent me tens of thousands of emails making me believe there were some things to look forward to in life.

I dedicate this book to all those who have never stopped searching for the truth, in the face of government lies, cheating, manipulation and deceit. To those who have intuitively felt that blasphemous lies we are told are but a vile whiff of hatred. All these people deserve to know the truth about our history and heritage. History teaches by analogy, not rigorous proof. The historical experience is not one of staying in the present and looking back. Rather it is one of going back into the past and returning to the present with a wider and more intense consciousness of the restrictions of our former outlook.

Finally, I owe the success of this book to Bonnie Toews, my first editor of this manuscript, and to TrineDay's own Russ Becker, without whose vision and sure hand this book would have been a pale version of its present, better self. And finally, to Kris Millegan. Kris, you defended this work and the truth, and the entire world owes you a debt of gratitude. Your belief that this book was important convinced others. They believed because you believed. And I believed because I saw you believe.

Mankind is yet to pass a final judgment. Miracles, as someone said, can happen without our permission. This book and all the people who made it happen are living proof of that.

Daniel Estulin
July 4, 2007

BILDERBERG MEETINGS SINCE 1954

1. May 29-31, 1954: Oosterbeek, Netherlands
2. March 18-20, 1955: Barbizon, France
3. September 23-25, 1955: Garmisch-Partenkirchen, West Germany
4. May 11-13, 1956: Fredensborg, Denmark
5. February 15-17, 1957: St Simons Island, Georgia, USA
6. October 4-6, 1957: Fiuggi, Italy
7. September 13-15, 1958: Buxton, England
8. September 18-20, 1959: Yesilköy, Turkey
9. May 28-29, 1960: Bürgenstock, Switzerland
10. April 21-23, 1961: St Castin, Canada
11. May 18-20, 1962: Saltsjöbaden, Sweden
12. May 29-31, 1963: Cannes, France
13. March 20-22, 1964: Williamsburg, Virginia, USA
14. April 2-4, 1965: Villa d'Este, Italy
15. March 25-27, 1966: Wiesbaden, West Germany
16. March 31-April 2, 1967: Cambridge, England
17. April 26-28, 1968: Mont Tremblant, Canada
18. May 9-11, 1969: Marienlyst, Denmark
19. April 17-19, 1970: Bad Ragaz, Switzerland
20. April 23-25, 1971: Woodstock, Vermont, USA
21. April 21-23, 1972: Knokke, Belgium
22. May 11-13, 1973: Saltsjöbaden, Sweden
23. April 19-21, 1974: Megève, France
24. April 25-27, 1975: Çesme, Turkey
25. April 22-25, 1976: Hot Springs, Virginia, USA CANCELLED [Prince Bernhard-Lockheed bribery scandal]
26. April 22-24, 1977: Torquay, England
27. April 21-23, 1978: Princeton, New Jersey, USA
28. April 27-29, 1979: Baden, Austria
29. April 18-20, 1980: Aachen, W. Germany
30. May 15-17, 1981: Bürgenstock, Switzerland
31. May 14-16, 1982: Sandefjord, Norway
32. May 13-15, 1983: Montebello, Canada
33. May 11-13, 1984: Saltsjöbaden, Sweden
34. May 10-12, 1985: Rye Brook, New York USA
35. April 25-27, 1986: Gleneagles, Scotland
36. April 24-26, 1987: Villa d'Este, Italy
37. June 3-5, 1988: Telfs-Buchen, Austria
38. May 12-14, 1989: La Toja, Spain
39. May 11-13, 1990: Glen Cove, New York, USA
40. June 6-9, 1991: Baden-Baden, Germany
41. May 21-24, 1992: Evian-les-Bains, France
42. April 22-25, 1993: Athens, Greece
43. June 3-5, 1994: Helsinki, Finland
44. June 8-11, 1995: Zurich, Switzerland
45. May 30-June 2, 1996: Toronto, Canada
46. June 12-15, 1997: Lake Lanier, Georgia, USA
47. May 14-17, 1998: Turnberry, Ayrshire, Scotland
48. June 3-6, 1999: Sintra, Portugal
49. June 1-4, 2000: Genval, Brussels, Belgium
50. May 24-27, 2001: Gothenburg, Sweden
51. May 30-June 2, 2002: Chantilly, Virginia, USA
52. May 15-18, 2003: Versailles, France
53. June 3-6, 2004: Stresa, Italy
54. May 5-8, 2005: Rottach-Egern, Germany
55. June 8-11, 2006: Ottawa, Canada
56. May 31-June 3, 2007: Istanbul, Turkey

BILDERBERG MEETING
Istanbul, Turkey
31 May – 3 June 2007

LIST OF PARTICIPANTS

Graham Allison, Professor of Government, Harvard University (USA);

George Alogoskoufis, Minister for Economy and Finance (Greece);

Ali Babacan, Minister for Economic Affairs (Turkey);

Francisco Balsemão, Chairman and CEO, IMPRESA SGPS, former Prime Minister (Portugal);

Michel Barnier, Vice President, Mérieux Alliance; former Minister for Foreign Affairs (France);

Michael Barone, Senior Writer, *US News & World Report* (USA);

Martin Bartenstein, Federal Minister of Economics and Labour (Austria);

Nicolas Baverez, Partner, Gibson, Dunn & Crutcher LLP (France);

Her Majesty Queen Beatrix, Queen of The Netherlands (The Netherlands);

Leonor Beleza, President, Champalimaud Foundation (Portugal);

Franco Bernabé, Vice Chairman, Rothschild Europe (Italy);

Rosina M. Bierbaum, Professor and Dean, School of Natural Resources and Environment, University of Michigan (USA);

Carl Bildt, Minister for Foreign Affairs, former Prime Minister (Sweden);

Mehmet A. Birand, Columnist (Turkey);

Lloyd C. Blankfein, Chairman and CEO, Goldman Sachs & Co. (USA);

Anders Borg, Minister for Finance (Sweden);

Charles G. Boyd, President and CEO, Business Executives for National Security (USA);

Ümit N. Boyner, Member, Executive Board, Boyner Holding (Turkey);

Vendeline A. H. von Bredow, Business Correspondent, *The Economist*; Rapporteur (Germany);

Ian Bremmer, President, Eurasia Group (USA);

Oscar Bronner, Publisher and Editor, *Der Standard* (Austria);

Hubert Burda, Publisher and CEO, Hubert Burda Media Holding (Belgium);

Gerald Butts, Principal Secretary, Office of the Prime Minister of Ontario (Canada);

Çengiz Candar, Journalist, Referans (Turkey);

Henri de Castries, Chairman of Management Board and CEO, AXA (France);

Juan Luis Cebrián, CEO, Grupo PRISA media group (Spain);

Hikmet Çetin, Former Minister for Foreign Affairs and former NATO Senior Civilian Representative in Afghanistan (Turkey);

Kenneth Clarke, Member of Parliament (UK);

Timothy C. Collins, Senior Managing Director and CEO, Ripplewood Holding, LLC (USA);

Frans van Daele, Permanent Representative of Belgium to NATO (Belgium);

George A. David, Chairman, Coca-Cola HBC SA (Greece);

Etienne Davignon, Vice-Chairman, Suez-Tractebel, Honorary Chairman, Bilderberg (Belgium);

Richard Dearlove, Master, Pembroke College, Cambridge (UK);

Kemal Dervis, Administrator, UNDP (Turkey);

Anna Diamantopoulou, Member of Parliament (Greece);

Thomas E. Donilon, Partner, O'Melveny & Myers LLP (USA);

Mathias Döpfner, Chairman and CEO, Axel Springer AG (Germany);

Cem Duna, Former Ambassador to the European Union (Turkey);

Esther Dyson, Chairman, EDventure Holdings, Inc. (USA);

Craig J. Mundie, Chief Research and Strategy Officer, Microsoft Corporation (USA);
Egil Myklebust, Chairman, SAS and Norsk Hydro ASA (Norway);
Matthias Nass, Deputy Editor, Die Zeit (Germany);
Ewald Nowotny, CEO, BAWAG PSK (Austria);
Christine Ockrent, Editor-in-Chief, France Télévision (France);
Jorma Ollila, Chairman, Royal Dutch Shell PLC, Nokia (Finland);
George Osborne, MP, Shadow Chancellor of the Exchequer (UK);
Laurence Parisot, President, MEDEF (Mouvement des Entreprises de France) (France);
Christopher Patten, Member, House of Lords (UK);
Richard N. Perle, Resident Fellow, American Enterprise Institute for Public Policy Research (USA);
Rick Perry, Governor of Texas (USA);
Volker Perthes, Director, Stiftung Wissenschaft und Politik (Germany);
HRH Prince Philippe (Belgium);
Rodrigo de Rato y Figaredo, Managing Director, IMF (International);
Olli Rehn, Commissioner, European Commission (International);
Heather Reisman, Chair and CEO, Indigo Books & Music Inc. (Canada);
Matías Rodríguez Inciarte, Executive Vice Chairman, Grupo Santander, Ciudad Grupo (Spain);
Olivier Roy, Senior Researcher, CNRS (France);
Paolo Scaroni, CEO, Eni SpA (Italy);
Eric Schmidt, Chairman of the Executive Committee and CEO, Google (USA);
Rudolf Scholten, on Board of Executive Directors, Oesterreichische Kontrollbank AG (Austria);
Jürgen E. Schrempp, former Chairman of the Boardt, DaimlerChrysler AG (Germany);
Klaus Schwab, Executive Chairman, World Economic Forum (Switzerland);
Robert W. Scully, Co-President, Morgan Stanley (USA);
Kathleen Sebelius, Governor of Kansas (USA);
Josette Sheeran, Executive Director, UN World Food Programme (USA);
Kristen Silverberg, Assistant Secretary of State, Bureau of International Organization Affairs (USA);
Domenico Siniscalco, Managing Director and Vice Chairman, Morgan Stanley (Italy);
Javier Solana,* High Representative for the Common Foreign and Security Policy, Secretary-General of the Council of the European Union and the Western European Union (International);
Her Majesty Queen Sophía, Queen of Spain (Spain);
Ayse Soysal, Rector, Bosphorus University (Turkey);
Lawrence H. Summers, Charles W. Eliot University Professor, Harvard University (USA);
Peter D. Sutherland, Chairman, BP PLC, and Chairman, Goldman Sachs International (Ireland);
Carl-Henric Svanberg, President and CEO, Telefonaktiebolaget LM Ericsson (Sweden);
Paul A. Taggart, Professor of Politics, University of Sussex (UK);
Sidney Taurel, Chairman and CEO, Eli Lilly and Company (USA);
J. Martin Taylor, Chairman, Syngenta International AG (UK);
Peter A. Thiel, President, Clarium Capital Management, LLC (USA);
Teija Tiilikainen, State Secretary, Ministry for Foreign Affairs (Finland);
Michel Tilmant, Chairman, ING NV (The Netherlands);
Jean-Claude Trichet, Governor, European Central Bank (France/International);
Jens Ulltveit-Moe, CEO, Umoe AS (Norway);

Daniel L. Vasella, Chairman and CEO, Novartis AG (Switzerland);
Jeroen van der Veer, Chief Executive, Royal Dutch Shell PLC (The Netherlands);
Jacob Wallenberg, Chairman, Investor AB (Sweden);
Vin (J. V.) Weber, Partner, Clark & Weinstock (USA);
Guido Westerwelle, Chairman, Free Democratic Party (Germany);
Ross Wilson, Ambassador to Turkey (USA);
James D. Wolfensohn, Chairman, Wolfensohn & Company, LLC (USA);
Paul Wolfowitz, President, The World Bank (International);
Joseph R. Wood, Deputy Assistant to the Vice President, National Security Affairs (USA);
Adrian D. Wooldridge, Foreign Correspondent, *The Economist*; Rapporteur (UK);
Arzuhan Dogan Yalçindag, President, TUSIAD (Turkey);
Erkut Yücaoglu, Chairman of the Board, MAP, former President, TUSIAD (Turkey);
Philip D. Zelikow, White Burkett Miller Professor of History, University of Virginia (USA);
Robert B. Zoellick, former US Trade Representative, former Deputy Secretary of State, Managing Director, Goldman Sachs (USA).

Rapport Builders
Vendeline A. H. von Bredow, Business Correspondent, *The Economist*; (Germany);
Adrian D. Wooldridge, Foreign Correspondent, *The Economist*; (UK)

Notable by his absence was David Rockefeller, who has been a virtual fixture at Bilderberg Group meetings.

TABLE OF CONTENTS

Hotel Bilderberg, Oosterbeek, Netherlands (circa May 1954)
site of first Bilderberg Group meeting.

Hotel des Iles Borromees, on the shores of Lake Maggiore
in Stresa, Italy, site of 2004 Bilderberg meeting.

INTRODUCTION

In 1954, the most powerful men in the world met for the first time under the auspices of the Dutch royal crown and the Rockefeller family at the luxurious Hotel Bilderberg in the small Dutch town of Oosterbeek. For an entire weekend, they debated the future of the world. When it was over, they decided to meet once every year to exchange ideas and analyze international affairs. They named themselves the Bilderberg Group. Since then, they have gathered yearly in a luxurious hotel somewhere in the world to try to decide the future of humanity. Among the select members of this club are Bill Clinton, Paul Wolfowitz, Henry Kissinger, David Rockefeller, Zbigniew Brzezinski, Tony Blair and many other heads of government, businessmen, politicians, bankers and journalists from all over the world.

Nevertheless, in the more than fifty years of their meetings, the press has never been allowed to attend, no statements have ever been released on the attendees' conclusions, nor has any agenda for a Bilderberg meeting been made public. Leaders of the Bilderberg Group argue that this discretion is necessary to allow participants in the debates to speak freely without being on the record, or reported publicly. Otherwise, Bilderbergers claim, they would be forced to speak in the language of a press release. No doubt, this discretion allows the Bilderberg Group to deliberate more freely. But that does not respond to the fundamental question: What do the world's most powerful people talk about in these meetings?

Any modern democratic system protects the right to privacy, but doesn't the public have a right to know what their political leaders are talking about when they meet the wealthiest business leaders of their respective countries? What guarantees do citizens have that the Bilderberg Group isn't merely a center for influence trafficking and lobbying if they aren't allowed to know what their representatives talk about at the Group's secret gatherings? Why are the Davos World Economic Forums and G8 meetings discussed in every newspaper, given front-page coverage, with thousands of journalists in attendance, while no one covers Bilderberg Group meetings? This blackout exists despite the fact that (or because?) they are annually attended by Presidents of the International Monetary Fund, the World Bank, and Federal Reserve; by chairmen of 100 of the most powerful corporations in the world such as Daimler Chrysler, Coca Cola, British Petroleum (BP), Chase Manhattan Bank, American Express, Goldman Sachs, and Microsoft; by Vice Presidents of the United States, Directors of the CIA and the FBI, Secretaries General of NATO, American Senators and members of Congress, European Prime Ministers, and leaders of opposition parties; and by top editors and CEOs of the leading newspapers in the world.

It is certainly curious that no mainstream media outlet considers a gathering of such figures, whose wealth far exceeds the combined wealth of all United States citizens, to be newsworthy, when a trip by any one of them on their own makes headline news on TV. This is the conundrum that I have pondered. Fifteen years ago it set me on an investigative journey that has become my life's work. Slowly, one by one, I have penetrated the layers of secrecy surrounding the Bilderberg Group, but I could not have done this without the help of "conscientious objectors" from inside, as well as outside, the Group's membership. To them, I extend my deepest gratitude for their priceless intelligence has made this book possible. You can understand then, that to protect them, I cannot mention these true heroes by name, only thank them for helping me find out what was being said behind the closed doors of the opulent hotels where the Bilderbergers hold their annual meetings.

Before we enter the realm of this exclusive club, it is important to recognize that neither people nor organizations are absolutely "evil," just as no one is absolutely "good." There are powerful people in the world guided by higher ideals, principles and beliefs than those of the manipulative secret club and its spin-offs that I describe in this book. The efforts of the original members to better our world were based on a "father-knows-best" autocracy similar to the Roman Catholic Church's paternalistic form of Christianity. Their intent was noble, at first.

Unfortunately, it seems that the Bilderberg Group has grown beyond its idealistic beginnings to become a shadow world government, which decides in total secrecy at annual meetings how their plans are to be carried out. They threaten to take away our right to direct our own destinies. And this is becoming easier, because the development of telecommunication technology, merged with profound instant impact of the Internet and new methods of behavior engineering to manipulate individual conduct, may convert what, at other epochs of history, were only evil intentions — into a disturbing reality.

Each new measure, viewed on its own, may seem only a slight aberration, but a whole host of changes, as part of an ongoing continuum, constitutes a shift towards total enslavement. This is why it is time to look behind the scenes. We are at a crossroads. And the roads we take from here will determine the very future of humanity. We have to wake up to the true objectives and actions of the Bilderberg Group and its parallel kin if we hope to retain the freedoms fought for by our grandfathers in World War II.

It is not up to God to bring us back from the "New Dark Age" planned for us. It is up to us! Whether we emerge from this century as an electronic global police state or as free human beings *depends on the actions we take now*. We will never find the right answers if we don't know the deep context.

This is what *The True Story of the Bilderberg Group* endeavors to provide.

Prince Bernhard presiding over first Bilderberg meeting in Oosterbeek, Netherlands, May 1954.

An invitation from Prince Bernhard to the 1957 Bilderberg Group meeting

Soestdijk Palace, December 1956

Dear Mr. Heuge

I have the honour to invite you to the next Bilderberg Conference which will take place on the 15th, 16th and 17th February 1957 at St. Simon's Island, Georgia, in the United States of America.

The object of this conference will be to study common and divergent elements in the policies of the Western World.

Prince of the Netherlands

R.S.V.P.: Dr. J. H. Retinger

27, The Vale, LONDON S. W. 3

Prince Bernhard 1911-2004

Prince Philip   Prince Bernhard

Prince Bernhard and Richard Nixon, 1955

PART ONE

THE BILDERBERG GROUP: MASTERS OF THE UNIVERSE

... a clique of the richest, economically and politically most powerful and influential men in the Western world, who meet secretly to plan events that later appear just to happen.
                              —*The Times* of London, 1977

It is difficult to re-educate people who have been brought up on nationalism to the idea of relinquishing part of their sovereignty to a supra-national body.
                    —Bilderberg Group founder, Prince Bernhard

World events do not occur by accident: They are made to happen, whether it is to do with national issues or commerce; and most of them are staged and managed by those who hold the purse strings.
                    —Denis Healey, former British Defence Minister

Top: Vernon Jordan; mega-investor Henry Kravis; his wife Marie-Josée, a senior fellow at the Hudson Institute; Richard Perle, a resident fellow at the American Enterprise Institute; and Jon Corzine (back to us) confab at Stresa.

Middle: Rodrigo de Rato announced his resignation in June 2007 as Managing Director, the top job at the International Monetary Fund, a position that has been held by Europeans since the Fund's beginning in 1945. Rato regularly attended Bilderberg meetings, here is shown with other Bilderberg attendees, former World Bank Presidents Paul Wolfowitz, and James Wolfensohn, and new British Prime Minister Gordon Brown.

Bottom: Bilderberg regular Vernon Jordan, Senior Managing Director, Lazard Frères & Co. and relative newcomer Fiat Vice Chairman John Elkann discuss the world's affairs at Rottach-Egern, Germany in 2005.

CHAPTER ONE

DEADLY DROP

In May 1996 I was in Toronto covering the annual Bilderberg meeting, but this time on my home ground in my adopted land of Canada. It felt good to be back, and I was reminded of so many reasons why I love this country.

Toronto, home to over five million people, is the largest financial center in Canada and the fourth largest city in North America. Only New York, Chicago and Los Angeles have larger economies. The Toronto Stock Exchange is here. It is the third largest in North America in trading value, ninth in the world in quoted market value, and it has the first fully computerized trading system in North America.

Within an hour's drive of Toronto are the greatest concentrations of automobile manufacturing and horse breeding in the country. I would be heading north to the site of this year's Bilderberg Conference in a short while, but first I wanted to enjoy wandering through the city streets, reacquainting myself with the wonderful sights so many Canadians take for granted.

Downtown, in the heart of Toronto's financial district, is Bay Street, which is Toronto's diminutive version of New York's famous Wall Street. At 161 Bay Street stands the Canada Trust Tower. This 53-story, 856-foot tower is one of the city's signature skyscrapers, and it has fascinated me since its construction in 1990 by a famed Spanish architect, Santiago Calatrava. This tower forms part of the 5.2 acre BCE Place, the second most distinctive sight on Toronto's skyline, after the CN Tower which, at 1,820 feet above the ground, is the world's highest freestanding structure.

BCE Place is actually several buildings connected by a shopping mall, but from a skyline perspective, it is the Canada Trust Tower and its sister, the Bay Wellington Tower, that steal the show. With tinted green windows and myriad jagged edges, the two towers present an artistic impression of staggered Lego blocks stacked at angles to defy gravity, giving the pair uniqueness among Toronto's more sedate skyscrapers.

Another jewel in the BCE crown is the Galleria, a five-story hall of light that runs along Front Street and faces south toward the waterfront district. The Galleria was designed as a "Crystal Cathedral" of commerce, with the roof providing cover for the Street Gallery, which connects Bay Street to Heritage Square. Also designed by Santiago Calatrava, it is 85 feet high, 46 feet wide, and 394 feet from end to end, and is composed of eight freestanding steel supports on either side of the Gallery. They branch out into parabolic shapes, which at that moment reminded me of a forest canopy.

Eventually I strolled up Yonge Street — the world's longest street, almost 1,200 miles long. Just up the road, 22 miles north by northwest of the downtown core, the Bilderberg elite were gathering at the CIBC Leadership Centre near the pristine town of King City, the site of the 1996 Bilderberg Conference. The CIBC retreat/resort is in King Township — a region of large, expensive horse farms, where members of the British Royal Family are hosted on their private visits to Canada. This marvellous center, privately owned by one of Canada's main banks, the Canadian Imperial Bank of Commerce, includes over three miles of nature trails through forested terrain and rolling hills.

It was no wonder that the Bilderbergers had decided on this exquisite location. From spa facilities and services featuring massage and skin-care/aesthetic treatments, saunas, and steam-rooms; to a unique 200-meter indoor fully heated track suspended roughly six feet above the ground; to indoor and outdoor swimming and whirlpools, the CIBC Leadership Centre has it all. It is also located near numerous golf courses, riding stables, hiking and cycling routes, museums and other recreation sites. In sum, there was little chance that the Bilderbergers would get bored.

The Toronto media and news services had been first alerted to this meeting by a series of faxes, phone calls and memos from me and Jim

Tucker, especially after it became known to me from deep undercover sources within the meeting that the 1996 conference was alledgedly to be used as a staging ground for the imminent breakup of Canada. This was to be secured through a Unilateral Declaration of Independence in Quebec, to be launched in early 1997. The declaration would fragment Canada, with the aim of achieving "Continental Union" with the U.S. by 2000, a date which has been pushed back at least twice since then.

As a general rule, Bilderberg meetings are never mentioned in the media, since the mainstream press is fully owned by the Bilderbergers. But the veil of secrecy was abruptly torn off on May 30, 1996, the first day of the conference.

A front-page story ran in one of Canada's most widely read and influential newspapers, the *Toronto Star*. Under the headline "BLACK PLAYS HOST TO WORLD LEADERS," John Deverell, a business reporter for the newspaper, noted that not only had Canadian publisher [Lord] Conrad Black offered $295 million to gain control of Canada's largest newspaper chain and then weathered the subsequent annual meeting of his Hollinger Inc., but also, to cap his week, he was now "the host for a four-day, closely guarded meeting of world leaders and royalty just north of Toronto."

Deverell named some of the more than 100 hand-picked attendees from around the world from the list we had supplied him: "U.S. Defence Secretary William Perry; Prime Minister Jean Chretien of Canada; former U.S. Secretary of State Henry Kissinger; Giovanni Agnelli, Honorary Chairman of Fiat; Finance Minister [and later Canada's Prime Minister] Paul Martin; Mario Monto, European Commissioner; David Rockefeller of Chase Manhattan Bank; George Soros, Prince of Belgium, the queens of the Netherlands and Spain as well as other business, political and academic elite."

That same day, the *Toronto Sun* headlined, "BIG HITTERS GATHER: VAST ARRAY OF INTERNATIONAL VIPs TALK THINGS OVER AT SECRETIVE BILDERBERG '96 IN KING CITY," and noted that "[Conrad] Black, media baron and chairman of Hollinger Inc., and other permanent members of the group, are unhappy at suggestions by extremists of the left and right that the private event is part of a system of secret government."

At 7:45 that morning, 680-NEWS' legendary radio journalist, Dick Smythe, who had the widest metro Toronto audience, presented the following report, which was re-aired at intervals as part of the station's news schedule:

> **Dick Smythe:** Well, this sounds like the plot from a conspiracy movie, as the world's movers and shakers meet in secret. Conrad Black is holding his annual Bilderberg Conference. Here's 680's Karen Parsons ...
>
> **Reporter:** About one hundred notables, including the Queens of the Netherlands and Spain, along with Henry Kissinger, the U.S. Defense Secretary William Perry and our Prime Minister, have gathered for the conference. Also along, the heads of Ford Motor Company, Xerox, the Bank of Commerce and Reuters. Black says there is a ban on reporters, so discussion will be intimate and candid. He says, "Exchanges can often be quite heated." Participants are required to take a vow of silence. Last year's conference was held in three mountaintop luxury hotels in Switzerland. This year, it's at a $60 million dollar luxury spa in King City. The Canadian Press has also distributed a brief report on the previously-secret meeting, which was published today by, among other newspapers, the *Toronto Sun*, with over 350,000 subscribers.

This was the first time in the history of the Bilderberg Conferences that they had ever been scrutinized in such a fashion. Bilderbergers are not accustomed to having to provide explanations to anyone, particularly since members own or control major metropolitan newspapers, newspaper chains and wire services.

However, 1996 was no ordinary conference. The Bilderbergers do not typically plot the overthrow of their host country's government during their meetings.

When the principal news outlets began checking our information through their own government and private sources, it became clear that Canada, one of the world's wealthiest countries, was scheduled to be ruthlessly partitioned by the Bilderbergers and the New World Order. They should have known that when their own freedom is at stake, no amount of ownership of the press would prevent secretaries, copy editors, writers, investigative journalists and, indeed, management of

Canada's television, radio and print media from disseminating the truth for public consumption.

The press coverage became so intense that Kissinger was overheard by one of the staff reporters screaming at the Canadian Prime Minister, Jean Chretien, that he would be damned if someone was going to screw this up for him. David Rockefeller pulled Conrad Black aside during a break to ask him if he could "lean" on some people in the press to get them to "shut up about this." Even then, the now disgraced and bankrupt Conrad Black was in way over his head.

What the Bilderbergers imagined being a trickle had quickly turned into a flood and then an avalanche. Not until the 1999 Conference in Sintra, Portugal, did the Bilderbergers relax the extraordinary security measures that followed in the footsteps of their worst defeat, the 1996 Conference in Toronto.

On June 1, "Big Jim" Tucker and I, along with a small cadre of part-time Bilderberg chasers, celebrated what was turning into an extraordinary success story. Every major newspaper in the country wanted an interview, television stations were constantly looking for updates, and radio stations were following us all over the city.

We gathered at the Horseshoe Tavern on Queen Street, Toronto's version of New York's Soho district. The Horseshoe Tavern, now some 60 years old, is one of the city's original music venues, the famous bar where Canadian singing legends Stompin' Tom, Blue Rodeo, The Tragically Hip and The Watchmen got their first breaks. In September 1997, the Rolling Stones would kick off their *No Security* tour there, with a 75-minute show for "Live on MTV." It is a good place to have a good time, and we felt well deserving of it.

As the festivities began to wind down, I pondered my approaching appointment, made during a phone call from one of my sources, who wanted urgently to see me before the end of the conference scheduled for the following day. We had agreed to meet in less than an hour at Calatrava's Galleria. BCE Place is one of the most inconspicuous places in all of Toronto precisely *because* of its immensity, with droves of tourist gawkers passing through the premises photographing and videotaping the sights and sounds of Toronto's premier architectural attraction.

Our party was now definitely breaking up, and I decided to walk to the Galleria through Kensington Market, a Toronto version of Madrid's

Rastro, located just west of Chinatown. It was Saturday, which is the busiest day of the week, when it becomes a bustling open-air market. If anyone were to follow me, I would surely lose the tail in this matrix of busy streets and densely packed crowds.

As I rounded the corner at the Galleria, I could see my contact browsing the newspaper stand, a plastic bag in left hand and his other holding a rolled up magazine. After a chance eye contact, and without acknowledging each other's presence, we moved silently towards the revolving entrance of the adjacent Canada Trust Tower, where a friend who worked for the real estate developer had arranged a room overlooking the city skyline on one of the top floors.

I walked into an elevator, nervously glancing behind me. My contact was to follow me five minutes later. As I entered the posh suite, the splendor of one of North America's most beautiful cities opened up and stood majestically before me. From 800 feet above ground, the city stood still. I was shut off from the bustle and sounds of this great metropolis by soundproof windows.

The Canada Trust Tower is an architectural marvel where a square meter of space rents out for 160 Canadian dollars. The building is equipped with 24-hour CCTV surveillance cameras, 24 elevators, eight levels of underground parking, seven security guards at the entrance, plus undercover police. The skyscraper is home to some of the most established and successful multinational corporations in the world.

All of a sudden, I once again felt on the outside looking in. Would all this continue to make a difference? Would people wake up to the imminent danger? Or would this, in the longer run, be just another cloak-and-dagger experience? After all, "Have a nice day, son" had been the reply of one passerby, after I had patiently explained to him just who was visiting and what they were up to.

Nonetheless, much had been accomplished in these last several days. For once, we clearly had the upper hand on the Bilderbergers. Press coverage was tremendous. Kissinger was royally pissed off: definitively a good sign. To their chagrin, attending European royalty were hounded by unwanted press. The plans for the imminent breakup of my adopted country were temporarily put on hold. What else could one hope to achieve in such a short time?

Still, I knew that this was a temporary reprieve. These people would be back, lessons learned and notes taken. They wanted to crush any resistance, to rule the world with or without its consent, with guns or butter, without ...

My thoughts were interrupted by a discreet knock on the heavy wooden door.

"Come in," I replied, only slightly raising my voice.

My Source, wearing leather gloves, slowly crossed the threshold that separated the lightly decorated hallway from the heavy art deco of the suite. Contemplating for a moment the extraordinary view of the downtown Harbour Front area surrounded by lakeside promenades and landscaped waterfront pathways, he moved appreciatively toward the window.

"You stopped them this time around," said the Source, weighing every syllable as if even a slight alteration in the register might have transmitted a different meaning. Despite his words, he projected an aura of resignation. "The breakup of Canada will go ahead as planned. It is only a matter of time."

"Maybe," I said. "But all is well, for now, until the next close encounter. Between now and then, quite a few of them will have died of old age, disease and fortuitous accidents."

"Fortuitous? For whom?" replied the Source.

He pulled out hand-written notes, or rather scribbles that I despaired of deciphering on my own, from the magazine he was tightly gripping with his right hand.

"I thought note taking wasn't allowed," I quipped, displaying a full smile at him.

"Note taking is discouraged, my friend," he corrected me.

I glanced at the page. The familiar hand of a fountain pen had left a blotchy imprint here and there, but, overall, I realized I could understand it. I knew quite well the Source's writing, his faint Ts and crooked Rs, diligently drawn out within the confines of a lined paper. I reflected momentarily upon what this courageous person was risking in meeting me and handing me this priceless information.

Why weren't there more people like this in the world? But perhaps there are. We may simply not know them, or the personal struggles they may be waging thousands of miles away. For example, there are the many everyday people who have enabled me to acquire much of my information.

I would arrive at the site of a Bilderberg meeting several days ahead of them, stay at the same five-star luxury hotel until their security forces along with the arrival of Bilderberg guests kicked me out one day before the start of their conference. During my time in the hotel, I would get to know the waitresses, waiters and general staff. Those who seemed more open I approached and explained how the Bilderberg meeting worked, what this secretive group was about and what would take place in the hotel over the next few days. Of course many didn't believe me, but I would beg them not to take me at my word, just to watch what happened in their hotel and to listen to the conversations of the Bilderberg guests as they served them. Then they could decide if they wanted to be my eyes and ears, for the good of humanity.

I was taking advantage of all five-star hotel policies: staff and employees must speak a minimum of four languages — English, French, German and one more — to accommodate guests. They could discreetly eavesdrop and understand most of what was discussed through the conference. As days went by, those I approached witnessed the police presence, secret service, and secrecy of the attendees, and came to believe that what I had told them was true. For the few who decided to help me, I would designate several local bars where we could meet inconspicuously. This insider, of course, required a more secure meeting place

"I have to go," the Source said quietly without looking up.

I mechanically extended my open hand in his direction, but just as the Source was about to clasp it with his outstretched palm, I found myself giving him a bear hug instead.

"I won't waste your time thanking you, because no amount of thanks can be enough for what you have been doing for us."

The Source looked away. "I have to leave."

"We'll leave as we came up," I said, "in five minute intervals. I'll go down first."

"Don't bother. I left my car in the underground parking. We can take the elevator down together," replied the Source.

Pulling on his leather gloves, he pressed the elevator button. A blue light shone through its transparent surface. I could hear the whooshing sounds of the hydraulic lift speeding towards us from the bowels of the building at six levels per second. I turned toward my informant.

"When will I see you next?"

With the sound of the bell, the doors opened, and I took a step in that direction. "Watch out!!" screamed the Source, grabbing my arm and yanking me back.

I stared at the elevator. In front of me, a chilling spectacle ... an empty elevator shaft with certain death awaiting me some 650 feet below, had the Source lacked the reflexes to pull me back from the abyss.

I shuddered all over. Cold chills ran up and down my spine in rapid succession.

"The floor," I muttered, barely perceiving. "Where is the floor?"

"We have to get out of here!" said the Source. "Someone has jimmied the system. They have been expecting you!

"Listen," he said. "Don't take the elevator. It isn't safe. Walk down the stairs and call the police. When they get here, I'll take advantage of the moment and take the elevator down to the garage. Go! Do it now!"

Skipping the stairs two at a time, I propelled myself around the stairwell corners with short pushes of my hands against the walls, galvanized with adrenaline, flying down the stairs in record time. I could feel my heart pounding against my chest wall and gasped for more oxygen. On one of the lower floors, I heard the garbled voice of a foreign-born security guard climbing the stairs towards me.

"...Er, ...ter, ...mister, sir. Are you all right? What happened? I was called on the intercom on the second floor ... someone manually to made elevator stop ... only in emergency can to do this."

I grabbed the man's forearm. "Could you please call the police as quickly as you can?" I said, while catching my breath between every other word. The man pulled out his walkie-talkie, and I could hear a high-pitched voice coming through from the other end of the line.

I ran on. Five, four, three, two, one ... ground level. I pushed open the heavy metal doors that opened on the main lobby. Two police cruisers were already parked outside. The first onlookers were beginning to gather on the other side of the revolving entrance doors.

"Are you the man who got stuck in the elevator?" asked the Toronto police constable, pointing at me with his fat index and middle finger.

"Not exactly," I muttered shaking my head in virtual disbelief. "I was about to enter into an elevator that was missing its principle component, the floor."

The cop gave a short cry. A stocky companion with sharp features, clipped moustache and hairy wrist glanced over.

"You know, son, you are very lucky to be alive." The policeman stood with his knees slightly opened, his shoe tips pointing outwards. "Usually only blind people survive these situations. A blind man would never step into an elevator without checking to see if it is there. Most of us take it for granted. When the Mafia want someone rubbed out, this is one of their preferred methods."

On June 1, 1996, I was about to turn thirty, too young to die.

Fuck them, I thought. *This is far from over. We can still win this.*

I gave the pertinent details to the constable, who looked at me incredulously from time to time, his eyes focused on the lower part of my face as if he were lip reading.

A security guard with an impeccably bald dome and slightly clipped hair asked me once again if I was all right. Several people on the sidewalk recalled seeing a stocky man in his forties walk out of the building some five minutes before the police had arrived.

A police van and two more policemen on motorcycles pulled up. Yes, yes, the show had begun. It was the crowd's turn to take center stage.

The wrong people remembered the right things, and vice versa. A fat lady, who refused a chocolate candy because she was "on a diet," gave a lurid account of how she saw someone, or maybe something, walk, or perhaps stumble.... A street violinist remembered two men carrying a medium-sized piano out of the building.... A young lady with a poodle....

But whatever these people may or may not have seen of relevance to the crime, their hopes were now to participate somehow. Yes, yes, and participate they did, that large crowd of well-wishers and onlookers and gawkers and charlatans.

Put the pen away. The show is over. You sir, downstage, put your glasses back on! Officer, stop scribbling into your pad! Ladies and gentlemen, please, could I have you all put your personal belongings back into your imaginary suitcases and leave the premises? The show is over!

A tramp stuck a half-eaten cigar into his mouth. A thin dapperish man with long sideburns slowly walked by pretending not to notice, not even turning his head. Two hotdog vendors gloomily pushed their sausages over some tram tracks, back across the street, shooed away by the beat cop with a deprecatory shake of his head.

I walked the other way, the same way I had approached. The first of June is summer in Andalusia, but here summer was still two months away.

A distinctly Russian man with a "hedgehog" haircut walked by hand-in-hand with a lady, complaining about the eating habits of someone named Vania. He reminded me of the land of my birth. He also reminded me of the man who had drawn me into all of this in the first place.

Top: Daniel Estulin trying to take a photograph of Richard Perle past two private security guards at the 2006 Bilderberg meeting in Canada.
Bottom: Armed guards making sure the 2004 Bilderberg meeting is private.

CHAPTER TWO

THE HIGHLANDER, 1992

My involvement with the secret society called the Bilderberg Group had begun on a fall day in October 1992, with a telephone call from a Russian émigré based in Paris. He had read an earlier story about my family's plight in a New York-based Russian daily newspaper, written on the tenth anniversary of our forced exile, and he wished to meet to discuss "a certain matter of great importance." Several weeks later, we met at Segovia, a well-known Spanish restaurant in Toronto located just off Yonge Street.

When I made that fateful decision to meet the man whose identity will remain anonymous, but whom we shall simply call "Vladimir," I entered into a parallel universe where red meant go and green meant shoot, and yellow and blue and orange and any other color simply didn't exist. It was a world utterly counterintuitive, and unfamiliar to all but a select few who somehow had had a brush or a connection with the underworld of spooks and counter-espionage. This parallel world remains unseen in the daily struggles of most of humanity, but, believe me, it is there: a cesspool of duplicity and lies and double-speak and innuendo and blackmail and bribery. It is a surreal world of double and triple agents, of changing loyalties, of professional psychotic assassins, brainwashed black ops agents, soldiers of fortune and mercenaries, whose primary sources of income are the dirtiest and most despicable government-run subversive missions — the kind that can never be exposed.

These people spend their entire lives dancing between raindrops and disappearing at the faintest whiff of danger. As much as most people would like to believe that this is only possible in James Bond films, please take my word for it: this parallel universe determines much of what you see, read and hear on a daily basis. To survive in the world of these men, one must do it on their terms, and must never judge them for their actions, nor believe what most of them are prepared to tell you. I have seen professional, award-winning investigative journalists so shell-shocked that they were unable to fathom the truth of what they had just witnessed.

In this shadow world, your only real weapon is a highly fine-tuned sixth sense, which may just keep you out of trouble long enough to survive and figure things out. When I stepped into that world, I immersed myself in a universe I found so perverse and evil that it has left an indelible mark on my soul. It is the price of involvement.

I arrived at Segovia first, ordered a drink, planted myself in the corner against the wall, and waited. Ten minutes later, Vladimir appeared — tall, lanky, elegantly dressed. He had twinkling eyes. As he walked by me, he placed two light fingers upon my shoulder, glanced downward and motioned to a waiter.

"Whiskey," he uttered in a hardly noticeable Russian accent, a mark of someone who had spent a considerable portion of his life abroad. He sat down in front of me. With a tip of his pen, Vladimir brushed an orange thread off his heavily-starched white shirt. I realized at once that this was no typical Russian émigré.

"Listen," he said as he pulled himself closer to the table edge. "How well do you know the guy who runs this place?"

"He is a good friend," I replied. "That's why I wanted us to meet here."

He flushed, hastily nodded and looked hopefully at me. Down at the other end of the room, an overweight businessman with a Chanel-scented handkerchief tried to seduce a sleek young woman.

Vladimir pulled out a heavy, worn black leather briefcase and set it carefully on his lap. Two barely noticeable clicks opened the lock. With his elongated thumbs, he carefully pushed it open. It was full of papers that were neatly kept in multi-colored folders. In turn, these had been carefully stored in a false bottom of his briefcase.

Over the course of the next two hours, Vladimir took me through a series of events that forever shattered my cozy universe. The documents

I saw erased all doubts about the veracity of what I was hearing and seeing. His openness and honesty, as well as his willingness to answer any questions I threw at him, endeared him to me. It was all there: a Trilateral Commission orchestrating the removal of the Philippines' President Ferdinand Marcos; minutes of secret meetings discussing JFK's assassination; the Club of Rome's December 5, 1980 meeting in Washington, D.C., endorsing and accepting their "Global 2000 Report" — a blueprint for global genocide; the KGB's "Kissinger files"; etc.

Nevertheless, before I could fully subscribe to Vladimir's evidence, I needed to be sure that this man wasn't a "honey pot" — an intelligence asset with legitimate material in hand, set loose by his controllers with the objective of attracting very dangerous characters to a free-for-all. I was new to the game, and to me black was still black, red was stop, green was go, and amber meant caution. It took me a long time to get accustomed to the fact that these people brought their own rulebooks to the game. And in order to survive, you had to follow them.

Years later, I found out why Vladimir had come to me. He was a double agent who had worked for the KGB and MI5. Or was it MI5 and the KGB? Somewhere along the line his cover was blown, and he had become desperate. He was in fear for his life, and when he saw that fateful newspaper article about my family, he had seen someone who might be able to help: my grandfather, a former KGB counterintelligence officer.

This gambit, Vladimir hoped, just might help him bluff his way back into the game. He had tried to shake off his controllers, and now they were after him. He needed something to trade with those who were trying to silence him. He felt that I, or rather my grandfather, could be his conduit, as I knew enough press people in Toronto to persuade them to run with his story, while my grandfather still held enough influence to keep the MI5 people at bay.

I heard back from Vladimir a week later. Our telephone conversation was insanely weird. Again, I found myself in that parallel universe, where nothing makes sense and every phrase is spoken in code. The only thing that I managed to remember from a barrage of numbers and dates he threw at me was UP AR 340-18-5. My intelligence contacts were able to trace this to a highly classified original OPERATION WATCHTOWER, a secret U.S. government drug trafficking operation that financed anti-Communist activities between 1975 and 1984. It also dealt with surveillance.

"Maybe he was trying to tell me that he was being watched," I surmised. I waited anxiously for him to call back, but he never did.

Instead, Vladimir vanished. But that murky universe of secret societies and off-the-book government operations didn't. His description of the Bilderberg Group turned my world upside down and changed my life forever. "Bilderberg" became synonymous with a One-World-Government takeover, and that distant parallel universe turned into my area of operations.

I converted into one of them, a spook, a spectre, a shade... dancing between raindrops and disappearing at the first sight of danger: a shadow dancer. In America, they simply called me "the Highlander."

CHAPTER THREE

BILDERBERG FOUNDATION

I magine a private club where presidents, prime ministers, international bankers and generals rub shoulders, where gracious royal chaperones ensure everyone gets along, and where the people running the wars, the markets and Europe say what they never dare say in public. This is the Bilderberg Group, and it is the most secretive of any organization worldwide. The reason that no one is willing to break the group's conspiracy of silence or stand up to it is revealed in the words of French broadcaster Thierry de Segonzac: "The Bilderbergers are too powerful and omnipresent to be exposed."

The secrecy of the Bilderbergers has captured the imaginations of novelists such as Robert Ludlum and Gayle Lynds. Their books model covert organizations based on the few facts published about the Bilderberg Group. These novels illustrate the fact that whenever a regime change is needed, anywhere worldwide — whether this be based on the need to sustain a welfare state or to correct destabilizing capital flows — it only happens when a world body of power brokers decides to address the issues and posts them on its agenda.[1]

The Netherlands' Prince Bernhard subscribed to the belief that severe economic dips like the Great Depression could be avoided if responsible and influential leaders could actually manage world events behind their necessary public posturing. For this reason, he was asked to organize the first meeting of "like-minded" representatives from all facets of the world's economic, political, industrial and military realms in 1954. They met at the Bilderberg Hotel in Oosterbeek, Holland between May 29th and May 31st. At the end of that meeting, the attendees agreed to form a secret association.

Most reports contend the original members named their alliance the Bilderberg Group after the hotel where they made their covenant. Author Gyeorgos C. Hatonn, however, discovered that German-born Prince Bernhard was an officer in the Reiter SS Corp in the early 1930s and was on the board of an I.G. subsidiary, Farben Bilder. In his book, *Rape of the Constitution; Death of Freedom,* Hatonn claims Prince Bernhard drew on his Nazi history in corporate management to encourage the "super secret policy-making group" to call themselves the Bilderbergers after Farben Bilder, in memory of the Farben executives' initiative to organize Heinrich Himmler's "Circle of Friends" — elite wealth-building leaders who amply rewarded Himmler for his protection under National Socialist programs, from the early days of Hitler's popularity through to Nazi Germany's defeat. The royal Dutch family discreetly buried this part of Prince Bernhard's background when, after the war, he became a top official in Royal Dutch Shell, a Dutch-British conglomerate. Today, this rich European oil company forms part of the inner circle of the Bilderberg elite.

During the first meeting of the Bilderbergers, the founding members drew up their mission and their goals. According to one observer, they have continued in the same vein: "The intention behind each and all of the Bilderberg meetings was about how to create an 'Aristocracy of purpose' between Europe and the United States, and how to come to agreement on questions of policy, economics, and strategy in jointly ruling the world. The NATO alliance was their crucial base of operation and subversion because it afforded them the backdrop for their plans of 'perpetual war,' or at least for their 'nuclear blackmail' policy."[2]

I will illustrate this amply, as we peel the layers of secrecy away and expose the Bilderbergers' true intentions, which incidentally were only too patently clear to then-French President, General Charles de Gaulle.

In his October 1967 newsletter, *Les Documents, Politiques, Diplomatiques et Franciers,* political investigator Roger Mennevee analyzed the Bilderbergers' relationship with de Gaulle. He began his report with an astonishing observation that "all of the French personalities who had associated themselves with the Bilderberg Group, such as Georges Pompidou, Antoine Pinay and Guy Mollet were also the strongest opponents of Charles de Gaulle's nuclear policy," known as the *force de frappe*. Pompidou was the Prime Minister. Pinay and Mollet were Ministers in the French government.

Why this alliance? Because one of the main objectives of the Group was to submit the sovereignty of the free nations of Europe to a Bilderberger-controlled British-American One World Government, using a nuclear threat as a battering ram against the rest of the unwilling world. And in order to control Europe, it was vital to eliminate France's nuclear deterrent, even when that deterrent was vital in containing the Soviet nuclear threat. General de Gaulle's biographer, Jean Lacouture wrote, "de Gaulle had to establish an incontrovertible position of strength in Europe against Britain's free trade orientation toward a New World Imperial Order. This is why France had to be one of the three pillars of the free world, as opposed to one of the columns of the European Temple."[3]

If we analyze the agenda items of Bilderberg meetings since 1954, what stands out remarkably is the attempt to manage and bring under control differences in ideology among American and European aristocracies with respect to how these two groups should go about looting the planet. For example, page seven of the 1955 Bilderberg meeting General Report speaks of "removal of misunderstanding and possible suspicion between the countries of Western Europe and the U.S.A. in the face of dangers, which beset the world."[4]

Since 1954, the Bilderbergers have represented the elite and the absolute wealth of all western nations — financiers, industrialists, bankers, politicians, business leaders of multinational corporations, presidents, prime ministers, finance ministers, state secretaries, World Bank and International Monetary Fund representatives, presidents of world media conglomerates, and military leaders.

In September 2005, in a precedent-setting gesture to countermand accusations of a Bilderberg Group conspiracy, the Group's seventy-three-year-old chairman, Viscount Etienne Davignon, gave an interview to the BBC's Bill Hayton. In it, he presented a more benign purpose for the Group's private meetings: "I simply think it's people who have influence interested to speak to other people who have influence in a forum that allows them to speak freely and to examine their differences of opinion without criticism and public debate over their views." Davignon has denied the Bilderbergers want to establish a global ruling class, "because I don't think a global ruling class exists." Instead, he contends, "Business influences society, and politics influences society — that's purely common sense. It's not that business contests the right of democratically elected leaders to lead."

Wars have usually been fought over expanding territory, but in this new era of globalization, where business and politics co-depend for survival, economic control dominates. Regardless of the Bilderberg chairman's claims, there is no doubt the Group wields economic control over world trade. The fact remains: the public is not privy to the proceedings of their annual meetings. They meet in secret to discuss global strategy and reach consensus on a wide range of issues. Such secrecy is suspect, and my goal is to uncloak the Bilderbergers' secrecy and show how this private club of world leaders and interlocking agencies keeps trying to subjugate all free nations to their rule through international laws, which they manipulate and have the United Nations administer.

Bilderberger members "run" the central banks and are therefore in a position to determine discount rates, money-supply levels, interest rates, and the price of gold, as well as which countries receive loans. By manipulating money up and down the business chain, the Bilderbergers create billions of dollars for themselves. The ideology of money and lust for power drives them.

Every U.S. president since "Ike" Eisenhower has belonged to the Bilderberg Group, not that they have all attended the meetings personally, but all have sent their representatives. Another member is now ex-Prime Minister Tony Blair, as well as most of the principal members of the British government. Even Canada's high-profile past Prime Minister, Pierre Trudeau, was a member. Past Bilderberg invitees are Alan Greenspan, former Chairman of the Federal Reserve; Hillary and Bill Clinton; John Kerry; Melinda and Bill Gates; and Richard Perle.[5]

Also members are the people who control what you watch and read — media barons like David Rockefeller, Conrad Black (the now disgraced ex-owner of over 440 media publications around the world from *The Jerusalem Post* to Canada's newest daily, *The National Post*), Edgar Bronfman, Rupert Murdoch, and Sumner Redstone, CEO of

Viacom, an international media conglomerate that touches virtually every major segment of the media industry. They have protected the secrecy of this secret society, and this may be why the name "Bilderberg" is new to you.

No matter where you look — government, big business and any other institution seeking to exercise power — their key to control is *secrecy*. Meetings such as those of the Organization for Economic Cooperation and Development (OECD), the G8, World Trade Organization, World Economic Forum, Central Banks, the European Union Council of Ministers and the EU Commission, EU summits, government cabinet meetings, numerous think tanks, etc. are always conducted behind closed doors. The only possible reason for this is that "they" don't want you and me to know what they are discussing. That well-worn excuse for keeping things under wraps — "It is not in the public's interest" — really means that it is not in the interest of the institutions in power for the public to know what they are discussing and deciding.

Beyond this common reluctance to reveal the proceedings of meetings, the secrecy principle extends to the forums and meetings themselves; i.e. by and large, we don't even know meetings are taking place, let alone what is being planned and discussed in them.[6] "There's the World Economic Forum at Davos in January/February, the Bilderberg and G8 meetings in April/May, and the IMF/World Bank annual conference in September. A kind of international consensus emerges and is carried over from one meeting to the next. But no one's really leading it. This consensus becomes the background for G8 economic communiqués; it becomes what informs the IMF when it imposes an adjustment programme on Argentina; and it becomes what the U.S. president proposes to Congress."[7]

According to the Bilderberger's draft document of 1989, their first meeting "grew out of the concern expressed by many leading citizens on both sides of the Atlantic that Western Europe and North America were not working together as closely as they should on matters of critical importance. It was felt that regular, off-the-record discussions would help create a better understanding of the complex forces and major trends affecting Western nations in the difficult post-war period."

Lord Rothschild and Laurence Rockefeller, key members of two of the most powerful families in the world, personally handpicked 100 of the world's elite for the secret purpose of regionalizing Europe, according to Giovanni Agnelli, the now-deceased head of Fiat, who also said, "European integration is our goal, and where the politicians have failed, we industrialists hope to succeed."

"No policy is made here; it is all talk, some of it banal and platitudinous," said Will Hutton, London editor of *The Observer*, who participated in the 1997 Bilderberg meeting. "But the consensus established is the backdrop against which policy is made worldwide."[8]

According to founder Prince Bernhard of Holland, as quoted in Alden Hatch's authorized biography of the Prince, each Bilderberg attendee is "magically stripped of his office" upon entering the meeting, becoming "a simple citizen of his country for the duration of the conference." Prince Bernhard, who died in 2004, was the father of Queen Beatrix of the Netherlands and a close friend and associate of Britain's Prince Philip. "When these representatives of the Western establishment leave a Bilderberg meeting," he said, "they carry the Group's consensus with them. The high-powered Bilderberg debates are intended to build unity by resolving differences, and therefore certainly have a significant influence on attendees."

Indeed, from the moment the Bilderberg Conference closes, what seems to happen — "almost by accident" — is that the consensus reached in different areas of discussion at the Bilderberg annual meeting are wholeheartedly promoted by these all-powerful political and commercial interests through the mainstream press, while simultaneously becoming common policy to governing international forces of seemingly different persuasions.

CONFERENCE PROTOCOL

Nobody can buy their way into a Bilderberg meeting, although many corporations have tried.[9] The Group's Steering Committee decides whom to invite — what the *Guardian* newspaper of London aptly calls a "Bilderberg person," and their qualifications haven't changed in fifty years of secret meetings. Essentially, they look for a One World Order enthusiast and a Fabian Socialist — Fabianists believe in what they describe as "the democratic control of society in all its activities." The key word is control, and control of the individual is best achieved through global government, a goal Fabianism shares with Communism.

According to a source within the Steering Committee, "the invited guests must come alone; no wives, girlfriends, husbands or boyfriends. Personal assistants [translation: heavily armed bodyguards, usually ex-CIA and Secret Intelligence Service (SIS aka MI6)] cannot attend the conference and must eat in a separate hall. Not even David Rockefeller's personal assistant can join him for lunch. The guests are explicitly forbidden from giving interviews to journalists."

To maintain their aura of hermeticism, Bilderbergers book a hotel for the duration of the conference, usually ranging from three to four days, with the whole building being cleared of all other guests by the CIA and local secret service to ensure complete privacy and safety for the delegates. All drawings of the layout of the hotel are classified, staff is thoroughly vetted, their loyalty questioned, their backgrounds verified, and political affiliations checked. Any suspect ones are removed for the duration.

During the 1998 meeting, "Police in combat blacks with sniffer dogs search every delivery vehicle, inside and outside, top and bottom, and then escort it to the tradesmen's entrance. Armed officers haunt the surrounding woods and square-jawed men with secret service earphones guard the entrances. Anyone approaching the hotel that did not have a stake in controlling the planet is turned back."[10]

The host national government takes care of all the security concerns of the attending guests and their entourage. It also pays the costs of the military protection, the secret service, national and local police presence, as well as all additional private security to protect the intimacy and the privacy of the all-powerful world elite. The attendees are not required to follow the established rules and regulations of the host country, such as having to go through customs, carrying proper identification, such as passports, which are not required on Bilderberg visits. When they meet, nobody who is not on the "in" is allowed to come near the hotel. The elite often bring their own chefs, cooks, waiters, secretaries, telephone operators, busboys, cleaning staff and security personnel.

The 2004 conference, for example, was held at Grand Hotel des Iles Borromees in Stresa with "174 stunning rooms that faithfully recreate the Belle Époque era; Impero or Maggiolini style, lavish drapes, warm, rich colors, fabrics and Murano chandeliers that enhance the authenticity. Most lake-facing rooms enjoy a private balcony, and all bathrooms are tiled in Italian marble and have a whirlpool. Suites are magnificent, boasting fine art, inlaid ceilings, statues, vast whirlpool baths and separate showers in imperial suites."[11]

The Bilderberg Group pays for delegate and guest accommodations, which are modestly priced at 1,200 euros per room. Michelin three-star chefs prepare the food. In fact, one of the criteria in choosing the hotel is the availability of the best and most renowned chefs. The other is the size of the town (always a small town, away from the spotlights of a big city and curious people). Small towns have the added advantage of allowing personal assistants with big guns to set up in full view of everyone with no questions asked. Telephone, room service and laundry bills are paid for by the participants.

A staff member at the Trianon Palace in Versailles told me in 2003 that David Rockefeller's telephone bill ran up to 14,000 euros in three days. According to sources who are also Bilderberg participants, it wouldn't be extravagant to put a price tag on the four-day "globalist festival" at 10 million euros. This is more than it would cost to protect the President of the United States or the Pope on one of his many international visits. Of course, neither the President nor the Pope is nearly as important as the Bilderberg Group.

There are four daily sessions — two in the morning and two in the afternoon, except for Saturdays, when there is only a morning session. On Saturday, between noon and 3 P.M., the Bilderbergers play golf, swim, accompanied by their "personal assistants," go on an organized boat cruise or a helicopter ride.

The seating plan is in rotatable alphabetical order. One year, Umberto Agnelli (the now deceased chairman of Fiat) might sit at the front. The next year, Klaus Zumwinkel, Chairman, Deutche Post Worldnet AG and Deutche Telekom, might take his place.

Each country sends a delegation of, typically, three persons: an industry or business leader, a top-level minister or a senator, and an intellectual or chief editor of the leading periodical. The United States has the most participants because of its size. Smaller countries like Greece and Denmark are afforded, at most, two seats. The conferences usually consist of a maximum of 130 delegates. Two thirds of the attendees are from Europe, and the rest come from the United States and Canada. (Mexican globalists belong to a less powerful sister organization, the Trilateral Commission.)

One-third of the delegates are from government and politics, and the remaining two-thirds from industry, finance, education, labor and communications. Most delegates are fluent in English, with French as their second language of choice.

BILDERBERG RULES OF PROCEDURE

The Bilderberg Group, from its inception, has been administered by a small nucleus of persons, appointed since 1954 by a committee of "wise men," which is made up of a European Chairman, both a European and a U.S. Secretary General, and a Treasurer. The annual invitations, according to a Bilderberger unofficial press release, are only sent out to "important and respected people who, through their special knowledge, personal contacts and influence in national and international circles, can amplify the objectives and resources of the Bilderberg Group."

Bilderberg meetings follow a traditional protocol founded in 1919 in the wake of the Paris Peace Conference held at Versailles for the Royal Institute of International Affairs (RIIA) based in Chatham House in London. While the name "Chatham House" is commonly used to refer to the Institute itself, the Royal Institute of International Affairs is the foreign policy executive arm of the British monarchy. According to RIIA procedures, "when a meeting, or part thereof, is held under the Chatham House Rule, participants are free to use the information received, but neither the identity nor the affiliation of the speaker(s), nor that of any other participant, may be revealed; nor may it be mentioned that the information was received at a meeting of the Institute."

The founders of the Bilderberg Group based their meetings on the Chatham House Rule because this allows people to speak as individuals and to express views that may not be those of their organizations, while encouraging free discussion. "People usually feel more relaxed if they don't have to worry about their reputation or the implications if they are publicly quoted."[12]

In 2002, the application of the Rule was clarified and its wording strengthened: "Meetings of Chatham House may be held 'on the record' or under the Chatham House Rule. In the latter case, it may be agreed with the speaker(s) that it would be conducive to free discussion that a given meeting, or part thereof, should be strictly private and thus held under the Chatham House Rule. The Chatham House Rule guarantees anonymity to those speaking within its walls in order that better international relations can be achieved. Chatham House can take disciplinary action against one of its members who breaks the Rule."[13]

The Bilderberg Group has taken this more emphatic rule to heart. Although participants attest that they attend the Group's annual meeting as private citizens and not in their official government capacity, that affirmation is dubious — particularly when you compare the Chatham House Rule to the Logan Act in the United States, where it is absolutely illegal for elected officials to meet in private with influential business executives to debate and design public policy.

The Logan Act was intended to prohibit unauthorized United States citizens from interfering in relations between the United States and foreign governments. There appear to have been no prosecutions under the Act in its almost 200-year history. However, there have been a number of judicial references to the Act, and it is not uncommon for it to be used as a political weapon.

None of which is to say that private citizens can get away with *anything* when visiting or interacting with foreign countries. They can't export or sell arms illegally, unless, of course, they belong to the Central Intelligence Agency, in which case not only are they allowed to profit from illegal arms and drug sales and influence peddling, but also to interfere in private affairs of independent states.

Among those who have attended Bilderberg Group meetings and flouted the Logan Act: Allen Dulles (CIA); Sen. William J. Fulbright (from Arkansas, a Rhodes Scholar); Dean Acheson (Secretary of State under Truman); Nelson Rockefeller and Laurence Rockefeller; Gerald Ford (former President); Henry J. Heinz II (Chairman of the H. J. Heinz Co.); Thomas L. Hughes (President of the Carnegie Endowment for International Peace); Robert S. McNamara (Kennedy's Secretary of Defense and former President of the World Bank); William P. Bundy (former President of the Ford Foundation, and editor of the Council on Foreign Relations' *Foreign Affairs* journal); John J. McCloy (former President of the Chase Manhattan Bank); George F. Kennan (former U.S. Ambassador to the Soviet Union); Paul H. Nitze (representative of Schroeder Bank — Nitze played a very prominent role in matters of Arms Control agreements, which have *always* been under the influence of the RIIA); Robert O. Anderson (Chairman of Atlantic-Richfield Co. and head of the Aspen Institute for Humanistic Studies); John D. Rockefeller IV (ex-Governor of West Virginia, U.S. Senator); Cyrus Vance (Secretary of State under Carter); Eugene Black (former President of the World Bank); Joseph Johnson (President of the Carnegie Endowment for International Peace); Henry Ford III (head of the Ford Motor Co.); Gen. Andrew J. Goodpaster (former Supreme Allied Commander in Europe, and later superintendent of the West Point Academy); Zbigniew Brzezinski (National Security Adviser to President Carter, founder of the Trilateral Commission); Gen. Alexander Haig (once European NATO Commander, former assistant to Henry Kissinger, and later Secretary of State under Reagan); and James Rockefeller (Chairman, First National City Bank).

Bilderberg meetings are always frank, but do not always conclude with consensus. For the past several years, French, British and Americans have almost come to blows over Iraq. In 2003, then-French Foreign Minister, Dominique de Villepin, openly told Henry Kissinger that if "only the Americans had told them the truth about Iraq" — that the real reason for the invasion was to gain control of oil and natural gas — perhaps they, the French, "would not have vetoed their UN resolutions. The rest of the world is not stupid, Henry." According to sources at the conference, Kissinger gloomily turned around and walked away.

British nationalism is another cause for Bilderberg concern. In 1998 at the Turnburry, Scotland meeting, British Prime Minister Tony Blair was lectured like a naughty schoolboy for not doing enough to bring Britain into the common currency. According to a source of investigative journalist Jim Tucker, "Blair assured Bilderberg members that Britain would join, but he first had to resolve 'political problems' because of a 'surge of nationalism' at home."

In the May 29, 1998 issue of *Spotlight*—a newspaper of dubious agendas—a German was reported to have told Blair, "You're a Maggie Thatcher in long pants." This was a crude reminder that Lady Thatcher had been dumped as head of state by her own Conservative Party on Bilderberg orders and replaced with trapeze artist John Major over the same issue.

John Williams, in his work, *Atlanticism: The Achilles' Heel of European Security, Self-Identity and Collective Will*, states that some of the Western elite attend Bilderberg meetings "to polish and reinforce a virtual consensus, an illusion that globalization, defined under their terms — *what's good for banking and big business is good for everybody else* — is inevitable and for the greater good of mankind."[14]

In a rare description of how Bilderberg Group discussions are structured, one of the founding members, Otto Wolff von Amerongen, the Chairman and CEO of Otto Wolff GmbH in Germany, noted how each meeting is set up with short introductions to the chosen topics, followed by a general debate.[15] It's interesting to note that von Amerongen is credited with reviving business ties between Germany and the old Soviet bloc. He served as Bonn's informal ambassador to Russia, but his past may link him to Nazi Germany's theft of Jewish holdings during World War II.

Werner Ruegemer, who co-directed a 2001 television documentary about Otto's family firm, alleged that von Amerongen was a Nazi spy in Portugal, involved in selling shares of stocks stolen from Jews and gold plundered from the central banks of European nations that Hitler had conquered. Ruegemer also claimed that von Amerongen exported tungsten — a key armaments metal used to harden steel in rifles and artillery — to Germany from Portugal, the only nation still trading tungsten with Germany through the war.

Two other delegates from the 2003 Bilderberg Conference in Versailles, who prefer to remain anonymous but are believed to be British, explain how each panel consists of a moderator and two or three people. Six "panels," with three members in each, lead the discussion. Each panel lasts for approximately two hours. After an introductory speech of about ten minutes, the rest of the participants choose when they want to enter into the debate or whether they want to speak for one, three or five minutes by raising one, three or five fingers. One-minute speakers get to speak first, etc., and then there are discussion questions lasting for five, three or two minutes. There are no introductory documents, and there are no records, although the delegates are required to prepare for the discussions in advance. The initial list of "proposed" participants is circulated as early as January, with the final selection being made in March.

To avoid infiltrations, the Bilderberg Steering Committee sets the date for the meeting four months in advance, but the name of the hotel is not announced till one week before. At the opening of the meeting, the Chairman recalls the Bilderberg Rules of Procedure, and then turns to the first item of the agenda. Bilderberg marks all distribution material to its members: *"personal and strictly confidential, and not for publication."*

Bilderberg regulars Henry Kissinger and Henry Kravis carried on extensive discussions at Bilderberg 2004. Henry's wife, Marie-Josée (shown here with Kissinger) is one of the very few wives that regularly attend the meetings. Do Kissinger and Kravis make investments based upon their insider knowledge of Bilderberg discussions and decisions?

DES ILL
BORROME

GIARDIN
PRIVAT

CHAPTER FOUR

BILDERBERG BEDFELLOWS

I t is important to distinguish between active members who assist annually and others who are only invited occasionally. About eighty members are regulars who have attended for many years. Fringe people, who are invited to report on subjects related to their sphere of influence or professional and academic knowledge, are clueless about the formal structure behind the Bilderberg Group, and remain in absolute ignorance of the Group's greater goals and universal objectives. A select few are invited because Bilderbergers think they may be useful tools in their globalist plan and are later helped to reach very powerful elected positions. One-time invitees who fail to impress, however, are cast aside.

The most dramatic example of a "useful recruit" was the obscure governor of Arkansas, Bill Clinton, who attended his first Bilderberg meeting at Baden-Baden, Germany, in 1991. There, David Rockefeller told Clinton why the North America Free Trade Agreement (NAFTA) was a Bilderberg priority and that the group needed him to support it. The next year, Clinton was elected President, and — guess what? — he was a strong proponent of NAFTA.

The following list tracks the coincidences between the dates of some major leaders' attendance at a Bilderberg meeting and the dates of their subsequent career moves:

• Bill Clinton: attended the Bilderberg meeting in 1991; won the Democratic Party's nomination and was elected President in 1992.

• Tony Blair: attended the Bilderberg meeting in 1993; became party leader in July 1994 and elected Prime Minister in May 1997.
• George Robertson: attended the Bilderberg meeting in 1998; appointed NATO Secretary-General in August 1999.
• Romano Prodi: attended the Bilderberg meeting in 1999; sworn in as the President of Europe in September 1999. His term lasted until January 2005; in 2006, Prodi was elected Prime Minister of Italy.

THE FRANCOIS MITTERRAND TEST

On December 10, 1980, the Bilderberg's "Committee of 300" ordered the official resurrection of Francois Mitterrand, a socialist discarded by the French establishment, as France's next president. According to John Coleman, whose book, *Conspirators' Hierarchy: The Story of the Committee of 300,* discusses these events, "Mitterrand was in the process of being picked up, dusted off and returned to power."[16]

Mitterand's comeback speech expressed his disdain for capitalism: "Industrial capitalist development is the opposite of freedom. We must put an end to it. The economic systems of the 20th and 21st century will use machines to crush man, first in the domain of nuclear energy, which is already producing formidable results."

Coleman's reflections make one shudder: "Mitterrand's return to the Elysee Palace was a great triumph for socialism. It proved that the 'Committee of 300' was powerful enough to predict happenings and then make them happen, by force, or by whatever means it took to make its point that it could crush any and all opposition even if, as in the case of Mitterrand, he had been totally rejected a few short days before by a discerning political power group in Paris."

This "discerning political power group," who rejected Mitterrand, along with a large segment of his own socialist party, was the far-right National Front led by Jean-Marie Le Pen, a fixture in French politics who campaigned for tight immigration controls long before President Jacques Chirac introduced stricter policies, which in November 2005 set off rioting in France among unemployed youth.

SHAPING TURKEY'S FUTURE

Four days after two Turkish attendees — Gazi Ercel, Governor of the Central Bank of Turkey, and Emre Gonensay, Turkish Foreign Minister — returned home from the 1996 King City Bilderberg meeting, the Turkish government fell.

In a surprise move, Mesut Yilmaz, Turkish Prime Minister, abruptly quit. His resignation effectively dissolved the coalition government patched together between the True Path Party, led by conservative ex-Prime Minister Tansue Cille, and his centrist Motherland Party. Yilmaz's resignation cleared the way for Necmettin Erbakan, head of the pro-Islamic Welfare Party, to form the next Turkish government. This change in government gave the Bilderbergers a golden opportunity to project Islamic influence into the soft underbelly of Christian Europe, thus creating ethnic tensions and destabilizing the region.

THE PORTUGUESE GAMBIT

According to a well-informed source, 2004's Bilderberg meeting in Stresa, Italy, set up wholesale promotion for Portuguese Bilderbergers. Following that session, major changes in leadership took place in Portugal.

> • Pedro M. Lopes Santana, the little-known Mayor of Lisbon was suddenly appointed Prime Minister by the republic's president.
> • José M. Durão Barroso, former Prime Minister, was appointed President of the European Commission.
> • José Sócrates, Member of Parliament, was elected leader of the Socialist Party after Eduardo Ferro Rodrigues resigned May 25, 2003, in a social/political crisis brought on by a police investigation into fifteen cases, allegedly involving him, of sexual violence against minors in state-run foster homes between 1999 and 2000. (Sources close to the investigation confirmed to me that the crisis was stage-managed from behind the scenes by Bilderberg members.) Sócrates became Portugal's Prime Minister in 2005.

THE BILDERBERGERS' VICE PRESIDENTIAL CANDIDATE

In July 2004, Bilderberg members literally chose Democratic presidential candidate John Kerry's former rival as his running mate, after John Edwards, in his first-time attendance at a Bilderberg gathering, impressed them with his vision for American politics. Various sources, whose names I cannot disclose, have independently corroborated that, after hearing John Edwards speak about NAFTA during the second day of the conference, Henry Kissinger telephoned John Kerry with the following comment: "John, this is Henry. We have found your Vice President."

In another momentary lifting of the veil the *New York Times* of July 8, 2004 also suggested the powerful group's involvement:

> **Did Bilderbergers Select Edwards?**
> Several people pointed to the secretive and exclusive Bilderberg conference of some 120 people that this year drew the likes of Henry A. Kissinger, Melinda Gates and Richard A. Perle to Stresa, Italy, in early June, as helping win Mr. Kerry's heart. Mr. Edwards spoke so well in a debate on American politics with the Republican Ralph Reed that participants broke Bilderberg rules to clap before the end of the session. Beforehand, Mr. Edwards traveled to Brussels to meet with NATO officials, brandishing his foreign-policy credentials.

POWERFUL BUDDIES

To understand who controls the leadership of NATO, the world's largest military operation or today's World Army, you only have to look at the NATO Secretaries General who have belonged to the Bilderberg Group: Joseph Luns (1971-1984), Lord Carrington ('84-'88), Manfred Wörner ('88-'94), Willy Claes ('94-'95), Javier Solana ('95-'99), Lord Robertson ('99-'04), Jaap G. de Hoop Scheffer ('04-). With such military connections, how much easier it becomes to initiate Bilderberg policy in areas like the Persian Gulf, Iraq, Serbia, Bosnia, Kosovo, Syria, North Korea, Afghanistan, and so on, with an army under one's control.

As a note of interest, in August 1956, Joseph Rettinger wrote on page 11 of the Bilderberg Report that this "group may be a factory of initiative; we decided, however, that none of the new ideas and initiatives would be developed by the group, but that they should be passed on to some persons or organization who would further develop them."

In fact, during the final day of the inaugural 1954 conference, a proposal was submitted (p.8 of the General Report) by the Bilderberg Steering Committee whereby the European Defence Community would be integrated into NATO with an objective of serving as a "central organ of decision, capable of action in the political and economic as well as in the military." Thus, it was decided that the Bilderbergers would use NATO to control European affairs.

Former U.S. Defense Secretary Donald Rumsfeld and Ireland's General Peter Sutherland (former European Union commissioner and chairman of Goldman Sachs and British Petroleum) are active Bilderbergers. In 2000, Rumsfeld and Sutherland earned a bit of pocket money by serving together on the board of the Swiss energy company, ABB. Their secret alliance became public knowledge when it was disclosed that ABB sold two light-water nuclear reactors to an active member of the "axis of evil" — North Korea. Needless to say, British Petroleum doesn't advertise this when the company promotes its "safety first" public initiatives.

Every British Prime Minister for the past thirty years has felt compelled to attend Bilderberg Conferences. In fact, some say the Bilderberg Group is really a creation of MI6 under the direction of the Royal Institute of International Affairs. "The plan of British Intelligence was to get Joseph Rettinger, who would later become one of the key founding fathers of the European Movement, to organize the Bilderberger Group as the real power brokers behind the different governments of Europe and of the United States."[17]

According to another observer, "Rettinger [a Jesuit] was funded with secret money from the U.S. State Department and kept afloat with massive subventions through Thomas Braden, head of the CIA's International Organization Division."[18]

John Coleman relates in *Conspirators' Hierarchy* that the idea came from Alastair Buchan (a board member of the RIIA and a member of the Round Table, as well as a son of Lord Tweedsmuir) and Duncan Sandys (a prominent politician, and son-in-law of the late Winston Churchill), who was a friend of Rettinger's, and himself also a Jesuit priest and a 33rd Degree Freemason.

The British newspaper *The Observer* reported the following in its April 7, 1963 edition: "These people [Bilderbergers] maintain that the future belongs to technocrats, because the rumour among them is that the grave questions of international affairs are too delicate to be left in the hands of diplomats. However, the 'clandestinity' of their debates shows that they only seek one thing: effective domination over the peoples of the world, but by dissimulating themselves and by leaving the responsibility of governments in the hands of petty politicians."

The Bilderberg Group may, in fact, be a natural extrapolation of Britain's Coefficients Club, founded in 1902. Lord Alfred Milner spoke of his vision for the future during a 1903 meeting at the St. Ermin's Hotel, over half a century before the Bilderbergers were founded. At that meeting, Milner stressed the point:

> We must have an aristocracy — not of privilege, but of understanding and purpose — or mankind will fail... And here my peculiar difficulty with democracy comes in. If humanity at large is capable of that high education and those creative freedoms our hope demands, much more must its better and more vigorous types be so capable. And if those who have power and leisure now, and freedom to respond to imaginative appeals, cannot be won to the idea of collective self-development, then the whole of humanity cannot be won to that. The solution does not lie in direct confrontation. We can defeat democracy because we understand the workings of the human mind, the mental hinterlands hidden behind the persona.
>
> We need constructive imagination working within the vast complex of powerful people, clever people, enterprising people, influential people, amidst whom power is diffused today, to produce that self-conscious highly selective, open-minded, devoted aristocratic culture, which seems to me to be the next necessary phase in the development of human affairs. I see human progress, not as the spontaneous product of crowds of raw minds swayed by elementary needs, but as a natural but elaborate result of intricate human interdependencies, of human energy and curiosity liberated and acting at leisure, of human passions and motives modified and redirected by literature and art.[19]

We can put the words of Lord Milner in perspective better by reviewing what Italian industrialist, the late chairman of Fiat, Giovanni Agnelli had to say: "European integration is our goal, and where the politicians have failed, we industrialists hope to succeed." Indeed they do.

If MI6 needed a royal face to give the Bilderbergers public support and promotional possibilities, then Prince Bernhard of the Netherlands, known for his numerous close ties to European Royalty and top industrialists, was an ideal contact-man, and thus was seemingly given the "diplomatic" presidency of the Group. But it was Rettinger who actually managed the group from behind the scenes until his death on June 12, 1960.

The 1957 Bilderberg Conference initiated Denis Healey into its ranks. Britain's Healey, who is often described as the best Labor politician never elected its leader (despite standing twice), was a founding member of the so-called "European Movement" promoting understanding and future cooperation of American and European politicians, businessmen, top bureaucrats and military leaders. The group received financial support from a New York-based organization, which called itself the "American Committee on United Europe." Healey did not know it at the time, but the group was a CIA front, whose leadership included General Donovan, wartime head of the OSS (precursor to the CIA), then-Secretary of State George Marshall and the ubiquitous Allen Dulles. Healey was later appointed as Chancellor of the Exchequer, or the British cabinet minister responsible for all financial matters, second only to the Prime Minister in power.

Many believe I am connecting a remarkable series of coincidences and seeing conspiracy. Perhaps, but the coincidences grow thicker.

Bilderberg Chairman Viscount Étienne Davignon and Paul Wolfowitz at Bilderberg 2005

Bilderberg Steering Committee member, Peter Sutherland Chairman of BP and Chairman of Goldman Sachs International, Director-General WTO, at Bilderberg 2004

David Rockefeller needs "no stinking badges," here at Bilderberg 2005.

At Bilderberg 2004, Rothschild representative Franco Bernabé talks with Henry Kravis, while Ruchard Haass, President of the Council on Foreign Relations (CFR) talks on the phone. Diplomat/nvestment banker Richard Holbrooke is in the back with a glass.

CHAPTER FIVE

BILDERBERG OBJECTIVES

The Bilderbergers are searching for the age of post-nationalism: when we won't have countries, but rather regions of Earth surrounded by Universal values. That is to say, a global economy, one World government (selected rather than elected) and a universal religion. To assure themselves of reaching these objectives, the Bilderbergers focus on a "greater technical approach and less awareness on behalf of the general public."[20]

—William Shannon

The Bilderberg Group's chief fear is organized resistance. Members do not want the common people of the world to figure out what they are planning for the world's future: mainly, a One World Government (World Company) with a single, global marketplace, policed by one world army, and financially regulated by one "World Bank" using one global currency.

How the Bilderbergers intend to achieve their One World vision is outlined in the following "wish list." They want:

- **One International Identity.** By empowering international bodies to completely destroy all national identity through subversion from within, they intend to establish one set of universal values. No others will be allowed to flourish in the future.
* **Centralized Control of the People.** By means of mind control, they plan to direct all humanity to obey their wishes. The blueprint of their plan is chillingly

described in Zbigniew Brzezinski's book, *Between Two Ages: America's Role in the Technetronic Era.* A man with a Ph.D. from Harvard in 1953 and a founder of the Rockefeller-controlled Trilateral Commission, Brzezinski has an impressive resume. Not only was he Carter's National Security Advisor, but also a member of Ronald Reagan's Foreign Intelligence Advisory Board and co-chair of George H.W. Bush's National Security Advisory Task Force in 1988. He is, as well, an associate of Henry Kissinger and well known for his presentations to several Bilderberg Conferences. He foresees, under the New World Order, no middle class, only rulers and servants.

• **A Zero-Growth Society.** In a post-industrial period, zero growth will be necessary to destroy vestiges of general prosperity. When there is prosperity, there is progress. Prosperity and progress make it impossible to implement repression, and you need repression if you hope to divide society into owners and slaves. The end of prosperity will bring an end to the production of nuclear-generated electric power and all industrialization (except for the computer and service industries.) The remaining Canadian and American industries would be exported to poor countries such as Bolivia, Peru, Ecuador, Nicaragua, where slave labor is cheap. One of the principal objectives for NAFTA will then be realized.

• **A State of Perpetual Imbalance.** By artificially manufacturing crises that will put people under continual duress — physically, mentally and emotionally — it is possible to keep people in a perpetual state of imbalance. Too tired and strung-out to decide their own destinies, populations will be confused and demoralized to the extent that, "faced with too many choices, apathy on a massive scale will result."[21]

• **Centralized Control of All Education.** One of the reasons for the European Community, "American Union" and the future Asian Union to seek greater control of education in general is to allow One World globalists to sterilize the world's true past. Their efforts are bearing "fantastic" fruit. Today's youth are almost completely ignorant of the lessons of history, individual liberties and the meaning of freedom. From the globalist point of view, this arrangement simplifies the program.

• **Centralized Control of All Foreign and Domestic Policies.** What the United States does affects the whole world. Right now the Bilderbergers seem to exercise some control over U.S. President Bush and his policies. Canada, while appearing to retain its own sovereignty, marches to U.S. demands. Europe, of course, is now influenced by the consensus of the European Community.

• **Empowerment of the United Nations.** By using what the United Nations already has in place, they plan to shape it into a *de jure,* and then *de facto*, world government and charge a direct UN tax on "world citizens."

• **Western Trading Bloc.** By expanding NAFTA throughout the Western Hemisphere into South America, an "American Union" will eventually form, similar to the European Union.

• **Expansion of NATO.** As the UN intervenes in more trouble-spots globally, as it is in Afghanistan now, NATO becomes the UN's world army.

• **One Legal System.** The International Court of Justice is to become the sole legal system for the world.

• **One Socialist Welfare State.** The Bilderbergers envision a socialist welfare state, where obedient slaves will be rewarded and non-conformists targeted for extermination.

The Bilderberg Group has the power and influence to impose its policies on any nation of the world. We've already seen how far-reaching their tentacles are — grasping to control the President of the U.S.A., the Prime Minister of Canada, all the main news media outlets in the free world, all the most important politicians, financiers and media as well as every central banker of every major country in the world, the U.S. Federal

Reserve, thus its money supply, the International Monetary Fund, the World Bank, and all the way to the UN. With such connections, they are capable of destroying anyone, big or small, who gets in the way of their plans to create a One World Order, as I will demonstrate through many hair-raising, and mind-boggling examples.

For example in *Adventures with Extremists* (Picador, 2001), Jon Ronson describes how, during the Falklands War, the British government requested international sanctions be implemented against Argentina, but "encountered stiff opposition. At a Bilderberg meeting in Sandefjord, Norway, however, David Owen, British MP stood up and gave the fieriest speech in favour of imposing them. Well, the speech changed a lot of minds. I'm sure that various foreign ministers went back to their respective countries and told their leaders what David Owen had said. And you know what? Sanctions were imposed."

Alas, this simple and beautiful story of international cooperation amongst nations falls far short of a complete account.

BILDERBERG TEST RUN

One Bilderberg objective is to de-industrialize the world by suppressing all scientific development, starting with the United States. Especially targeted are the fusion experiments as a future source of nuclear energy for peaceful purposes. "Development of the fusion torch would blow the Bilderberger conception of 'limited natural resources' right out of the window. A fusion torch properly used could create unlimited untapped natural resources from the most ordinary substances, thus benefiting mankind in a manner, which is, as yet, not even remotely comprehended by the public."[22]

Why is nuclear energy hated so much by the New World Order? According to John Coleman, a former British MI6 secret agent, nuclear power stations generating abundant cheap electricity are "*The* key to bringing Third World countries out of their backward state. With nuclear energy generating electricity in cheap and abundant supplies, Third World countries would gradually become independent of U.S. foreign aid, which keeps them in servitude, and begin to assert their sovereignty."

Less foreign aid means less control of a country's natural resources by the IMF, and greater freedom and independence for the people. It is this idea of developing nations taking charge of their own destinies that is repugnant to the Bilderbergers and their surrogates.

This was confirmed on page 13 of the Bilderberg 1955 General Report: "In the field of atomic energy, scientific discovery was continually overtaking itself.... It could not be excluded that the scientists would put the bomb into the hands of more and more people and soon 'the atomic bomb would become the arm of the poor.' The same applied to the development of atomic energy for peaceful purposes, where we had almost to foresee the unforeseeable."

Nuclear energy, according to the Bilderberger ideals, is not for the poor nations of the planet. Rather, it is the definitive weapon to threaten unwilling-to-submit Third and Fourth World nations, as illustrated by the Falklands War.

According to my own investigative channels, a top-ranking member of the Bilderberg council made a claim also confirmed by Coleman: "The subsequent overthrow of the Argentine government, followed by economic chaos and political upheavals, were planned by Kissinger Associates acting in concert with Lord Carrington,"[23] (former British Foreign Secretary and another top-ranking member of the Bilderberg council). We also learned that the Argentine operation was planned by the Rockefeller-controlled Aspen Institute of Colorado.

The reason this action became so important is that the Bilderbergers saw their post-industrial zero-growth goal disintegrating, and acted accordingly by making "an example of Argentina as a warning to other Latin American nations to forget any ideas they may have had to promote nationalism, independence and sovereign integrity."[24]

The choice of Argentina was deliberate, because the richest nation in South America was providing most of Mexico's nuclear power technology, against the wishes of the Bilderbergers. The Falklands War ended that mutually beneficial collaboration in a hurry. Without a doubt, the Group prefers to have Mexico as an outlet of cheap, sweatshop slave labor, rather than to have it assert itself as a full-fledged trading partner.

Moreover, because of a constant barrage of negative media propaganda, few Americans realize, even today, just how vital the Latin America market is to the interests of the United States, ranging from technology to heavy industrial equipment. Healthy trade with Latin

America would "galvanize many faltering American companies and provide thousands of new jobs."[25]

The Bilderbergers sought to prevent this at all costs.

BILDERBERG MEDDLING IN FOREIGN AFFAIRS OF SOVEREIGN NATIONS

These are just some of the ways the Bilderberg Group has sought to intervene in countries' affairs:

- The Bilderbergers took the decision for the U.S. to establish formal relations with China before Nixon's administration made it a public policy.
- At a meeting in Saltsjöbaden, Sweden, in 1973, the Bilderbergers agreed to increase the price of oil to $12 a barrel, a 350% jump meant to create economic chaos in the United States and Western Europe, in order to prop up the oil corporations' sagging fortunes. The perceived oil shortage formed part of the backdrop of the staged Arab-Israeli war, and provided a cover for the formal endorsement of major price agreements negotiated prior to the outbreak of war.
- In 1983, the Bilderbergers got a secret promise out of the then "ultraconservative" President Ronald Reagan to transfer 50 billion dollars of American taxpayers' money to Third World and Communist countries through its favorite conduits, the IMF and the World Bank. That pledge was more than kept, and became known as the "Brady plan."
- The Bilderbergers orchestrated the decision to get rid of Margaret Thatcher as British Prime Minister, because she opposed the willing hand-over of British sovereignty to the European Super State designed by the Bilderbergers. And we all watched incredulously as her own party sold her out in favor of the Bilderberg poodle, John Major.
- In 1985, the Bilderbergers agreed to give full support to the Strategic Defence Initiative (Star Wars), long before it became the official policy of the U.S. government.

• At their 1990 meeting at Glen Cove, Long Island, New York, they decided that taxes had to be raised to pay more towards the debt owed to the international bankers. Bilderberg luminary, President George H.W. Bush, signed off on the tax-hiking "budget agreement" in 1990, and it lost him the election.

• At the 1992 meeting, the group debated the possibility of conditioning the public into accepting the idea of a UN Army that could, through the use of force, interfere in the internal policy and conflict resolution of sovereign nations. This Bilderberger proposal was given front-page coverage by two of Canada's leading periodicals, the *Toronto Star* and the *National Post*, during the 2006 meeting in Ottawa.

• The multimillion-dollar sale of Ontario Hydro, owned at the time by the Canadian government, was discussed for the first time at the Bilderberg meeting in King City in 1996. Shortly after, Ontario Hydro was broken up into five independent companies and privatized.

• Starting at the 1996 meeting and continuing through 1998, Kosovo fell under the microscope of the Bilderbergers when they discussed the formation of a greater Albanian state following "trusteeship" of an "independent" Kosovo, the dismemberment of Yugoslavia (by the return of its northern province, which has 350,000 ethnic Hungarians, to Hungary) as part of a general re-drawing of borders in the region (calculated to continue regional instability and conflict), and the reconstruction of billions of dollars of destroyed regional infrastructure at western taxpayers' expense.

• Leaked reports from the 2002 meeting stated that the war in Iraq had been delayed until March 2003, at a time when every newspaper in the world was expecting the attack to be launched in the summer/fall of 2002.

• In 1999, Kenneth Clarke MP, Martin S. Feldstein, president of the National Bureau of Economic Research, Stanley Fisher, deputy managing director of the International Monetary Fund (IMF), Ottmar Issing, board member of the European Central Bank and Jean-Claude Trichet, governor of the Bank of France, discussed "Dollarization" as the next step after the single European currency.

• The Bilderbergers have discussed the formation of an Asian bloc under the leadership of Japan, with free trade, a single currency and a political union similar to the European Union.

• The splintering of Canada as a step toward an American Union was originally scheduled for 1997, but unexpected media coverage in the *Toronto Star*, Canada's most popular daily newspaper, during the 1996 meeting in King City, at least forced the group to postpone their plan. The proposed breakup of Canada was described in several books on the subject, including *New World Order Corruption in Canada*, a collection of essays edited by Robert O'Driscoll and Elizabeth Elliott (Saigon Press, 1994).

CHAPTER SIX

BILDERBERG PUPPETS

From the start of his political career as governor of California, Ronald Reagan distanced himself from tough, old-time traditionalists and put Rockefeller men in as his key advisors. By his 1980 presidential election, those who thought "conservative, traditional America" had won could not have imagined how wrong they were. Though Reagan promised, if elected, to dismiss the Chairman of the Federal Reserve, Paul A. Volcker, because of his anti-inflation policy, Reagan broke his word, to the disbelief of the conservative wing of the Republican Party, once he took office.

By coincidence or not, Anthony Wedgewood Benn, a member of the British Parliament told members of the Socialist International meeting in Washington on December 8, 1980, "You can thrive under Volcker's credit collapse if you *profile* [translation: brainwash] Reagan to intensify the credit collapse."

These comments bring several questions immediately to mind: What did Benn mean? Was he implying someone had influence over Ronald Reagan? Why would Reagan break his word to his own party? Why did he favor Rockefeller advisors to the exclusion of others on his personal team?

One of Reagan's "insiders" was Peter Vickers Hall, a man known to be a top Fabianist in the U.S., and a member of the Tavistock Institute for Human Relations, a Bilderberg-affiliated organization. In 1981, Hall made this speech: "There are two Americas. One is the nineteenth century, heavy, industry-based society. The other is the growing post-industrial society, in some cases built on the shards of the old America. It is the crisis between these two worlds which will produce the economic and social catastrophe of the next decade. The two worlds are in fundamental opposition; they cannot coexist. In the end, the post industrial world must crush and obliterate the other one."

He was predicting the demise of the U.S economy and industry. How alarming is that to hear from a man so closely connected to the President of the United States twenty-five years ago? Is it possible Reagan was a Bilderberg foil placed in the White House to fulfill a specific role for his sponsors?

In his book, *Conspirators' Hierarchy: The Story of the Committee of 300*, John Coleman, makes this claim: "That the advice [Peter Vickers Hall's] was taken and applied to the Reagan administration can be seen in the collapse of the savings and loan, and banking industries, which accelerated under Reagan economic policies." Coleman also notes, in passing, that Milton Friedman presided over the Bilderberg plans to de-industrialize America "using the Reagan presidency to accelerate the collapse of first the steel industry, and then the auto and housing industries."

It is upsetting to consider that the Bilderbergers often appear to be a nearly omnipotent force with no counterweight capable of standing up to them. After losing her prime ministership to John Major, Lady Thatcher told Jim Tucker at the *Spotlight* newspaper that she considered being denounced by the Bilderbergers a "tribute," because neither Britain nor any country should surrender its sovereignty. At least Lady Thatcher was only forced out of office and kept her life. The same can't be said for Aldo Moro, Italian Prime Minister.

BILDERBERG CONNECTION TO THE ALDO MORO ASSASSINATION

In 1982, John Coleman, a former intelligence operative with access to top echelons of power and secrets, revealed that Italy's former Prime Minister, Aldo Moro, "a loyal member of the Christian Democrat Party, who opposed 'zero growth' and population reductions planned for his country was murdered by assassins controlled by P2 Masonry with the object of bringing Italy into line with Club of Rome and Bilderberg orders to de-industrialize the country and considerably reduce its population."

Coleman claims in *Conspirators' Hierarchy* that the globalists wanted to use Italy to destabilize the Middle East, their main objective. "Moro's plans to stabilize Italy, through full employment and industrial and political peace, would have strengthened Catholic opposition to Communism and made the destabilization of the Middle East — a prime goal — that much harder."

Coleman described with meticulous detail the sequence of events that paralyzed the Italian nation: how Moro was kidnapped by the Red Brigades in the spring of 1978 in broad daylight and subsequently brutally shot to death, with all of his bodyguards murdered in cold blood. On November 10th, 1982, in a Rome courtroom, Gorrado Guerzoni, a close friend of the deceased, testified that Aldo Moro, who had been a leading politician for decades, was "threatened by an agent of the Royal Institute for International Affairs (RIIA) while he was still the U.S. Secretary of State."

Coleman recounts how, at the trial of members of the Red Brigades, "several of them testified that they knew of high-level U.S. involvement in the plot to kill Moro." In June and July of 1982, "Aldo Moro's widow testified that her husband's murder came about as a result of serious threats against his life, made by what she called a *high ranking United States political figure.*"

Asked by the judge if she could tell the court what was said by this person, Eleanora Moro repeated the exact phrase given by Guerzoni in his prior testimony: "Either you stop your political line or you will pay dearly for it."

In one of the more chilling pages of his book, Coleman writes the following: "Recalled by the judge, Guerzoni was asked if he could identify the person Mrs. Moro was talking about. Guerzoni replied that it was Henry Kissinger, as he had previously intimated."

Why would a high-ranking U.S. diplomat threaten a leading politician of an independent European nation? Guerzoni's sensational and potentially damaging testimony to U.S.-Italian relations was instantly broadcast all across Western Europe on November 10th, 1982. Yet, apparently, not one television station in America thought the news worthy of anyone's attention, and this despite the fact that Kissinger had been condemned as an accomplice to these murders.

That blackout wasn't really surprising, as we shall see in Part Two concerning the Council on Foreign Relations.

BILDERBERG BAPTISM OF BILL CLINTON

As a final illustration of Bilderberg influence, President Bill Clinton was "anointed" for the presidency at the 1991 Bilderberg Conference in Baden-Baden, which he attended. What was completely unknown to most of the U.S. and world media was that Clinton then took an unexpected, unannounced trip to Moscow, directly from this Bilderberg meeting.

On Tuesday, June 9th, he met for ninety minutes with Soviet Interior Minister Vadim Bakatin. Mr. Bakatin, a minister in the doomed cabinet of President Mikhail Gorbachev, was in the middle of campaigning in the fiercely-contested Presidential election, the vote for which was a mere six days away. Yet, he took time out of his crowded schedule to meet unexpectedly with the internationally-unknown Governor of Arkansas. Why?

Mr. Bakatin's subsequent career might provide a clue. Although Gorbachev lost the Presidential election, Bakatin, a "reformer," was rewarded by President Yeltsin with the top spot at the KGB. It appears that President Clinton was sent by the Bilderbergers directly to Moscow to get his KGB student-era, anti-Viet Nam War files "buried" before he announced his candidacy for the U.S. Presidency, which occurred some two-and-a-half months later.

One of the few U.S. papers to run this story was the *Arkansas Democrat*, which did so under the headline: "CLINTON HAS POWERFUL BUDDY IN U.S.S.R. – NEW HEAD OF KGB."

It may come as no surprise, therefore, that, according to sources, Bilderberger-backed candidate Clinton promised President Yeltsin that, if he won the election, Russian warships would be given full refuelling and other port privileges at all U.S. Navy bases. This promise was more than kept once Clinton was sworn in as the U.S. President.

According to Samuel "Sandy" Berger, formerly Bill Clinton's national security advisor, speaking at the Brookings Institution, "Globalization – economic, technological, cultural and political integration – is not a choice. It's a growing fact. It's a fact that will proceed inexorably, with or without our approval. It's a fact we ignore to our peril."

He is right. As Jim Tucker once told me, "God may have created the universe, but as far as planet earth is concerned, the message to

God from the Bilderberg Group is simply this: *Thanks, but we'll take it from here.*"

CHAPTER SEVEN

WATERGATE CON GAME

The Watergate crisis is a case of mistaken identity and a travesty of justice. The truth behind Watergate has never been revealed, but those who orchestrated the overthrow of the Shah, the war in the Falklands, the death of Aldo Moro and the downfall of Margaret Thatcher are again implicated. Do we know for sure that Richard Nixon abused his presidential powers? What if the "smoking gun" and the "damning" evidence of "abuse" were manufactured? Pat Nixon always claimed her husband was framed, and believed history will eventually vindicate him.

According to my sources, who attended Bilderberg conferences in the early 1970s, the role of the *Washington Post* newspaper was to keep the heat on Nixon by releasing one "revelation" after another, thereby engendering a climate of public distrust of President Nixon.

Top level British Secret Intelligence Service intelligence analyst, John Coleman, in his book, *Conspirators' Hierarchy*, directly pointed his finger at Katherine Graham, the publisher of the *Washington Post* from 1963 to 1993, and accused her of murdering her husband, Philip L. Graham, a case the FBI has officially classed as "suicide." He alleges that she killed her husband just so she could take control of the newspaper. What's more interesting is that such a grave accusation never garnered a civil suit for libeling the now dead multimillionairess (and confirmed Bilderberg member). Those who have studied the Bilderbergers and their system of protections believe that to address the charges would give Coleman more credence, and Katherine Graham's family, friends and associates have no intention of doing that. They have chosen the path of "discretion is the better part of truth," to adapt a familiar cliché.

Yet, the *Washington Post*'s part in the Watergate crisis demonstrates the immense power of the press, as was quite properly anticipated by the controllers of the U.S. media, better known as Council on Foreign Relations (CFR) — a group we shall examine in Part Two. The scandal involving Nixon and his administration mortally wounded the Office of the Presidency and assaulted the institutions upon which the republic of the United States stands. How did this benefit the Bilderberg Group? Certainly, an independent and strong America with an incorruptible head of state (I do not mean Richard Nixon) would have made it impossible for the New World Order to realize their plans of global conquest.

Who played a significant role in humiliating President Nixon?

One of the most visible players was David Young, head of the "Plumbers," an interagency spy group with a Gestapo mentality working for the White House Special Investigations Unit, which Nixon created under John Ehrlichman. Young, who originally worked under one of the founding Bilderberg members, Henry Kissinger, at the National Security Council, "bugged" the White House. His tapes were the "smoking gun" that felled Nixon. In these incriminating tapes, Nixon is heard admitting he ordered the cover-up of the Watergate break-ins as he discusses ways to frustrate the Watergate investigations. The recordings further proved that the President had lied to the American public for nine months.

Another key player was ex-CIA and FBI officer, James W. McCord, who was the security director of the Committee for the Re-election of the President (Nixon). It seems he "accidentally" left the infamous piece of tape on a door in the Watergate building that alerted a security guard to the break-in. McCord was arrested the night of the burglary along with four other men. He pleaded guilty and was convicted on six counts. He later wrote a letter to Judge John J. Sirica, the judge of the Watergate case, in which he claimed perjury had been committed. McCord's allegations — that the White House knew of the burglary and attempted to cover it up — drove the investigators to push harder to seize the secret tape-recording system in the White House. After McCord confessed, he accused CIA operatives of burning his personal papers in his home. McCord still feared the CIA would kill him once he was locked up in the penitentiary to serve his sentence.

The pivotal player in the Watergate affair, however, was none other than General Alexander Haig. The general was a product of the Round Table, the Bilderberg's parallel group. In *The Tavistock Institute: Sinister and Deadly*, the ground-breaking book on the sinister plans of the world's foremost brainwashing institute, John Coleman untangled the secret arrangements between the shadow government, U.S. politicians in the service of the New World Order and the obliging press. He notes how Haig came to the attention of Joseph Califano, an American member of the Queen of England's Round Table. Califano, legal council of the Democratic National Convention, actually interviewed Alfred Baldwin, one of the "plumbers" in the Watergate break-in, and made notes on McCord's background and why McCord selected Baldwin to be on his "team."

"Even more damaging," writes Coleman, "Califano's memorandum contained all details of transcripts of wiretaps of conversations between Nixon and the re-election committee, all this *before* the break-in occurred."

Why wasn't Califano arraigned for withholding evidence?

Coleman got his hands on priceless Tavistock secret manuals that spelled out the methodology used to destroy President Richard Nixon: "The way President Nixon was first isolated, surrounded by traitors and then confused, followed to the letter the Tavistock-method of gaining full control of a person according to the methodology laid down by Tavistock's chief theoretician, Dr. Kurt Lewin."

That methodology included the following: "One of the main techniques for breaking morale through a strategy of terror consists in exactly this tactic — keep the person hazy as to where he stands and just what he may expect. In addition, if frequent vacillations between severe disciplinary measures and promises of good treatment together with the spreading of contradictory news, make the cognitive structure of this situation utterly unclear, then the individual may cease even to know a particular plan would lead toward or away from his goal. Under these conditions, even those individuals who have definite goals and are ready to take risks are paralyzed by severe inner conflict in regard to what to do."

So successfully were Tavistock terror tactics and brainwashing used to remove the President of the United States that Americans began to believe the plethora of lies, distortions and Orwellian double-talk mounted by the conspirators as truth, when in fact, "Watergate" was an outright lie from beginning to end.

Nixon and his two closest aides, Haldeman and Ehrlichman, had no clue as to what was going on. They were no match for the combined forces of the Bilderberg/RIIA/Tavistock Institute under the direction of the British MI6, with a secret annual budget, unknown to the public, of around $350-500 million. (As a side note, the British Parliament has no effective jurisdiction over MI6.) They were completely overwhelmed and never knew that "David Young, a graduate of Oxford and a long-time Kissinger associate through Round Table assets such as the law firm of Milbank Tweed, was working in the basement of the White House, supervising leaks."

James McCord's confession of perjury to Judge John Sirica should have warned Nixon that he was being set up for a downfall. But, the confused and emotionally paralysed Nixon followed, to the letter, the Tavistock profiling of how a person's morale can be broken through a strategy of terror.

Kissinger was responsible for brainwashing and confusing President Nixon, while, in effect, it was Haig who ran the U.S. government during this "orientation period" of the President.

Coleman writes that "on the insistence of the RIIA, Haig virtually took over the management of the Government of the United States after the April 1973 coup d'etat."

Haig filled the top one hundred posts in Washington with men from the Brookings Institution, Institute for Policy Studies (IPS) and the Council on Foreign Relations, men who were loyal to the superimposed interests of the Bilderberg's World Order above those of the United States of America.

According to Coleman's intelligence sources, in the spring of 1970, William McDermott of the FBI went to see the top security officer at the RAND Corporation in Santa Monica, California, to warn him that Daniel Ellsberg was suspected of stealing, for the U.S. military, RAND study papers on Viet Nam and copying them before returning them to the RAND office. RAND is a non-profit organization created to connect military planning with research and development decisions. RAND is also referred to as the U.S. Brainwashing Institution, for its experiments in methodology for social planning and psychological response to stress. In the subsequent meeting with RAND's director, Dr. Henry Rowan, McDermott was told by Rowan that a Department of Defense (DOD) inquiry was already in progress. Because of Rowan's assurance, the FBI dropped its investigation of Ellsberg. What the FBI didn't know was that Rowan was Ellsberg's best friend, and Coleman discovered that "no inquiry was in progress, nor did the DOD ever conduct one. Ellsberg retained his security clearance at RAND and blatantly went on removing and copying Viet Nam War documents right up to the time of his exposure during the Pentagon Papers affair, which rocked the Nixon Administration to its foundations."

At that stage, Nixon's Atomic Energy Commission was dismantled, so Chairman James Schlesinger could then be drafted to serve as the government's Secretary of Defense. It would be Schlesinger's task to require all military commanders to refuse orders from the White House prior to top Republicans' threatening to impeach the President. Instead, Nixon voluntarily resigned August 8, 1974.

Was the humiliation of Nixon a lesson and a warning to future Presidents of the United States not to imagine they could defy the direction or manipulation of the Shadow World Government and win?

More specifically, the collapse of Nixon's presidency led to the reduction of the armed services after U.S. withdrawal from Viet Nam and the de-industrializing of the United States with the signing of the General Agreement on Tariffs and Trade (GATT), which Nixon vehemently opposed — two results that directly fulfilled the *Post-Industrial-Zero-Growth Strategies* of the Bilderberg Group.

John Coleman added in *Conspirators' Hierarchy*, "From this beginning, we can trace the roots of the 1991 recession/depression which... cost the jobs of 30 million Americans."

By far the most influential player in the Watergate Crisis was Nixon's National Security Adviser — Henry Kissinger. As far back as the mid-1960s, the Bilderbergers placed Kissinger in charge of a small group consisting of James Schlesinger, Alexander Haig and Daniel Ellsberg. Working with them was the Institute of Policy Studies chief theoretician, Noam Chomsky. While the IPS was the brainchild of the British Round Table, the Tavistock Institute determined its agenda, and together they developed programmed-learning techniques. In the '60s, Kissinger's team and Chomsky were creating the "New Left" as a grassroots movement in the U.S. to engender strife and unrest. Their goal was to spread chaos and to proliferate the "ideals" of left-wing nihilistic socialism. From this position, they could engineer the "big stick" with which to beat the United States' political establishment.

Once Kissinger was installed as National Security Advisor, he, Ellsberg and Haig were then able to set in motion the RIIA's Watergate plan to oust President Nixon after he publicly declared he did not approve of the General Agreement on Tariffs and Trade (GATT), a statement that infuriated David Rockefeller. In fact, Nixon was right. The GATT has since proved to be a further erosion of America's national sovereignty, as Sir James Goldsmith, a billionaire member of the European Parliament, testified it would to the U.S. Senate in 1994, just before he died.

As Nixon's National Security Advisor, Kissinger and his staff received all intelligence, foreign and domestic, law enforcement information, including FBI top-clearance and most-secret information before any of it was released to Nixon. No wonder that Haldeman and Ehrlichman, the two men that Nixon trusted with his life, could not understand what was going on around them.

For Kissinger, it was the zenith of his career. Disgracing Nixon and drumming him out of office handed Kissinger unprecedented powers, the likes of which have never been seen since. With Nixon's resignation, the Bilderbergers finally saw "their" president, Gerald Ford, move into the White House. The New World Order's yes man took direct orders from Henry Kissinger, an agent of David Rockefeller, a servant to the Bilderbergers.

CHAPTER EIGHT

BILDERBERG UNMASKED

Thomas Jefferson, one of the Founding Fathers of American democracy explained it this way: "Single acts of tyranny may be ascribed to the accidental opinion of a day; but a series of oppressions, begun at a distinguished period, and pursued unalterably through every change of ministers [Presidents], too plainly prove a deliberate systematical plan of reducing us to slavery."

The deep attitude of the global, mostly male, corporate gang was expressed by David Rockefeller at the June 1991 Bilderberg meeting in Baden-Baden, Germany, where he argued for "supranational sovereignty of an intellectual elite and world bankers, which is surely preferable to the national auto determination practiced in past centuries."[26]

On December 9, 2001, Professor John McMurtry of the University of Guelph in Canada said this in his opening address at a Forum entitled "How Should Canada Respond To Terrorism and War?": "As such a structure of world rule, it is accomplished by the same financial and media system deciders as put Tony Blair into office in Britain and George W. Bush into the White House against a majority vote. Trans-national corporations have marketed and financed these political leaders to ensure that captive states serve them rather than the peoples governments are elected by, guaranteeing through state plenipotentiaries and trans-national trade edicts that governments can no longer govern them in common interest without infringing the new trade and investment laws in which trans-national corporations alone are granted rights."

What perplexes me most is that other people don't see the dangers. Is it because knowledge brings responsibility and clamors for a decisive response? If we acknowledge that, in fact, there does exist a power far greater than the elected office of the President, a "moral" authority far more powerful than the Christian Pope, an invisible power that controls the world's military apparatus and intelligence systems, controls the international banking system, controls the most effective propaganda system in history, we might be then forced to conclude that democracy is, at best, an illusion, and at worst, a prelude to a dictatorship that will become known as the *New World Order*.

Michael Thomas, a Wall Street investment banker who has won wide acclaim as an author, and is regarded by many as the Reagan-Bush era's most incisive commentator, said in *SCH News*, May 28, 1999, "If the Bilderbergers seem more publicity-shy than ever, that is, among other reasons, because their proposals, implemented by subservient agencies such as the IMF and the World Bank have caused more mass devastation in recent years than World War II ever did."

"The unhappy result," as ex-BBC journalist Tony Gosling reports at his Web site, www.bilderberg.org, "is a picture of Western democracy subverted, with decision makers getting together not for reasons important to ordinary people — social justice, common interest, and quality of life — but to strengthen economic austerity and bring even more private gain for the world's political and corporate elite."

Despite the evidence at hand, the majority still believe that with all the day-to-day problems they have to face, they can't be bothered to take the "conspiracy theories" seriously. That is exactly what the Tavistock profiling has done to us. Faced with chaos, we are reacting as Nixon did when he was first isolated, confused and later destroyed by the global planners. Demoralized and confused, lacking self-esteem, unsure of the future, people are far more ready to welcome the sudden appearance of a "Messiah," a *New Order* that promises to eliminate drugs, pornography, child prostitution, rampant crime, wars, famine and suffering, and guarantee a well-ordered society in which people live in harmony.

But this newly hatched "harmony" will encroach on our freedoms, human rights, thoughts and our very existence. "Harmony" will mean a welfare society; we will become just a number in the vast bureaucratic system of the New World Order. Non-conformists, such as myself, will be interned in Guantanamo-like concentration camps. All this will happen unless we, the people of (what is left of) the free world, stand up to defend our national ideals, rather than leave it in the hand of the governments, the EU commissioners, the UN representatives and the royalty who have betrayed us.

These nice, proper members of European royal families, the sweet-talking elderly ladies and the debonair gentlemen are, in reality, utterly ruthless. They will use the suffering of every nation and exploit its wealth to protect their privileged way of life. The aristocracy's fortunes are "inextricably woven and intertwined with the drug trade, the gold, diamond and arms trades, banking, commerce and industry, oil, the news media and entertainment industry."[27]

How can these facts be verified, given that it is virtually impossible to penetrate the Bilderberg Group? Some of it cannot be checked, because the information comes straight out of intelligence files, with only a privileged minority ever seeing it. Don't expect the news media to ever mention the conspiracy on the nightly news bulletins. The press is under the total control of the nice ladies and gentlemen who spend so much of their time in philanthropic endeavors. Most people believe that, as they can't see a *motivation* for the things I have described (and it doesn't appear on the TV or radio news or in their newspapers) it must be a "conspiracy theory" — to be ignored or mocked and, either way, rejected. Hard evidence is what they want, and hard evidence is difficult to come by. This is what Tavistock-type psychological profiling has done to the human race. The New World Order has striven to neutralize the only real threat that we, the people, can pose to their plans.

I am attempting to rip the mask off the New World Order and show it for what it is. There are many sources and documents in this book which can corroborate, at least, a good number of the facts, and which will leave, I hope, an intelligent reader wondering if there is more to all of this than might seem plausible.

Richard Rubin

Richard Haass,
Current President CFR

Dennis Ross, Counselor, the Washington
Institute for Near East Policy with Richard
Haass, Bilderberg 2005

The Pratt House
East 68th Street
New York, NY

Leslie Gelb

Winston Lord

David
Rockefeller

CFR secretary
(non-member)

Peter G. Peterson

Alton Frye

John Swing

Bayless
Manning

All except the secretary have been
President or Chairman of CFR.

PART TWO

THE COUNCIL ON FOREIGN RELATIONS (CFR)

The Trilateral Commission doesn't secretly run the world. The Council on Foreign Relations does that.

—Sir Winston Lord,
President of Council on Foreign Relations, 1978
Assistant Secretary of State, the U. S. State Department
Member of the Order of Skull & Bones
Aid & Abet, Vol. 2, No. 2, Pg. 7

Non-member, George W. Bush

Members of the CFR meet with George W. Bush on January 5, 2006. From left to right: Harold Brown, Lawrence Eagleburger, James Baker, Colin Powell, James Schlesinger, Donald Rumsfeld, Dick Cheney, non-member George W. Bush, Condoleezza Rice, George Shultz, Melvin Laird, Robert McNamara, Madeleine Albright, Alexander Haig, Frank Carlucci, William Perry, and William Cohen.

John Kerry

Leslie Gelb, Richard Helms, James R. Schlesinger, Kenneth A. Moskow, William Webster, R. James Woolsey, John Deutch

Kissinger, Brezinski, Albright

Dick Cheney

Hamilton Fish, Kissinger 1957

David Rockefeller and Peter G. Peterson (CFR Chairman & Senior Chairman of the Blackstone Group) speak with Fidel Castro in Havana in February 2001.

David Rockefeller presents Boris Yeltsin as a guest speaker to the CFR at the Pratt House in New York on September 11, 1989.

CHAPTER NINE

HIT OR MISS, 1999

E mpires, as any Russian can readily attest, come and go. About twenty-five hundred years ago, one such upstart venture we call "Roman" began as a swindle of its sister states, known to history as the "Latin League." Eventually, most of the Latins received a second-class form of citizenship: the so-called "Latin rights." The original region of *Latium* is now known as Lazio, where my family and I had lived, in Ladispoli.

In the first week of November 1999 I received what looked to be a postcard from an acquaintance from that small town on the Mediterranean coast in the province of Rome. The card simply said,

"Having a good time. Wish you were here."

It was dated November 29, 1999, and signed, "Fashoda."

Obviously there was something terribly wrong with this apparently innocent holiday memento. In addition, the Italian postcard was posted with a French stamp... and sealed with a March 30, 1980 seal!

Anyone in the intelligence business will tell you immediately that dates and places hold a tremendous significance to spooks and their couriers. March 30, 1980 was the date my family officially left the Soviet Union. While in Italy, we had settled in Ladispoli, which would serve as our home for the next year.

"This was hand-delivered and left in my mailbox by someone who had something important to tell me." I thought. "Italian postcard with a French stamp. Interesting....

"November 29, 1999. That's three-and-a-half weeks from now," I said out loud. I turned the postcard over and examined the non-descript photograph. It was a typical summer holiday scene: an endless sea of bathers and a barely distinct line of blue water on the horizon. I was able to make out two people, a mother, most likely, and her son all in white, staring straight ahead while a toddler innocently hugged his knee.

I walked out into the street. Rain fell lightly. Two small children jumped and squealed delightfully from puddle to puddle, leaving a print of their soles on the edge of the road. I crossed the slick street beneath the dark rushing clouds and pushed open the door of a corner pub.

November 29, 1999. What the hell did it all mean?

I re-read the text.

"Having a good time. Wish you were here. Fashoda."

"Who the hell is this guy?" I racked my brain for any intelligence contact I had nurtured over the past decade. I must admit there were some strange names and nicknames in that long list, but no Fashoda.

I ordered a coffee while mechanically twirling the postcard in my hand.

"Sounds African," I thought to myself. But with the exception of half a dozen key SASS operatives, members of the South African Secret Service, I had not been able to establish a stable relationship with a single member of the security apparatus of any African nation.

"Could this be a code?" I mumbled to myself.

"Fashoda, Fashoda, Fashoda." I turned the postcard over again and stared aimlessly at the mother and her children.

Then, suddenly, in a flash, it came. "Fashoda!!!"

Once an obscure dot on the map of Sudanese Egypt, the fort at Fashoda was built on a dusty peninsula connected by a narrow strip of land to a ridge which runs parallel to the water. The surrounding country is mostly deep swamp; mosquitoes are present in the millions. The climate is always humid and the temperature rarely below ninety-five in the shade.

The name and the place have since disappeared into the mists of history, but in September 1898, Britain and France seemed on the verge of war, the closest the two countries have been to armed confrontation since the battle of Waterloo in 1815, because at Fashoda, half a world away, French officers leading African troops confronted British officers leading African troops, each commander claiming sovereignty and demanding the withdrawal of the other.

At the end of the century both the British and the French believed that if a French scouting party could claim a tributary on the Upper Nile at Fashoda, France could build a dam there, block the flow of the Nile, trigger chaos in Egypt that would force Britain out of the Suez Canal, cut Britain's strategic lifeline to India, and thus topple the Empire that depended on India's wealth and manpower.

After a tense confrontation, face was saved for all parties by an agreement that three flags — Egyptian, British and French — would fly over the fort. The following year, the French and British governments agreed that the watersheds of the Nile and the Congo should mark the boundaries between their spheres of influence. Much of the map of modern Africa derives from this agreement. It also began a warming of relations that led to the Anglo-French Entente of 1904, a major step on the road to World War I.

"Fashoda is not a person but a place!" I could feel my heart pumping.

November 29, 1999. Ladispoli. Lazio, Rome, Italy, Fashoda, March 30, 1980, France... March 30, November 29, 1980, 1999, France, Italy, Rome, Lazio, Ladispoli, Fashoda... FIFRLL...FRILLF...FFRILL

Again and again, I kept looking for a pattern, but I just couldn't nail it down.

The rain had stopped and a purplish-green rainbow had extricated itself from behind a three-story building. A glum waitress finally appeared and clumsily set my full-to-the-brim café crème on the table. An elderly gentleman settled at an adjacent table, bumping his knee. Several vociferous men at the bar were discussing money, interrupting each other with a heavy thump on a victim's shoulder or forearm.

I suddenly sat up. "Fashoda. Travis Read!!!"

Travis Read was a hoodlum I had met during King City's 1996 Bilderberg conference. He appeared to be an undisciplined and obnoxious small-time thief who hung around with Garik S., an Israeli high school dropout. Garik later turned out to be a highly-trained Mossad operative working out of a basement apartment in Etobicoke, a non-descript suburb of Toronto.

Travis had a penchant for getting arrested and almost as quickly of getting let go. He also had a penchant of somehow always "sharing" a prison cell with a major criminal or a valued government informant, an extremely unusual coincidence, keeping in mind that government informants are high-value targets whose lives are jealously protected by the cops. As I later found out, Travis Read had become a criminal in order to work with the criminals. That was his cover. That was his rain dance.

He was sent to Sudan by liaisons working for both the CIA and Canada's national police force, the RCMP, an outfit involved with criminal intelligence. Travis was your typical shit disturber — cocky, a congenital liar, almost always intoxicated, rude... and almost always hard up for cash. The details of his Sudan trip were never revealed, but just as in 1898, this God-forsaken place was attracting all the wrong characters for all the right reasons. It was a hotbed of drugs and guns and oil, and a staging grounds for destabilizing efforts against a number of African nations too tired to fight protracted wars and too weak to resist U.S. and French and British and Russian and Chinese "friendly" political overtures. All of these African nations shared one common denominator — oil.

Travis hated the hypocrisy of the system that had created and used him. Yet paradoxically, because he possessed so many secrets which he took great care to hide from prying eyes, he was still alive.

"If Travis wants to see me," I thought to myself, "this is going to get extremely messy."

Travis was an intelligence junkyard dog. He knew too much, had pissed off too many people over the years, and had unnecessarily threatened some heavy high rollers. This man was bad news. And yet, I was at once both fearful and fascinated.

"What does he have that could possibly interest me?" I muttered to myself.

I caught the silhouette of a stunning woman against the windowpane. Her graceful thin, long neck seemed to extend into infinity. An expression of mild melancholy lent a mysterious beauty to her Botticellian face, while a wiggly-bottomed teenager clad in her school uniform noisily sucked back her milkshake at a corner table facing the street.

In order to get to the bottom of what was up, it was clear that I had to go to Rome. As I pushed open the pub door and walked out onto a noisy street, the idea did not appeal to me. Travis Read was trouble, and even if he had genuine information to pass along, he could easily have been set up by his controllers, who always kept him on a long enough leash that allowed him to do things most civilians could never do. After Canada and Bilderberg 1996, I could think of enough people who would have been happy to see me out of the picture.

The more I thought of it, the more I expected that a trap was being set up for me. I just didn't know who was behind the setup. To pull this off, I needed help.

On November 7, 1999, I participated in a four-way satellite, secure network phone conversation with several former members of the Soviet Union's security apparatus. I must admit that when the chips are down, I have always been able to rely on former Soviet officers. They inherently do not trust the West and are not easily bought, contrary to what mainstream newspapers and press reports want you to believe. This makes them trustworthy in my eyes.

These were no ordinary men. One of them was an expert on short- and medium-range nuclear and bacteriological weapons and their delivery systems. Another was a key staff officer under General Valery Manilov, Deputy Chief of Staff of the Russian Armed Forces. One year later, Manilov would become the most outspoken Russian military figure to denounce the Kursk "accident" as a deliberate U.S. provocation.

We quickly agreed that I could not walk into this alone, and one of the men volunteered names of former KGB contacts and security people stationed in Rome as my back-ups. To my surprise, one of the names was a well-known Vatican clergyman, whose apparent anti-Communist posture was a well-concealed mirage. Out of the list of some dozen names, I quickly settled on three, two of whom I personally knew, with the third a unanimous choice amongst the rest of the group.

Travis was going to meet me on November 29. That, at least, was obvious. If he knew where to find me, he obviously knew my telephone number and many another pertinent piece of information.

"He is either setting me up or he is in trouble," I thought. "If Travis is being set up with his full knowledge by his controllers, he must have pushed the wrong people too far." To survive himself, he was most likely told to deliver me to the other side. Loyalty was definitely not Travis Read's strong suit.

"But then again," I thought, "it is his life that is on the line, most likely ..." And when one lacks friends, as he did, all one can hope for are temporary business associates. They just may be your ticket to another round. I understood his predicament.

After several more short telephone conversations via a secure line, I agreed to meet my contacts in Rome, at Hotel Tefi.

Hotel Tefi, owned by an old acquaintance of my grandfather, for years served as a hideout for secret service operatives from the former Soviet Union who used Rome as a home base for counter-intelligence activities. It is strategically located just off the Piazza della Repubblica, some three hundred meters from where Gogol, one of Russia's giants of literature, in 1842 wrote his immortal work *Dead Souls*. Among Tefi's original owners was my grandfather's childhood friend, both having been born in Karasubazar, Belogorsk in the Crimea.

The men who appeared on November 26 at Hotel Tefi were seasoned veterans with a number of top-secret assignments in their resumes. These were veterans of "irregular warfare" — surveillance, psychological intimidation, blackmail. Watching them handle their weapons, I concluded that among their numerous "skills" they were also likely contract killers. These were not the type of people you would ever wish to double-cross.

Yet I knew that I was safe in their company. My grandfather had put his own life on the line in the early 1950s to save the lives of these men's fathers, all KGB officers, just as Stalin, months from death, launched his final purge of the top Red Army officer corps and secret service high command. They were my invisible army with a web of contacts that extended to every secret service agency on the planet. The NSA, CIA and FBI were no exceptions. Russian intelligence has always been surprisingly effective in penetrating U.S. agencies.

Alexander Ivanovitch was born in the small town of Chesis, near Riga. During WWII, it had been completely wiped out by German artillery. Konstantin was from the town of Borisov in Belorussia. Anatolii from Moscow. All were highly decorated former intelligence officers who had a heavy axe to grind with the West.

After a brief and heart warming *Kak dela dorogoy?* (How are you my dear?) and *Privet chelovek!* (Hi guy!), we got down to business.

Konstantin pulled out a pistol and laid it gently on the table.

Znaesh Shto Eto? (You know what this is?), he asked me looking over to his right as he placed special emphasis on the *know*. I looked down at a dark object in front of me.

I know my guns, and it wasn't difficult to see by the non-metallic polymer frame that I was staring at a Glock semiautomatic pistol.

"G36," said Anatolii, "still a full year away from public consumption." He was obviously enjoying himself. It was the first time I had seen the new Glock — compact .45 ACP with a 3.78-inch barrel and six-round single-stack magazine that was 0.36 centimetres narrower, and a full four ounces lighter to carry, than the antecedent double-stack 10-round Glock G30. Those who used it called it "poetry in motion."

"You may need to use it," barked Anatolii in a staccato-like rhythm.

"Piazza della Repubblica, at dusk," said Konstantin.

"Whatever you do, don't let him dictate the place and time of meeting," said Anatolii insistently, holding my forearm in his enormous hand. "Otherwise, we can't protect you."

On November 27, late in the afternoon, my cell phone rang. It was Travis. He was staying at some dive on the outskirts of Rome. He asked me to meet him near the Coliseum at 10 A.M. on November 29.

"Piazza della Repubblica at 5:30 P.M.," I interrupted him.

"I make the rules," barked Travis.

"Piazza della Repubblica at 5:30 P.M.," I repeated, raising my voice.

"Do you want the info or don't you?" said Travis.

"Not enough to get killed," I said coldly.

He hung up the telephone. Some twenty minutes later Travis rang back. He swore, he threatened, he pleaded, swore some more. Then, he agreed.

"All right, Piazza della Repubblica at 5:30 P.M."

"Travis," I said. "I know you are in trouble. I just hope you are not using me as a honey pot. That would be quite unfortunate." He hung up.

Piazza della Repubblica is strategically situated some 50 meters from Hotel Tefi. In the middle of the Piazza is Gian Lorenzo Bernini's masterpiece fountain in honor of his great protector Urbanus VIII. Four dolphins support two valves which in turn support a triton blowing water through a shell held up in his hands.

I phoned Konstantin from a public phone booth.

"Good," was all he said before hanging up.

Back at the hotel the plan was quickly put together.

"That Volvo is your getaway car," said Anatolii, pointing at a black car parked in the shade next to an ice-cream parlor.

"If there is trouble," said Konstantin, "it would take Sasha [Alexander] less than five seconds to get to you."

"If they ever got near you," noted Anatolii pensively.

I sincerely doubted that my adversaries — should there be any — would have any inkling of what they were in for.

On the morning of November 29, Anatolii and Konstantin, expert marksmen and former members of the Russian Special Forces, took up their positions on the roofs of adjacent buildings. Around four in the afternoon I ordered a drink at one of the outdoor terraces around the piazza. Anatolii and Konstantin had a clear shot at anyone approaching me from any direction. Both held custom made necked-down rifles. These were no off-the-shelf things. The rifles were specially manufactured to shoot a small caliber bullet at the extremely high speed of over 1,500 meters per second. The trajectory of the bullet is thus very flat, with little drop due to gravity over long ranges. Only those with very deep pockets could afford such expensive toys.

As I sat waiting for my contact to appear, a large group of French school children on a field trip walked by, blissfully and almost in unison licking their gelatos. Alexander Ivanovitch sat waiting in the black Volvo across the piazza.

Five-thirty came and went. There were no signs of Travis. Six P.M. Six-fifteen. Nothing. He finally called me around seven to tell me that he had decided to pass on to me sealed diplomatic pouches with incriminating evidence detailing the U.S. government's involvement in sectarian warfare in Sudan. This fitted tightly with the Bilderberger long-term objectives of profits from never-ending war and oil scarcity.

I told him that if this was his intention, and if he was talking to me over an open cell phone, it was unlikely he would ever make it to the piazza alive. I told him to stay put if he felt there was little chance of being found.

Then, the phone went dead.

You are probably not surprised to learn that Travis never showed up for our meeting. Around 8:30 P.M. we rushed into Travis' residence, if you could call it that, guns drawn. The one-bedroom dump had been completely ransacked. Yet, there were no other signs of foul play, no bloodstains. And no Travis Read.

To the best of my knowledge, he has never been heard from again. There were no doubts in my mind that I had in fact spoken to Travis. I recognised his unmistakable manner of speech, his particular way of chewing his words and regurgitating them before spewing them out. He was the only man I had ever met who spoke that way.

Driving to the airport, I kept looking behind me, but there were no signs of Travis. What I wouldn't give to find out what happened to him.

"Careful what you wish for," my sixth sense warns me. "You might just get what you may have no stomach for."

In this line of work, you learn not to get too sentimental or too keen. Either one could be construed as a weakness; and either one could put you on the wrong end of a gun barrel.

Once in a while, Travis' ghost appears in the deepest recesses of my memory, a morbid reminder of the fragility and fallibility of the human spirit.

Edward M. House and President Woodrow Wilson worked together to establish a world government through a League of Nations. House would go on to co-found the Council on Foreign Relations in 1921. House was the author of *Philip Dru: Administrator*, a book he wrote anonymously. In the novel *Philip Dru*, America becomes ruled by a dictator, who throws out the Constitution and introduces reform. Wilson once said, "Mr. House is my second personality. He is my independent self. His thoughts and mine are one. If I were in his place I would do just as he suggested... If anyone thinks he is reflecting my opinion by whatever action he takes, they are welcome to the conclusion."

CHAPTER TEN

CROSSOVER PARTNERS

A s in a conventional teleplay, there are actually secret spin-off organizations similar to the Bilderberg Group. The largest is the Round Table, whose branches include Britain's Royal Institute of International Affairs, Institutes of International Affairs of Canada, Australia, South Africa, India and Holland, as well as Institutes of Pacific Relations for China, Russia and Japan. One of the Round Table's branches in the United States is called the Council on Foreign Relations, or CFR.

Part of the origins of the CFR go back to 1921 and one of its founders, Edward Mandell House, who was President Woodrow Wilson's chief advisor and rumored to be the power behind the Wilson administration from 1913 to 1921. Ironically, House was a known Marxist. He idealized socialism, and under his watch in the White House, he lobbied for a state-controlled central bank empowered to make U.S. money. In 1913, the United States Congress still controlled the country's currency, but that year passage of the Federal Reserve Act transferred Congress' power to a private central bank. House also proposed the 16th Amendment to the United States Constitution, which introduced the graduated income tax, another idea he borrowed from Karl Marx.[28]

House also wrote the plan for the League of Nations, which was President Wilson's prized proposal at the 1919 Paris Peace Conference. Charles Seymour, House's official biographer, said that Wilson "approved the House draft almost in its entirety, and his own rewriting of it was practically confined to phraseology."

At the end of Wilson's term in 1921, House and like-minded sympathizers established the Council on Foreign Relations. From the outset, their commitment to form a one-world government based on a centralized global financing system attracted the strangest mix of capitalist and socialist, opportunist and idealist. Among the potpourri of American elitists at that first meeting were the rich and famous.

Within a year, the Rockefeller and Carnegie Foundations agreed to finance the CFR's agenda and growth. President Franklin Roosevelt is responsible for filling the State Department with CFR members in 1940, and subsequent generations of CFR-placed staff have run it ever since.

The CFR is headquartered in New York in the Harold Pratt House, a four-story mansion on the corner of Park Avenue and 68th Street. The widow of an heir to the Standard Oil Rockefeller fortune — Charles Pratt — donated the building to their use in 1929. In 2006, over 4,000 of America's leading Establishment are members (term or life) of the CFR. Although the CFR is very influential in government, it remains off the radar screen to most Americans. Only one person in five thousand knows about the organization, while even fewer are aware of its real purposes.

During the first fifty years of its existence, the CFR received rare media coverage. Such anonymity might seem strange until you view a CFR membership list. It includes top executives from the *New York Times*, the *Washington Post*, the *Los Angeles Times*, the *Wall Street Journal*, NBC, CBS, ABC, FOX, *Time*, *Fortune*, *Business Week*, *U.S. News and World Report*, along with many others. Since the media are part of the group's think-tank sessions, we have to question their "discretion." If it is overdone, why? Why would they censor themselves?

When asked this question at a CIA gathering nearly 25 years ago, CFR member Katherine Graham, the legendary *Washington Post* publisher, told the audience, "There are some things the general public does not need to know about us and shouldn't."

In fact, the CFR's systemic conspiracy has been mentioned more than once in the past by some of America's leading individuals. As early as March 26, 1922, John F. Hylan, Mayor of New York, in a speech said, "The real menace of our republic is the invisible government, which, like a giant octopus, sprawls its slimy length over our city, state and nation. At the head is a small group of banking houses generally referred to as 'international bankers.' This little coterie of powerful international bankers virtually run our government for their own selfish ends."

On February 23, 1954, Senator William Jenner warned, in a speech, "Today the path to total dictatorship in the United States can be laid by strictly legal means; unseen and unheard by the Congress, the President, or the people.... Outwardly we have a Constitutional government. We have operating within our government and political system another body representing another form of government, a bureaucratic elite which believes our Constitution is outmoded and is sure that it is the winning side.... All the strange developments in foreign policy agreements may be traced to this group who are going to make us over to suit their pleasure."

Historian Arthur Schlesinger, Jr. has called the CFR a "front organization" for "the heart of the American Establishment." *Newsweek* has referred to the CFR's leaders as "the foreign-policy establishment of the U.S." Richard Rovere, writing in *Esquire* magazine, saw them as "a sort of Presidium for that part of the Establishment that guides our destiny as a nation."

The 200-plus journalists, correspondents, and communications executives who belong to the CFR defend the group's right to private discussion on the basis of a supposed need for a forum where concerned leaders can speak freely to analyze critical events affecting U.S. political directions in a world economy, if they are to have any hope of developing solutions and/or policies. Once these solutions and policies are announced, then the CFR welcomes press coverage and public debate. This implies that we should accept the 1987 CFR Report that is posted on the CFR's Web site at face value. But, when any organization does not tolerate open publication of their discussions and activities, we have to wonder at the information we're provided. Does such reporting represent the facts or is it what the Council wants us to see and believe?

In Jim Marrs' *Rule by Secrecy*, economist John Kenneth Galbraith, himself a former member, called the CFR's practices a scandal. "Why," he asked, "should businessmen be briefed by Government officials on information not available to the general public, especially since it can be financially advantageous?" To add further confusion, there is another coexisting organization with the same one-world government objective, except its members represent global trade alliances: North America,

Western Europe and Pacific Asia. It's called the Trilateral Commission (TC) and was founded, and financed, by David Rockefeller in 1973. Before establishing this organization, he tested the idea for forming the commission at the 1972 Bilderberg Group meeting in Knokke, Belgium.

And guess what?

Many of the same individuals who belonged to the CFR and the Bilderbergers also joined the Trilateral Commission. CFR members comprise Americans only. The Bilderberg Group is limited to members from the United States, Canada and Western Europe. The Trilateral Commission brings together global power brokers, as I discuss in Part Three of this book. David Rockefeller, whose family financed the CFR, is a common denominator among these parallel groups. Not only is he the CFR Chairman Emeritus, but he also continues to provide financial and personal support to the TC, CFR and Bilderberg Group.

It's no wonder, then, that critics see these three organizations as comprising self-interested elitists protecting their wealth and the investments of multinational banks and corporations in the growing world economy at the expense of developing nations and third-world countries. The policies they develop benefit them as well as move us towards a one-world government.

To appreciate the extent of power the Bilderbergers, CFR and TC exercise, it is enough to recall that almost all of the presidential candidates for both parties have belonged to at least one of these organizations, many of the U.S. congressmen and senators, most major policy-making positions, especially in the field of foreign relations, much of the press, most of the leadership of the CIA, FBI, IRS (Internal Revenue Service), and many of the remaining governmental organizations in Washington. CFR members occupy nearly all White House cabinet positions.

Of CIA directors, only James R. Schlesinger, who briefly headed it in 1973, was not a CFR member. He was, however, a protégé of CFR member Daniel Ellsberg, famous for the release of the Viet Nam era "Pentagon Papers," and his appointment was approved by Henry Kissinger, a key Bilderberg, CFR and TC leader.

Of U.S. presidents, we have seen a string of CFR members winning the elections every four years. In 1952 and 1956, CFR Adlai Stevenson challenged CFR Eisenhower. In 1960, it was CFR Nixon vs. CFR Kennedy. In 1964, the conservative wing of the Republican Party "stunned the Establishment" by nominating its candidate, Barry Goldwater, over

Nelson Rockefeller. Rockefeller and the CFR wing portrayed Barry Goldwater as "a dangerous radical who would abolish Social Security, drop atom bombs on Hanoi, and in general be a reincarnation of the Fascist dictator Mussolini."[29] Goldwater was humiliated, and Johnson won in a landslide.

In 1968, it was CFR Nixon's turn against CFR Democrat Hubert Humphrey. In 1972, CFR President Nixon took on CFR Democratic challenger George McGovern. In 1976, CFR Republican President/ contender Gerald Ford opposed CFR/TC challenger Carter. In 1980, President Carter was defeated by Ronald Reagan, who, although not a CFR member, had in George H.W. Bush a CFR Vice President. Reagan, after becoming President, quickly staffed his office with 313 CFR members. As an interesting side note, the independent third-party candidate in the 1980 elections, John Anderson, was also a CFR member.

In 1984, President Reagan contested Democratic CFR member, Walter Mondale. In 1988, Republican contender for the office of the President, George H.W. Bush, ex-CIA boss and a CFR member took on Michael Dukakis, the little-known CFR Governor of Massachusetts. In 1992, President Bush faced an obscure governor from the backward state of Arkansas as his competitor for the presidency. This was Bill Clinton, a Bilderberger as well as a member of the CFR and the Trilateral Commission. When Clinton became President, he employed almost 100 CFR members in his administration. Furthermore, the team of Clinton and Gore was financed and supported by the CFR membership and agenda.

In 1996, Clinton fought off a challenge from a Republican veteran and another CFR member, Robert Dole. In 2000, CFR Democrat Al Gore squared off against Texas Governor George W. Bush, son of the former President George H.W. Bush. George W. Bush, who won, was not a CFR member, but as is always the case, he was surrounded by the Establishment in the corridors of power. Bush's insider team included Condoleezza Rice, Dick Cheney, Richard Perle, Paul Wolfowitz, Lewis Libby, Colin Powell and Robert Zoellick — all CFR members. In 2004, incumbent Bush won, against the CFR and Bilderberg challenger, Democrat John Kerry.

In fact, from 1928 to 1972, a CFR member has won every presidential election (except Lyndon Johnson who more than compensated the Establishment by filling most of the top positions in Government with

CFR members). George H.W. Bush had 387 members of the CFR and TC in his Administration. Nixon, at the beginning of his Administration, placed 115 CFR members in key positions in the Executive Branch. Of the first 82 names on a list prepared to help President Kennedy staff his State Department, 63 belonged to the CFR, according to Arnold Beichman's report in the September 1, 1961 edition of the *Christian Science Monitor*. It was simply titled, "Council on Foreign Relations." Indeed, the CFR has served as a virtual employment agency for the federal government under both Democrats and Republicans.

Columnist Edith Kermit Roosevelt, granddaughter of President Theodore Roosevelt, had this to say about them: "Most people are unaware of the existence of this legitimate Mafia. Yet, the power of the Establishment makes itself felt from the professor, who seeks a foundation grant, to the candidate for a cabinet post or State department job. It affects the nation's policies in almost every area."

George Wallace, American Democratic presidential candidate on four occasions in the 1960s and '70s, made famous a slogan: "There is not a dime's worth of difference between the Democrat and Republican parties." And he was right. Governmental policies never seem to change even though significant "philosophical" differences have taken place within the ruling government. The reason for this, claims Gary Allen, one of America's "conspiracy-niched" investigative reporters, in his brilliant and now out-of-print best seller, *The Rockefeller File*, is that "while grassroots Democrats and Republicans generally have greatly differing views on the economy, political policies, and federal activities, as you climb the sides of the political pyramid, the two parties become more and more alike."

Whether a Democrat, a Republican, a Conservative or a Liberal is in power, the opposing rhetorics spouted by the candidates apparently have little to do with who actually wins the elections: the decision makers who pull the strings stay the same, because cabinet seats are always held by CFR members. Even as U.S. presidents come and go, the CFR's power and agenda remain the same.

And the average voter is no fool. The public realizes something is amiss. Political surveys illustrate a growing perception that nothing changes in government no matter how you vote. This widespread observation has led to reduced voter turnout at election time and a restless cynicism among citizens.

No matter how the public feels, the objective of the hardcore inner circle of the CFR has not changed since its founding in 1921 at the Majestic Hotel in Paris. In the 50th anniversary issue of the CFR's official quarterly publication, *Foreign Affairs*, Kingman Brewster, Jr., U.S. Ambassador to Great Britain and president of Yale University, contributed the leading article: "Reflections on Our National Purpose." As a CFR member, Brewster did not back away from stating the Council's goal: "Our national purpose should be to abolish American nationality and to take some risks in order to invite others to pool their sovereignty with ours."

These *risks* include disarming to the point where America would be helpless against the "peace-keeping" forces of a global UN government. Rather, America would happily surrender its sovereignty to the world government in the interests of what he called the "world community," or what today's media likes to call "the international community."

These secret proposals reflect the work of dozens of different agencies and commissions, and are now being vigorously advanced by the Commission on Global Governance. Its report, entitled *Our Global Neighbourhood*, is a blueprint for the UN's future role as a global super-government.[30]

Another contributor to *Foreign Affairs*, Richard N. Gardner, former deputy assistant Secretary of State, in April 1974 wrote, "In short, the 'house of world order' will have to be built from the bottom up rather than from the top down.... An end run around national sovereignty, eroding it piece by piece, will accomplish much more than the old fashioned assault."

James Warburg, son of CFR founder Paul Warburg, and a member of Franklin D. Roosevelt's "brain trust," which was made up of individuals from outside government, including professors, lawyers, and others who came to Washington to advise him on economic affairs, delivered blunt testimony before the Senate Foreign Relations Committee on February 17, 1950: "We shall have world government whether or not you like it — by conquest or consent."

And most tellingly, in an address to the Bilderberg Group at Evian, France, May 21, 1992 — and transcribed from a tape recording made by a Swiss delegate, Michael Ringier, Publisher and CEO of Ringier Inc. — Henry Kissinger said, "Today, Americans would be outraged if UN troops entered Los Angeles to restore order; tomorrow, they will be grateful. This is especially true if they were told there was an outside threat from beyond, whether real or promulgated, that threatened our very existence. It is then that all people of the world will plead with world leaders to deliver them from this evil. The one thing every man fears is the unknown. When presented with this scenario, individual rights will be willingly relinquished for the guarantee of their well-being granted to them by their world government."

In his book, *The Future of Federalism*, Nelson Rockefeller proclaimed, "No nation today can defend its freedom, or fulfill the needs and aspirations of its own people, from within its own borders or through its own resources alone.... And so the nation-state, standing alone, threatens, in many ways, to seem as anachronistic as the Greek city-states eventually became in ancient times."

Rockefeller might have been referring to the wrong-headed strategic policies under Pericles and Alcibiades, which got Athens into the disastrous Peloponnesian War that brought on the collapse and the self-ruin of its Golden Age. These stratagems are easily comparable to the current U.S. foreign policy in its calamitous advance.

In fact, the CFR was apparently planning the New World Order before 1942. An editorial on page two in the *Baltimore News-Post*, Monday December 8, 1941 — the day after Pearl Harbor was bombed — predicted there would be a new world league, which would formulate a "basic declaration of the rights of man ... and to protect *those rights, the system will have the power to deal with and punish individuals in some cases*" [emphasis added].

Furthermore, "The UN began with a group of CFR members called the Informal Agenda Group. They drafted the original proposal for the UN, and called in three CFR attorneys, who declared it was Constitutional. They then presented the proposal to President Roosevelt, who announced it the very next day to the public. When the United Nations held its founding conference in San Francisco, more than forty of the American delegates were CFR members."[31]

Later, the United Nations did adopt a declaration of human rights. Then, international law was only concerned with how national authorities exercised regulation of their own individual citizens. Now, the UN has the right to kidnap individuals within their own national borders and bring them to trial at The Hague. Though war crimes are heinous, it is up to each nation victimized by such crimes to try its own people under its own laws. Yet, there have been no protests of this blatant travesty of international justice.

Again in 1941, Quincy Wright, Ph.D., a CFR member and a specialist in international law at the University of Chicago, made the earliest and clearest statement of how he viewed the "New World Order" — one government over the entire world that would limit national sovereignty and the independence of individual nations. That this declaration at the outset of World War II received no criticism nor comparison to Hitler's feared "New Order" demonstrates how deep-rooted American isolation was at the time. No one recognized the similarity in the goals of the Nazi state to this ideology.

In discussing Dr. Wright's ideas in his lecture on the "New World Order," Terry Boardman told a packed auditorium of almost 1,500 people at Rudolf Steiner House in London in October 1998 that Wright envisioned three continental systems: a "United States of Europe," an Asiatic system and a Pan-American union. Wright also forecast that each continental system would have a common military force and that national military forces would be greatly reduced or outlawed.

Still, with the advent of a world government, a world army and a world currency, why would the Rockefeller family want to surrender U.S. sovereignty and government power, which they already control, as well as their wealth, to the controls and dictates of a World Government? Wouldn't such a World Government threaten their financial power and therefore be the last thing on earth they would wish to support?

Yes, of course, unless the Rockefellers, the Bilderberg Group, the Council on Foreign Relations and the Trilateral Commission expect the coming World Government to be under their control. In a letter to an associate on November 21, 1933, President Franklin D. Roosevelt wrote, "The real truth of the matter is, as you and I know, that a financial element in the large centers has owned the government ever since the days of Andrew Jackson."

If this is their ultimate goal — to create a single globalized marketplace, ruled by a world government (which in turn controls its courts, schools, and the people's reading habits and very thoughts), policed by a world army, financially regulated by a world bank (via a single global currency) — then we can ill afford to ignore what is happening to us and the world we live in.

It is imperative to understand that the conferences and meetings of the Council on Foreign Relations, Council of the Americas, Royal Institute for International Affairs, Institute of Pacific Relations, Trilateral Commission, Gorbachev Foundation, Bill Gates Foundation, etc. are not places where major decisions are made or new strategies embraced. Rather, these social gatherings capitalize on the CFR's use of its special discussion groups and study groups to advance its policies.

According to G. William Domhoff, a writer and an investigator of methods used by the elite organizations to strive to develop consensus, the CFR has historically operated in "small groups of about twenty-five, who bring together leaders from the six conspirator categories (industrialists, financiers, ideologues, military, professional specialists — lawyers, medical doctors, etc. — and organized labor) for detailed discussions of specific topics in the area of foreign affairs." In his 1970 book, *The Higher Circles*, he discussed "how the power elite make foreign policy": "Discussion groups explore problems in a general way, trying to define issues and alternatives. Such groups often lead to a study group as the next stage. Study groups revolve around the work of a Council research fellow (financed by Carnegie, Ford and Rockefeller) or a staff member."

In a 1968 discussion group, former CIA Director of Plans Richard Bissell, who was also a Ford Foundation consultant, laid out increasing needs for the interplay between CFR members and covert actions to be more discreet when the CIA turned to Council members to act as covers for clandestine operations. "If the agency is to be effective, it will have to make use of private institutions on an expanding scale, though those relations which have been 'blown' cannot be resurrected. We need to operate under deeper cover, with increased attention to the use of 'cut-outs' [intermediaries]. The CIA's interface with the rest of the world needs to be better protected. If various groups hadn't been aware of the source of their funding, the damage subsequent to disclosure might have been far less than occurred. The CIA interface with various private groups, including business and student groups, must be remedied."

The CFR's influence seamlessly extends throughout the American way of life. In *The Higher Circles*, Domhoff also quotes political scientist Lester Milbrath on how well this is being achieved: "The Council on Foreign Relations, while not financed by government, works so closely with it that it is difficult to distinguish Council actions stimulated by government from autonomous actions... the most important sources of income are leading corporations and major foundations."

As to the foundations Milbrath mentions, the major contributors over the years have been the Rockefeller Foundation, the Carnegie Foundation, and the Ford Foundation. "All foundations, which support the CFR," Domhoff concludes in *The Higher Circles*, "are in turn directed by men from Bechtel Construction, Chase Manhattan, Kimberly-Clark, Monsanto Chemical, and dozens of other corporations. Further, to complete the circle, most foundation directors are members of the CFR. In the early 1960s, Dan Smoot found that twelve of twenty Rockefeller Foundation trustees, ten of fifteen Ford Foundation trustees, and ten of fourteen Carnegie Foundation trustees were members of the CFR."[32]

Henry and Barbara

Henry and gals

Henry and Fareed Zakaria

William Buckley, Jr. and Clare Booth-Luce

Katie Couric

Michael Bloomberg

Hillary Clinton is not a CFR member. Her husband is.

Vernon Jordan

Paula Zahn

Henry and Andrea

Gerald Ford

David Brinkley

Peter G. Peterson and Leslie Stahl

Andrea Mitchell and her husband, Alan Greenspan

Archibald MacLiesh, Edward R. Murrow & Willaim S. Paley

Dan Rather

Tom Brokaw

CHAPTER ELEVEN

JOURNALISTIC COURTESANS?

Our job is to give people not what they want, but what we decide they ought to have.

—Former President of CBS News, Richard Salant.

One of the best kept secrets is the degree to which a handful of giant conglomerates, all belonging to the secret Bilderberg Group, Council on Foreign Relations, NATO, the Club of Rome, and the Trilateral Commission, control the world's flow of information. They determine what we see on television, hear on the radio and read in newspapers, magazines, books, or on the Internet.

Bilderberg has, at one time or another, had representatives of all major U.S. and European newspapers and network news outlets attend meetings. These media people are invited on the condition that they promise to report nothing. This is how the Bilderbergers sustain their news blackouts throughout the United States and Europe.

Doing a cursory check of the Web pages of the principal international news outlets, we will not find even one reference to the most important group that counts among its members all the most important politicians, businessmen and financiers. Worse, there was no hint of the beginning of the Iraq hostilities, even from the press who attended a 2002 Bilderberg meeting. We're talking about the *Washington Post, Newsweek, Time* magazine, *Wall Street Journal,* the *Economist* — the world's leading newspapers knew exactly when the war was to begin and did not fulfill the very minimum of their journalistic duty.

One of the more serious altercations among Bilderberg members took place at the annual 2002 meeting in a suburb of Washington D.C., between May 30 and June 2. European Bilderbergers demanded the immediate presence of U.S. Defense Secretary Donald Rumsfeld. They wanted to hear firsthand from the Secretary about U.S. war plans. Rumsfeld, compelled to change his appointments for the day, appeared May 31 before outraged European Bilderbergers to promise, in the name of the Bush government, that no attack was to take place against Iraq before February or March 2003. Wasn't this story sufficiently important to broadcast to the world as front-page news?

I must address an issue that dogged me through my research, investigations and actions to uncover the truth about the Bilderberg Group. I found that some of my "allies" came from "interesting" camps. When I commenced my investigation there was a dearth of information, with next to no mainstream news coverage of the Bilderberg Group. The *American Free Press* and before that the *Spotlight* were two of the very few newspapers that have covered these secret meetings. I do not agree with most of their political views, but I found their reporting and coverage of the Bilderberg meetings to be professional, competent and unique.

It was left to the *American Free Press* to inform its readers in June 2002 that, according to its sources within Bilderberg, the war in Iraq had been postponed until March 2003, when at the time the entire world press was screaming of an impending attack programmed for the summer or early fall of 2002.[33]

How is it possible that Nicolas Beytout, Editor-in-Chief of *Les Echos* didn't know it? Or that Phillipe Camus, CEO of EADS, and Henri de Castries, Chairman of AXA Insurance, *might* not have heard of it? Did Camus and de Castries use the inside information to profit from it? How much did Donald Graham, the *Washington Post* CEO, know? Did he profit in any way from being party to such valuable information?

It seems the largest periodicals such as the *New York Times* and the *Washington Post*, whose members form the very fiber of the Bilderberg Group, had explicit orders not to cover what would have undoubtedly been the story of summer 2002. Instead of the Iraq war, as if in unison, we got these stories:

"Rumsfeld Cautions Nuclear Foes"

Abstract - Defense Secretary Donald H. Rumsfeld said today he will try to persuade the leaders of India and Pakistan to step back from the brink of war by reminding them that nuclear weapons are "distinctively different" from any other tool of war.

Washington Post, June 6, 2002 pg. A.20

"Taking the Offensive"

Abstract - Many observers interpreted Mr. Bush's talk of taking "the battle to the enemy" as stage-setting for a possible military campaign against Iraq, which clearly fits in his category of "evil and lawless regimes" for which "containment is not possible."

Washington Post, June 4, 2002. pg. A.16
Jim Hoagland [journalist, Bilderberg member]

"What Else Are We Missing?"

Abstract - Op-Ed column says Mr. Bush should match his oratory with speedy action to remove Saddam Hussein's terrorist threat in Iraq.

New York Times, June 6, 2002 Section A, Page 31, Column 1
William Safire, [journalist, Bilderberg member]

"The Land of Denial"

Abstract - Op-Ed column says best thing that Pres. Hosni Mubarak of Egypt could do to achieve peace in Israel and fight global terrorism is to return Egypt to the mission it had in 19th and early 20th centuries, which was to lead Arab-Muslim world into modernity.

New York Times, June 5, 2002, Section A, Page 27, Column 5
* Thomas L. Friedman, [journalist, Bilderberg member]

"U.S. must act first to battle terror, Bush tells cadets"

Abstract - Pres. Bush delivers toughly worded speech to 1,000 graduates at United States Military Academy that seems aimed at preparing Americans for potential war with Iraq.

New York Times, June 2, 2002, Section 1, Page 1, Column 6
Elisabeth Bumiller

As an interesting aside, Jim Hoagland, William Safire and Tomas L. Friedman are all Pulitzer Prize-winning journalists as well as members of the Bilderberger-interlocked Council on Foreign Relations. In the past, they have attended Bilderberger Conferences but are sworn to secrecy. It appears they will never reveal what has transpired at the Bilderberg meetings to the American public.

The *American Free Press'* diplomatic correspondent at the UN, Christopher Bollen, asked a group of journalists waiting for a routine conference to start, "Why is anything related to Bilderberg edited out by the most 'respectable' editors of national newspapers?" His question was met with ironic laughter in the pressroom.

"The Bilderbergers have been removed from our assignment list years ago by executive order," said Anthony Holder, a former UN correspondent for the London *Economist*, the leading international business weekly.

"We are barely aware of the Bilderbergers' existence, and we don't report on their activities," asserted William Glasgow, senior writer responsible for covering such international organizations at *Business Week*. "One cannot help but be a little suspicious when priorities for the future of mankind are being considered by those who have real influence over that future, in total secret."[34]

"The involvement of the Rockefellers with the media has multiple implications. One is that the Rockefeller gang's plans for monopolistic World Government are never, but never, discussed in the machines of mass disinformation. The media decides what the issues will be in the country. They can turn on the poverty issue or turn it off. The same holds true for population explosion, pollution, peace, détente, or whatever," wrote American investigative journalist, the now-deceased Gary Allen, in *The Rockefeller File*. "The media can take a man like Ralph Nader and make him an instant folk hero. Or they can take an enemy of the Rockefellers (like Goldwater) and create the image that he is a cretin, a buffoon, a bigot, or a dangerous paranoid."

It is interesting to note that Ralph Nader, a perennial "independent" presidential candidate, "much admired for his anti-establishment stance," is financed by the Rockefeller network in his attempt to destroy the free enterprise system. Principal Nader financiers are the Ford Foundation and the Field Foundation, both CFR-interlocked. According to a *Business Week* article reprinted in the *Congressional Record* of March 10, 1971, "John D. Rockefeller IV is an advisor to Nader."

With money, the Rockefellers gained great influence over the media. With the media, the family gained sway over public opinion. With the pulse of public opinion, they gained deep influence in politics. And with this politics of subtle corruption, they are taking control of the nation.

According to several sources, David Rockefeller made the following comments at the 1991 Baden-Baden meeting: "We are grateful to the

Washington Post, the *New York Times*, *Time* magazine and other great publications, whose directors have attended our meetings and respected their promises of discretion for almost forty years." He went on to explain: "It would have been impossible for us to develop our plan for the world if we had been subjected to the lights of publicity during those years. But, the world is more sophisticated and prepared to march towards a world government. The supranational sovereignty of an intellectual elite and world bankers is surely preferable to the national auto determination practiced in past centuries."

Is it really, Mr. Rockefeller? Can Etienne Davignon's words be taken at face value? Remember what Mr. Davignon had to say during a 2005 BBC interview: "I don't think a global ruling class exists. Business influences society, and politics influences society — that's purely common sense. It's not that business contests the right of democratically elected leaders to lead."

However, a comment made to the Bilderberger elite by George Ball during a presentation titled "Internationalization of Business" at the April 26-28, 1968, Bilderberg meeting at Mont Tremblant, Canada, provides a far more truthful and insightful glimpse into the Group's economic orientation. Ball, who was the Undersecretary of State for Economic Affairs under JFK and Lyndon Johnson, a Steering Committee member of the Bilderberg Group as well as a Senior Managing Director for Lehman Brothers and Kuhn Loeb Inc., defined what the new Bilderberger policy of globalization was going to be, and how it would shape the Group's policy.

"In essence," writes Pierre Beaudry in *Synarchy Movement of Empire*, "Ball presented an outline of the advantages of a new-colonial world economic order based on the concept of a *world company*, and described some of the obstacles that needed to be eliminated for its success. According to Ball, the first and most important thing that had to be eliminated was *the archaic political structure of the nation state*."

In other words, Ball was calling for a return to the old colonial system but this time built on the concept of a *world company*. "To be productive," Beaudry quotes Ball, "we must begin our inquiry by explicitly recognizing the lack of phasing between *development of the world company* — a concept responding to modern needs — and the continued existence of an *archaic political structure of nation states*, mostly small or of only medium size, which is evolving only at glacier pace in response to new world requirements of scope and scale."

Beaudry cuts to the chase in summarizing Ball's speech: "For Ball, the very structure of the nation state, and the idea of the commonwealth, or of a general welfare of a people, represented the main obstacle against any attempt of freely looting the planet, especially the weak and poor nations of the world, and represented the most important impediment to the creation of a neo-colonial world empire. The priority of the world company is obviously based on international free trade without restraint; that is, trade measured by the British standards of profit of buying cheap and selling dear. The problem is that national governments have priorities, which are different from and contrary to those of a looting company."[35]

Mr. Ball let a *big* rabbit out of the hat when, according to page 39 of a Bilderberg transcript from the 1968 meeting at Mont Tremblant, he wistfully asked, "Where does one find a legitimate base for the power of corporate managements to make decisions that can profoundly affect the economic life of nations to whose governments they have only limited responsibility?"

In other words, Mssrs. Rockefeller and Davignon, what Mr. Ball would like to know is how does one establish a Halliburton type of world company, which would greatly surpass, in authority, any government on the planet? How *does* one establish David Rockefeller's Utopian ideal of the world, where "supranational sovereignty of world bankers supersedes national auto-determination practiced in past centuries"?

In fact, it is quite simple.

Current representative democracy works on the basis of an "elected" government — a Head of State and a sizable deliberative body — which can be dumped any time it may be decided by "orchestrating a crisis," along with a third power (called an "independent central banking system") in charge of its finances.

In the United States, this "independent" banking system is known as the Federal Reserve System, a privately owned bank system interlocked with the Bilderbergers. In Europe, the independent banking system is run through the European Central Bank, whose monetary policies are put together by the leading members of the Bilderberg elite, including Jean Claude Trichet.

In Britain, this "independent" system is run by the Bank of England, whose members are also full-time members of the Bilderberger inner circle.

The "independent central banking system" controls the issuance of currency; controls national credit and interest rates; and, any time the government displeases it, it uses its power to orchestrate the overthrow of the government. Margaret Thatcher, British Prime Minister, was removed from her post by her own Tory party because she opposed the transfer of British sovereignty to the European Super-State designed by the Bilderbergers.

According to Beaudry, "This is what Kuhn Loeb and Lehman Brothers have been building worldwide, by ways of merger and acquisitions, from the 1960s until today. In the past decades, the entire deregulation policy of U.S. industries and banking was precisely set up in response to this blueprint scenario for creating giant corporations for a new empire whose intention is nothing short of perpetual war."[36]

The Media

Past media invitees included Katharine Graham, now deceased, owner and chairwoman of the executive committee of the *Washington Post*; Donald E. Graham, Publisher, the *Washington Post*; Jim Hoagland and Charles Krauthammer, both columnists for the *Washington Post*; Andrew Knight, News Corporation director of Knight-Ridder; Arthur Sulzberger, *New York Times* editor and Council on Foreign Relations member; Robert L. Bartley, vice president of the *Wall Street Journal* and member of both the Council on Foreign Relations and the Trilateral Commission; Mortimer B. Zuckerman, chairman and editor-in-chief of *U.S. News and World Report,* New York's *Daily News*, and *Atlantic Monthly*, also a Council on Foreign Relations member; William F. Buckley, Jr., editor-in-chief of the *National Review*, Thomas L. Friedman, *New York Times* columnist; Bill Moyers, executive director of Public Affairs TV and former Director of the Council on Foreign Relations. A more extensive list is provided in an endnote.[37]

The ideas and policies that come out of the Bilderberg annual meetings are used to generate news in the leading periodicals and news groups of the world. The point is to make the prevalent opinions of the Bilderbergers so appealing that they become public policy and to pressure world leaders into submitting to the "needs of the Masters of the Universe." The "free world press" is completely at the mercy of the Bilderbergers disseminating the agreed-upon propaganda.

What is most disturbing is that publicly traded corporations try to keep the Bilderberger guest-list a secret, and the corporate press scarcely reports on the event at all. The likes of Microsoft, AT&T, Bechtel, Cisco, Compaq and Price Waterhouse Coopers have nothing to fear from the press. Never mind that Microsoft and NBC co-own MSNBC cable network. In fact, among the frequently invited Bilderberg guests can be found the name of Anthony Ridder of Knight-Ridder, Inc., America's second-largest newspaper chain, which owns such publications as the *Detroit Free Press*, the *Miami Herald* and the *Philadelphia Inquirer*.

In the 1993 August/September edition, the prestigious Dutch magazine *Exposure* outlined disturbing details about how the Tavistock Institute for Behavioural Analysis, premier behavioural research center in the world, planned to control the boards of the three major and most prestigious television networks in the United States: NBC, CBS and ABC. All three television networks came as spin-offs from the Radio Corporation of America (RCA). These organizations and institutions that theoretically are in "competition" with each other — this is part of the "independence" that ensures Americans enjoy unbiased news — are in fact closely interfaced and interlocked with countless companies and banks, making it an almost impossible task to untangle them.

According to then-U.S. Representative Bernie Sanders, NBC's owner General Electric is "one of the largest corporations in the world — and one with a long history of anti-union activity. GE, a major contributor to the Republican Party, has substantial financial interests in weapons manufacturing, finance, nuclear power and many other industries. Former CEO Jack Welch was one of the leaders in shutting down American plants and moving them to low-wage countries like China and Mexico."[38]

NBC is a subsidiary of RCA, a media conglomerate. On RCA's board sits Thornton Bradshaw, president of Atlantic Richfield Oil, and member of the World Wildlife Fund, the Club of Rome, the Aspen Institute for Humanistic Studies, and the Council on Foreign Relations. Bradshaw is also chairman of NBC.

RCA's most legendary role, however, was the service it provided to British Intelligence during World War II. Of particular note: RCA's President David Sarnoff moved to London at the same time Sir William Stephenson (of *Intrepid* fame) moved into the RCA building in New

York. During the war, Sarnoff was Eisenhower's top communications expert, overseeing the construction of a radio transmitter that was powerful enough to reach all of the allied forces in Europe. He campaigned for, and received, the honorary title of Brigadier General, and thereafter preferred to be known as "General Sarnoff." Today, the RCA directorate is made up of British-American establishment figures that belong to other organizations such as the CFR, NATO, the Club of Rome, the Trilateral Commission, Bilderbergers, Round Table, etc.

Among the NBC directors named in the *Exposure* article were John Brademas (CFR, TC, Bilderberg), a director of the Rockefeller Foundation; Peter G. Peterson (CFR), a former head of Kuhn, Loeb & Co. (Rothschild), and a former U.S. Secretary of Commerce; Robert Cizik, chairman of RCA and of First City Bancorp, which was identified in Congressional testimony as a Rothschild bank; Thomas O. Paine, president of Northrup Co. (the big defense contractor) and director of the Institute of Strategic Studies in London; Donald Smiley, a director of two Morgan Companies, Metropolitan Life and U.S. Steel; and the above-mentioned Thornton Bradshaw, chairman of RCA, director of the Rockefeller Brothers Fund, Atlantic Richfield, and the Aspen Institute for Humanistic Studies (both of the latter headed by a Bilderberger, Robert O. Anderson). Clearly the NBC board is considerably influenced by the Rockefeller-Rothschild-Morgan *troika*, leading exponents of the New World Order initiative.

ABC is owned by the Disney Corporation, "which produces toys and products in developing countries where they provide their workers with atrocious wages and working conditions."[39] It has 153 TV stations. Chase Manhattan Bank controls 6.7% of ABC's stock — enough to give it a controlling interest. Chase, through its trust department, controls 14% of CBS and 4.5% of RCA. Instead of three competing television networks called NBC, CBS, and ABC, what we really have is the Rockefeller Broadcasting Company, the Rockefeller Broadcasting System, and the Rockefeller Broadcasting Consortium.

On the ABC board of directors is Ray Adam, director of J.P. Morgan, Metropolitan Life (Morgan), and Morgan Guaranty Trust; Frank Cary, chairman of IBM, and director of J.P. Morgan and the Morgan Guaranty Trust; Donald C. Cook (CFR, Bilderberg), general partner of Lazard Freres banking house, whose executives frequently attend Bilderberg meetings; John T. Connor (CFR) of the Kuhn,

Loeb (Rothschild) law firm, Gravath, Swaine and Moore, former Secretary of the Navy, U.S. Secretary of Commerce, director of the Chase Manhattan Bank (Rockefeller/ Rothschild), General Motors, and chairman of the J. Henry Schroder Bank; Thomas M. Macioce, director of Manufacturers Hanover Trust (Rothschild); George Jenkins, chairman of Metropolitan Life (Morgan) and Citibank (Rothschild connections); Martin J. Schwab, director of Manufacturers Hanover (Rothschild); Alan Greenspan (CFR, Trilateral Commission, Bilderberg), chairman of the Federal Reserve Board, director of J.P. Morgan, Morgan Guaranty Trust, Hoover Institute, *Time* magazine, and General Foods; Ulric Haynes, Jr., director of the Ford Foundation and Marine Midland Bank.

Isn't it strange how the same Rockefeller-Rothschild-Morgan characters on the board of the ABC network, which, we are told, is independent of NBC, appear to represent the competition? ABC was taken over by Cities Communications, whose most prominent director is Robert Roosa (CFR, Bilderberg), senior partner of Brown Brothers Harriman, which has close ties with the Bank of England. Roosa and David Rockefeller are credited with selecting Paul Volcker to chair the Federal Reserve Board.

CBS is owned by Viacom, which has over 200 TV and 255 radio affiliates nationwide. This huge media conglomerate owns, among other companies, MTV, Showtime, Nickelodeon, VH1, TNN, CMT, 39 broadcast television stations, 184 radio stations, Paramount Pictures and Blockbuster Inc. As an American intelligence officer, CBS founder William Paley was trained in mass brainwashing techniques during World War II at the Tavistock Institute in England.

The financial expansion of CBS was supervised for a long time by Brown Brothers Harriman and its senior partner, Prescott Bush (father and grandfather to Presidents), who was a CBS director. The CBS board included Chairman Paley, for whom Prescott Bush personally organized the money to buy the company; Harold Brown (CFR), executive director of the Trilateral Commission, and former Secretary of the Air Force and of Defense of the U.S.; Roswell Gilpatric (CFR, Bilderberg), from the Kuhn, Loeb (Rothschild) law firm, Cravath, Swaine, and Moore, and former director of the Federal Reserve Bank of New York; Henry B. Schnacht, director of the Chase Manhattan Bank (Rockefeller/Rothschild), the Council on Foreign Relations, Brookings

Institution, and Committee for Economic Development; Michel C. Bergerac, chairman of Revlon, and director of Manufacturers Hanover Bank (Rothschild); James D. Wolfensohn (CFR, Trilateral Commission, Bilderberg), former head of J. Henry Schroder Bank, who has close links with the Rothschilds and the Rockefellers, and who in 1995 was successfully nominated to head the World Bank by Bill Clinton; Franklin A. Thomas (CFR), head of the Rockefeller-controlled Ford Foundation; Newton D. Minow (CFR), director of the Rand Corporation and, among many others, the Ditchley Foundation, which is closely linked with the Tavistock Institute in London and the Bilderberg Group. The former president of CBS was Dr. Frank Stanton (CFR), who is also a trustee of the Rockefeller Foundation and Carnegie Institution. So, are the Rothschild and the Rockefeller families, who are leading groups in the tightly controlled field of communications, answering directly to the Bilderbergers?

FOX News Channel, part of the FOX network, is owned by Rupert Murdoch, who owns a significant portion of the world's media. His network has close ties to the Republican Party and among his "fair and balanced" commentators is Newt Gingrich, former GOP Republican House speaker. Murdoch, needless to say, is a luminary in the secret Bilderberg Group. He has most recently added the *Wall Street Journal* to his empire.

All these networks are closely interlocked with Bilderberg, the Council on Foreign Relations and the Trilateral Commission. How, then, can it possibly be claimed that the majority of Americans get their news from independent sources?

The Logan Act:

§ 953. Private correspondence with foreign governments.

Any citizen of the United States, wherever he may be, who, without authority of the United States, directly or indirectly commences or carries on any correspondence or intercourse with any foreign government or any officer or agent thereof, with intent to influence the measures or conduct of any foreign government or of any officer or agent thereof, in relation to any disputes or controversies with the United States, or to defeat the measures of the United States, shall be fined under this title or imprisoned not more than three years, or both.

This section shall not abridge the right of a citizen to apply himself, or his agent, to any foreign government, or the agents thereof, for redress of any injury which he may have sustained from such government or any of its agents or subjects.

1 Stat. 613, January 30, 1799, codified at 18 U.S.C. § 953 (2004)

CHAPTER TWELVE

ENFORCED DISARMAMENT

Unknown to almost everyone, the U.S. government, sponsored by the Council on Foreign Relations, has made a secret commitment to surrender irrevocably to the United Nations the means of protecting its national sovereignty, and, ultimately, to confiscate all of the weapons owned by its own citizens, as part of a planned future global disarmament program. Except that the "future," as far as this particular program is concerned, appears to be very near indeed.

Some prestigious members of the American political community fully agree with this policy. CFR fellow Walter Rostow, JFK's adviser in the Viet Nam War, wrote in his book *The United States in the World Arena*, that "it is a legitimate American national objective to see removed from all nations — including the United States — the right to use substantial military force to pursue their own interests. Since this right is the root of national sovereignty, it is therefore an American interest to see an end to nationhood as it has been historically defined."

As a State Department official, heading its policy-planning council, Walt Rostow authored the infamous *Rostow Papers*, which laid out these goals for American foreign policy: unilateral disarmament, world government and accommodation with the Communist world. Was Walter Whitman Rostow a Communist, an anti-American or a one-world globalist? His father was a Marxist revolutionary in Russia. His brother, Eugene Debs Rostow, was named after prominent labor organizer and Socialist leader Eugene Debs. Two of his aunts were members of the Communist Party. Walter Rostow, on three separate occasions was rejected for employment in the State Department by the Eisenhower administration. U.S. Air Force intelligence branded him a security risk. The CIA had dropped him from a sensitive contract. He had long consorted with Communist Party members, including known Soviet spies. To get him on board as an adviser, the Kennedy administration had to fire Otto Otepka, head of security for the State Department.

As startling as these assertions may appear, they are fully supported by U.S. government documents.

Although "officially" released in September 1961, one document — DEPARTMENT OF STATE PUBLICATION 7277, published in unabridged form in the 35-page "BLUEPRINT FOR THE PEACE RACE" by the U.S. ARMS CONTROL AND DISARMAMENT AGENCY (PUBLICATION #4, GENERAL SERIES #3, MAY 1962) — had long been extremely difficult to track down, due to its sensitive nature and far-reaching consequences. Since its 1962 publication, the document has become "unavailable," according to numerous responses to inquiries I made to the U.S. Navy, CIA, Army, etc. I was finally shown it by a captain of the United States counter-intelligence division, who risked his job and his life in getting in touch with me and later showing them to me. Ironically, it is now easily found on the Internet.

FREEDOM FROM WAR: THE UNITED STATES PROGRAM FOR GENERAL AND COMPLETE DISARMAMENT IN A PEACEFUL WORLD DEPARTMENT OF STATE PUBLICATION 7277, Released September 1961

INTRODUCTION
This new program provides for the progressive reduction of the war-making capabilities of nations and the simultaneous strengthening of international institutions to settle disputes and maintain the peace. It is based on three principles deemed essential to the achievement of practical progress in the disarmament field:
First, there must be immediate disarmament action.
A strenuous and uninterrupted effort must be made toward the goal of general and complete disarmament; at the same time, it is important that specific measures be

put into effect as soon as possible.

Second, all disarmament obligations must be subject to effective international controls.

The control organization must have the manpower, facilities, and effectiveness to assure that limitations or reductions take place as agreed.

Third, adequate peace-keeping machinery must be established.

There is an inseparable relationship between the *scaling down of national armaments* on the one hand and the building up of international peace-keeping machinery and institutions on the other. Nations are unlikely to shed their means of self-protection in the absence of alternative ways to safeguard their legitimate interests. *This can only be achieved through the progressive strengthening of international institutions under the United Nations and by creating a United Nations Peace force to enforce the peace as the disarmament process proceeds.*

DISARMAMENT GOAL AND OBJECTIVES

The overall goal of the United States is a free, secure, and peaceful world of independent states adhering to common standards of justice and international conduct and subjecting the use of force to the rule of law; *a world that has achieved general and complete disarmament under effective international control; and a world in which adjustment to change takes place in accordance with the principles of the United Nations.*

In order to make possible the achievement of that goal, the program sets forth the following specific objectives toward which nations should direct their efforts:

• The disbanding of all national armed forces and the prohibition of their re-establishment in any form whatsoever other than those required to preserve internal order and for contributions to a United Nations Peace Force.

• The elimination from national arsenals of *all armaments*, including all weapons of mass destruction and the means for their delivery, other than those required for a United Nations Peace Force and for maintaining internal order:

• The institution of effective means for the enforcement of international agreements, for the enforcement of international disputes, and for the principles of the United Nations;

• The establishment and effective operation of an International Disarmament within the framework of the United Nations to insure compliance at all times with all disarmament obligations.

GOVERNING PRINCIPLES

• As states relinquish their arms, the United Nations must be progressively strengthened in order to improve its capacity to assure international security and the peaceful settlement of disputes.

DISARMAMENT STAGES

The program provides for progressive disarmament steps to take place in three stages and for the simultaneous strengthening of international institutions.

FIRST STAGE

The first stage contains measures which would significantly reduce the capabilities of nations to wage aggressive war.

• Arms and armed forces would be reduced: The armed forces of the United States and the Soviet Union would be limited to 2.1 million men each (with appropriate levels not exceeding that amount for other militarily significant states); levels of armaments would be correspondingly reduced and their production would be limited.

• UN peace-keeping powers would be strengthened: Measures would be taken to develop and strengthen United Nations arrangements for arbitration, for the development of international law, and for the establishment in Stage II of a permanent UN Peace Force.

• An International Disarmament Organization would be established for effective verification of the disarmament program: Its functions would be expanded progressively as disarmament proceeds. It would certify to all states that agreed reductions have taken place and that retained forces and armaments do not exceed permitted levels.

It would determine the transition from one stage to the next.

• Further substantial reductions in the armed forces, armaments, and military establishments of states, including strategic nuclear weapons delivery vehicles and countering weapons;

• The manufacture of armaments would be prohibited except for those of agreed types and quantities to be used by the UN Peace Force and those required to maintain internal order. All other armaments would be destroyed or converted to peaceful purposes.

• The peace-keeping capabilities of the United Nations would be sufficiently strong and the obligations of all states under such arrangements sufficiently far-reaching as to assure peace and the just settlement of differences in a disarmed world.

Set forth as the objectives of a program of general and complete disarmament, in a peaceful world:

(a) The disbanding of all national armed forces and the prohibition of their reestablishment in any form whatsoever, other than those required to preserve internal order and for contributions to a United Nations Peace Force;

(b) As states relinquish arms, the United Nations shall be progressively strengthened in order to improve its capacity to assure international security and the peaceful settlement of differences as well as to facilitate the development of international cooperation in common tasks for the benefit of mankind.

[emphases added]

Under Presidential Decision Directive No. 25, and in conjunction with the Department of State Publication 7277, the United Nations "Partnership for Peace" program serves to cement people to relationships between the citizens of the United States and the global military of the UN establishments.

TOP SECRET MILITARY PLANS

Page 554 of 1982 edition of the U.S. Code, Volume 9, Public Law #87-297 (1961) was signed by President Kennedy in 1962; it has received eighteen subsequent updates, and its provisions have been steadily implemented by every President since.

Public Law # 87-297 (1961) calls for the elimination of U.S. national forces and further declares that "no one may possess a firearm or lethal weapon except police or military personnel." This law is taught and explained in the National War College and various U.S. Armed Forces Academies.

What does it imply? That the New World Order will require an Army, and it will be formed under the UN banner.

On page 555 of Public Law #87-297 (1961), "disarmament" is defined as elimination of U.S. Forces and absolute restrictions on privately-owned "deadly weapons"; again, on page 557, Sections (a) and (d) require the U.S. to eliminate its Armed Forces; page 558 deals with "policy formulation," i.e. the accomplishment of these goals.[40]

Ironically, it was Alger Hiss, who would be convicted as a Soviet spy, who set up the United Nations with his U.S. State Department colleagues. He served as a temporary UN Secretary-General as well as resident of the Carnegie Endowment for International Peace and is credited with establishing the UN Department of Political and Security Affairs, which would have jurisdiction over all future UN military operations.

Hiss' influence shows up in the fine print of the rules and regulations governing UN military operations. One rule stated that the head of this UN department would always be a Soviet citizen, military officer, or person designated by the Soviets. This was the case for the first 53 years, in which the following fourteen Communists chaired the vital UN position of Undersecretary-General of Political and Security Council Affairs. The first selected to hold the post at the 35th plenary meeting on October 24, 1946, was Arkady Sobolev:

1946-49 Arkady Sobolev
1949-53 Konstantin Zinchenko
1953-54 Ilya Tchernychev
1954-57 Dragoslav Protitch
1960-62 Georgy Arkadev
1962-63 E.D. Kiselyv
1963-65 V.P. Suslov
1965-68 Alexei E. Nesterenko
1968-73 Leonid N. Kutakov
1973-78 Arkady N. Shevchenko
1978-81 Mikhail D. Sytenko
1981-86 Viacheslav A. Ustinov
1987-92 Vasilly S. Safronchuk
1992-97 Vladimir Petrovsky

The only appointee with no Soviet ties is the present chairman, Kieran Prendergast of the United Kingdom, who was appointed in 1997. Shortly thereafter, he became a Bilderberg Group member at the Turnburry meeting in Scotland in 1998.

Averell Harriman, Dean Acheson, John McCloy and David E. Bruce

Ogden Mills

Andrew Mellon

Condi Rice

Paul Wolfowitz

Brent Scrowcroft, Colin Powell, George Schultz, Henry Kissinger & non-CFR member George W. Bush

Donald Rumsfeld, Gerald Ford & Dick Cheney

Condi Rice and McGeorge Bundy

William Donaldson

Henry Stimson, John McCloy and Robert Lovett

Al Haig, Lawrence Eagleburger and Kissinger

CHAPTER THIRTEEN

CFR CABINET CONTROL

T he National Security Act of 1947 established the office of Secretary of Defense. Since 1947 there have been 14 Secretaries of Defense on the Council on Foreign Relations and/or Trilateral Commission membership list.

One undercover FBI agent once explained it to me this way: "President Clinton has appointed three Secretaries of Defense – William Cohen, William Perry, and Les Aspin. Under Secretary for International Security Affairs Lynn Etheridge Davis has been coordinating Psychological Operations under all three. Davis has been involved with the U.S. Intelligence community and a part of every Administration from the '70s through the '90s. Davis, Clinton and Perry are Trilateral Commission members. Davis, Clinton, Cohen, and Aspin all belong to the Council on Foreign Relations. Davis is also a Vice President at David Rockefeller's Chase Manhattan Bank.

"Now," my FBI source continued, "with whom do you suppose Lynn Etheridge Davis' loyalties lie?"

Davis once published a book, in 1974, titled, *The Cold War Begins: Soviet-American Conflict Over Eastern Europe*. It contained this chilling sentence: "The most important step would be for government to place *volunteer* military forces under UN command."

Is it any wonder that so many honest and patriotic men and women of the American spy community are helping to fight the menace of the New World Order?

Since 1940, every U.S. Secretary of State (with the sole exception of James Byrnes, who later became Governor of South Carolina) has been a member of the Council on Foreign Relations and/or its offshoot, the Trilateral Commission. Also since 1940, almost every Secretary of War/ Defense has been a CFR member. Virtually every key U.S. National Security and Foreign Policy Adviser has been a CFR member for the past 80 years. Almost all of the ranking generals and admirals, including those on the Joint Chiefs of Staff, plus many line officers are or have been members of the Council on Foreign Relations. The following lists include both present and former members.

PRESIDENTIAL CANDIDATES (CFR MEMBERS)

Selected by their respective parties as official candidates to the Office of the Presidency

John W. Davis (24), Herbert Hoover (28-32), Wendell Wilkie (40), Thomas Dewey (44-48), Adlai Stevenson (52-56), Dwight Eisenhower (52-56), John F. Kennedy (60), Richard Nixon (60,68,72), Hubert Humphrey (68), George McGovern (72), Gerald Ford (76), Jimmy Carter (76-80), John Anderson (80), George W. Bush (80,88-92), Walter Mondale (84), Michael Dukakis (88), Bill Clinton (92-96)

CIA DIRECTORS (CFR MEMBERS)

Richard Helms (66-73 Johnson), James R. Schlesinger (73 Nixon), William E. Colby (73-76 Nixon), George W. Bush (76-77 Ford), Stansfield Turner (77-81 Carter), William J. Casey (81-87 Reagan), William H. Webster (87-91 Reagan), Robert M. Gates (91-93 Bush), R. James Woolsey (93-95 Bush), John Deutsch (95-96 Clinton), George Tenet (97-04 Bush)

SECRETARIES OF DEFENSE (CFR MEMBERS)

Neil McElroy (57-59 Eisenhower), Thomas S. Gates (59-61 Eisenhower), Robert S. McNamara (61-68 Kennedy, Johnson), Melvin Laird (69-73 Nixon), Elliot Richardson (73 Nixon), Donald Rumsfeld (75-77 Ford), Harold Brown (77-81 Carter), Casper Weinberger (81-87 Reagan), Frank C. Carlucci (87-89 Reagan), Richard Cheney, (89-93

G.H.W. Bush), Les Aspin (93-94 Clinton), William J. Perry (94-97 Clinton), William Cohen (97-01 Clinton), Donald Rumsfeld (01-06 G.W. Bush) Robert M. Gates (06- G.W. Bush).

SECRETARIES OF THE TREASURY (CFR MEMBERS)

The Secretary of the Treasury is the chief economic and financial advisor to the government appointed by the President of the United States. The following Secretaries of the Treasury had membership on the Council on Foreign Relations:

Robert B. Anderson (Eisenhower), Douglas C. Dillon (Kennedy/Johnson), Henry Hamill Fowler (Johnson), David M. Kennedy and George P. Schultz (Nixon), William Edward Simon (Nixon/Ford), W. Michael Blumenthal (Carter), G. William Miller (Carter), James A. Baker III (Reagan), Nicholas F. Brady (Reagan/Bush), Lloyd M. Bentsen (Clinton), Robert E. Rubin (Clinton), Paul H. O'Neill (G.W. Bush), John W. Snow (G.W. Bush), Henry Paulson (G.W. Bush).

The Secretary of the Treasury relies heavily on the classified information he receives from the National Security Council. This classified information permits the Department of the Treasury to contribute fully to the "attainment of national security objectives and to the particular climate of opinion the United States is seeking to achieve in the world," explains Dr. Richard J. Boylan, behavioral scientist, university associate professor (emeritus) and researcher in the summer 2001 issue of *True Democracy*.

As the late Gary Allen noted in his international best-seller, *The Rockefeller File*: "The Rockefellers have made the Treasury Department virtually a branch of the Chase Manhattan Bank."

APPOINTMENTS TO THE SUPREME COURT

When a Justice retires from the Supreme Court, the general public sees the sitting President nominate a replacement who closely reflects his own thinking, including political and religious beliefs. His nominee is then usually approved by the U.S. Senate. What the general public does not see is how the President short-lists his candidates. If the President is a CFR member, the possibilities are screened by 100 or more Council members working together as the "Special Group" or the "Secret Team" behind closed doors. Each one is vetted to see which choice will best promote decisions that advance the opinion that Council on Foreign Relations members are seeking to promote in the world.

If the President is not a CFR member, the odd status of George W. Bush, this selected nominee is still influenced by advisers who are CFR members. This ensures continuity in the Supreme Court through various presidential terms; for instance, the Roe v. Wade watershed case, which established women's right to abortion, was decided by nine Justices chosen by Presidents who belonged to the CFR: Burger (Nixon 1969), Douglas (Roosevelt 1939), Brennan (Eisenhower 1956), Stewart (Eisenhower 1958), White (Kennedy 1962), Marshall (Johnson 1967), Blackmun (Nixon 1970), Powell (Nixon 1971), Rehnquist (Nixon 1971).[41] In this case, many people would agree the decision reached was the right one. But, the decision may also open the door for selective breeding in the future.

It is most distressing to learn that the President does not actually decide on the choice, but is told whom to select for the vacant seat. This not only compromises the American justice system as we believe it should be; it also suggests that the final custodians of our individual rights are, in fact, looking after the interests of the CFR.

CHAPTER FOURTEEN

CFR AND PSYCHO-POLITICAL OPERATIONS

According to Department of the Army Pamphlet No. 525-7-1, *The Art and Science of Psychological Operations,* "the Secretary of Defense is the principal assistant to the president in all matters relating to Department of Defense, and exercises direction, authority, and control over the department. He serves as a member of the National Security Council. Among the several principal military and civilian advisor and staff assistants to the secretary, his assistant secretary for International Security Affairs has major Psychological Operations (PSYOP) related responsibilities."[42]

Hadley Cantril, a successful 1940s sociologist and public opinion researcher explained this in his 1967 book, *The Human Dimension: Experiences in Policy Research,* published by Rutgers University Press: "Psycho-political operations are propaganda campaigns designed to create perpetual tensions and to manipulate different groups of people to accept the particular climate of opinion the CFR seeks to achieve in the world."

As Ken Adachi has noted, "What most Americans believe to be 'Public Opinion' is in reality *carefully crafted and scripted propaganda* designed to elicit a *desired behavioral response* from the public."[43] Getting people to behave the way you hope they will behave by persuading them that it is ultimately in their interest to do so is achieving a desired behavioral response. Public opinion polls are qualitative studies that investigate in depth the motivations, the feelings, and the reactions of selected social groups towards *acceptance* of the CFR's planned programs. Implementation of the insidious propaganda and public opinion manipulations (including mind-control agendas) is executed in the United States by well over 200 "think tanks" such as the RAND Corporation, Planning Research Corporation, Hudson Institute, International Institute for Applied Behavioral Sciences, Heritage Foundation and the Brookings Institution, which are overseen and directed *in the United States*, by the Stanford Research Institute (SRI) in Menlo Park, California.[44]

As John Coleman in *Conspirators' Hierarchy* writes, "Today, the Tavistock Institute operates a $6 billion a year network of Foundations in the U.S., all of it funded by U.S. taxpayers' money. Ten major institutions are under its direct control, with 400 subsidiaries, and 3000 other study groups and think tanks that originate many types of programs to increase control over the American people. The Stanford Research Institute, adjoining the Hoover Institute, is a $150-million-a-year operation with 3,300 employees. It carries on program surveillance for Bechtel, Kaiser, and 400 other companies, and extensive intelligence operations for the CIA. It is the largest institution on the West Coast promoting mind control and the behavioural sciences."

The Rockefeller-funded RAND Institute and the Rockefeller-financed Tavistock Institute in England investigate the "dynamics of evolution"; that is the logic behind *why* people of various backgrounds, interests, loyalties, and information levels hold certain opinions. The Establishment elitists refer to it as "the engineering of consent." As Coleman makes absolutely clear in his book: "Tavistock and like-minded American foundations have a single goal in mind — to break down the psychological strength of the individual and render him helpless to oppose the dictators of the World Order."

In *Educating for the New World Order* (Halcyon House, 1991), B.K. Eakman, noted the impact of one Establishment think tank: "Specific RAND policies that became operative include U.S. nuclear policies, corporate analyses, hundreds of projects for the military, the Central Intelligence Agency in relation to the use of mind altering drugs like peyote, LSD." One such project was code-named MK-ULTRA.

The covert MK-ULTRA operation, which lasted for 20 years, was the brainchild of Richard Helms, later to become CIA director. ULTRA was the code name for a CIA mind-control research program lasting from the 1950s through the 1970s. The "doctors," headed by psychiatrist Dr. Ewen Cameron and former Nazi scientists, used some of the same techniques as concentration camps, including electro-shock, sleep deprivation, memory implantation, memory erasure, sensory modification, and psychoactive drug experiments. Ironically, Dr. Cameron had served as a member of the Nuremberg tribunal that heard the war-crime cases against Nazi doctors.

"The ideology of American foundations," writes Dr. Byron T. Weeks, retired Colonel of the U.S. Air Force, "was created by the Tavistock Institute of Human Relations in London. In 1921, the Duke of Bedford, Marquess of Tavistock gave a building to the Institute to study the effect of shellshock on British soldiers who survived World War I. Its purpose was to establish the *breaking point* of men under stress, under the direction of the British Army Bureau of Psychological Warfare, commanded by Sir John Rawlings-Reese."[45]

The February 1971 edition of a Moscow-based Russian magazine, *International Affairs*, carried an article titled, "Ways and Means of U.S. Ideological Expansion." It analyzed America's propaganda efforts: "Psycho-political operations are further subdivided into *strategic psycho-political operations* that focus propaganda at small groups of people, such as the academics or experts, capable of influencing public opinion and *tactical psycho-political operations* that focus propaganda at the masses through mass communication media (i.e. newspapers, radio, television, textbooks, educational material, art, entertainment, etc.)."[46]

"Our" side evidently saw themselves the same way: "Both forms of propaganda are used to manipulate public opinion to attain foreign policy goals in a given period." So said a group of experts in a pamphlet entitled *The Art and Science of Psychological Operations: Case Studies of Military Application Volume One*, published in 1976 by the Headquarters Department of the U.S. Army.[47]

That same year, Thomas R. Dye, one of the most prolific American authors on the inner-workings of modern day America, described the process by which "public opinion" is established: "This opinion is formulated by the dominant Council on Foreign Relations members who belong to an inner circle called the 'Special Group' that plan and coordinate the psycho-political operations used to manipulate the American public, and through a vast intergovernmental undercover infrastructure called the 'Secret Team' that include the legislative, executive, and judicial branches of government, such as the Secretary of State, the Secretary of Defense, the Secretary of the Treasury and the Director of the CIA; those who control television, radio, and newspaper corporations; who head the largest law firms; who run the largest and most prestigious universities and think tanks; who direct the largest private foundations and who direct the largest public corporations."[48]

The Council on Foreign Relations' "Secret Team" follows the pattern of leadership of all secret societies. The organization is structured as circles within circles, with the exterior layer (Secret Team) always protecting the more dominant inner membership (Special Group) that coordinates the psycho-political operations. By keeping the objectives, the identities and the roles played by members of a "Secret Team" hidden from other team members, the CFR "Special Group" protects itself from hypothetical prosecution by denying its participation in the operation. To further protect itself from possible prosecution, the CFR does not reveal to every Council member what psycho-political operations are being planned or what their exact role in the operation is. The more exclusive Bilderberg Group operates under identical criteria.

The CFR has long been convinced that "absolute behavior control is imminent... without mankind's self-conscious realization that a crisis is at hand."[49]

The Association for Supervision and Curriculum Development of the liberal National Education Association, points to the effectiveness of today's sophisticated version of the old Hegelian dialectic process — the heart of the Soviet brainwashing system.

There are three ground rules:

1) The carefully crafted deception must contain a glimmer of the truth;

2) It must be convoluted enough, rendering simple fact-finding impossible. This can be accomplished by withholding key information from the public. According to Dale Keiger, a senior writer at *Johns Hopkins Magazine* covering humanities, international affairs and public policy issues in *A Different Form of Capitalism,* "The side meant to lose withholds key information that would cause public opinion to go against Council plans. In the Marshall Plan psycho-political operation, Kennan was for the plan and Lippmann against it. Kennan's side won. Years latter in his memoirs Kennan would say that upon reflection Lippmann was right."

3) The use of deception should not discredit a source which may have valuable future potential. This means that the media, largely owned by CFR-controlled corporations, must play the credibility card. With help from the media, for example, the CFR has already persuaded people around the world that "the resurgence of nationalism, the growth of fundamentalisms and of religious intolerance" is a global threat.[50]

The Council on Foreign Relations creates and delivers psycho-political operations by manipulating people's reality through a "tactic of deception," placing Council members on both sides of an issue. The deception is complete when the public is led to believe that its own best interests are being served while the CFR policy is being carried out.

Since the CFR has major leverage within the legal, legislative and court systems, it has little to fear from any "official" inquiry. Thus, it is free to create the perception in the general public, unable to comprehend the extent of the deceit, that laws are being followed. Lawyers, Legislators, and Judges elected, supported and protected by the Council are committing blatant illegalities to further CFR aims or to hide improprieties which, if exposed, would cause great public outcry.

For example, according to the Executive Summary of the Iran-Contra Investigation of the United States Government, available from U.S. National Archives & Records Administration for the years 1986-1993:

> In October and November 1986, two secret U.S. Government operations were publicly exposed implicating Reagan Administration officials in illegal activities: the provision of assistance to the military activities of Nicaraguan Contra rebels during an October 1984 to October 1986 prohibition on such aid, and the sale of U.S. arms to Iran in contravention of stated U.S. policy and in possible violation of arms-export controls. These operations became known as the Iran-Contra Affair. The Iran operation involved efforts in 1985 and 1986 to obtain the release of Americans held hostage in the Middle East through the sale of U.S. weapons to Iran, despite an embargo on such sales. The Contra operations from 1984 through most of 1986 involved the secret governmental support of Contra military and paramilitary activities in Nicaragua, despite Congressional prohibition of this support.
>
> The Iran and Contra operations were merged when funds generated from the sale of weapons to Iran were diverted to support the Contra effort in Nicaragua. Although this "diversion"

may be the most dramatic aspect of Iran/Contra, it is important
to emphasize that both the Iran and Contra operations, separately,
violated United States policy and law that is Arms Export Control
Act. In late November 1986, Reagan administration officials
announced that some of the proceeds from the sale of U.S. arms
to Iran had been diverted to the Contras.

On November 26, 1986, the Attorney General ordered the
Federal Bureau of Investigation to begin an investigation of the
Iran/Contra episode. On December 19, 1986, Lawrence Walsh was
appointed Independent Counsel to proceed with the investigation.
Did Lawrence Walsh play a constitutionally defined role as an
Independent Council, or might he, too, have been part of a much
greater conspiracy?

The record shows Walsh to have joined Henry Kissinger's team in
Paris during Viet Nam talks in 1969. In 1981, Walsh worked for one
of the oldest law firms in Oklahoma, Crowe and Dunlevy founded in
1902; the firm represented oil and insurance companies run by CFR
members.

CFR members of the "Special Group" — George H.W. Bush (Vice
President), Donald T. Regan (Chief of Staff to the President), Elliot
Abrams (Assistant Secretary of State for International Organization
Affairs), John Poindexter (U.S. National Security Advisor), Casper
Weinberger (Secretary of Defense), Robert M. Gates (Deputy Director
CIA), William J. Casey (CIA Director), and Robert C. McFarlane
(Assistant to the President for National Security Affairs) — all had
advised Reagan to go ahead with Iran-Contra.

On December 24, 1992, reports Associated Press, six years after the
Iran-Contra affair broke, President George H.W. Bush took advantage
of Christmas and the subsequent lack of attention from the media
to pardon fellow CFR members Weinberger, McFarlane, Abrams,
and three CIA chiefs named Fiers, George, and Clarridge. Why didn't
the "free press" bring this travesty of justice into the living rooms of
America? By remaining silent (another tactic of deception), the press
further demonstrated that it is part of the operation, part of the system,
part of the shadow government.

After a seven-year investigation that cost American taxpayers millions
of dollars, only one person, a second tier no-name, was convicted and
sent to prison... for not paying his income taxes.

An additional "tactic of deception" used to achieve the aims of the Council on Foreign Relations is to finance and "oversee" a legitimate study by a respected organization, with the express aim of manipulating public opinion by clever use of the right language.

Kai Bird, contributing editor and foreign affairs columnist for *The Nation* magazine, explained how this is accomplished in *The Color of Truth: McGeorge Bundy and William Bundy: Brothers in Arms*: "William L. Langer... organized the CIA's Office of National Estimates (known as ONE in 1950).... Langer had gone to Washington at the call of the CIA and promptly hired McGeorge's brother Bill as one of his top aides. They were old friends and political allies.... McGeorge had published a review in *The Reporter* of a massive two volume study of America's entry into World War II written by Langer and S. Everett Gleason. Langer had finished the project while at the CIA and Gleason was a high-ranking official in the National Security Council. McGeorge Bundy called it a 'magnificent achievement... so thorough that it will never be done again....' Funded by the Rockefeller Foundation and the Council on Foreign Relations to the tune of $139,000 — an extraordinary sum in those years — and written with privileged access to classified documents, the Langer-Gleason volumes were official history parading as independent scholarship."

William (Bill) Bundy, the man hired by Langer, was responsible for drafting the Tonkin Gulf Resolution. He was also an editor of the CFR's *Foreign Affairs* magazine. Furthermore, Bill Bundy was CFR Dean Acheson's son-in-law. Acheson's law partner was Donald Hiss — brother of the Soviet spy Alger Hiss. In the late 1940s, the Polish Communist Party hired Acheson's law firm to help win U.S. recognition. Also it was Acheson, the former Secretary of State, along with the aforementioned Walt Rostow, who persuaded Johnson to escalate the Viet Nam War.

The Council on Foreign Relations uses tax-free foundations as principal conduits to funnel money into favorable policy-making processes. Thomas R. Dye stated that nearly 40% of all foundation assets were controlled by the top ten or eleven foundations, who in turn were controlled by the Council on Foreign Relations.[51] Furthermore, "The directors or trustees have great latitude in directing the use of foundation monies to underwrite research, investigate social problems, create or assist universities, establish 'think tanks,' endow museums, etc."[52]

In 1993, Rene Wormser found that "the RAND National Defense Research Institute is a federally-funded Council on Foreign Relations 'think-tank' sponsored by the Office of the Secretary of Defense and headed by Council on Foreign Relations member Michael D. Rich. Clients include the Pentagon, AT&T, Chase Manhattan Bank, IBM, Republican Party, U.S. Air Force, U.S. Department of Energy and NASA. The interlocking leadership between the trustees at RAND, and the Ford, Rockefeller, and Carnegie foundations is a classic case of CFR/Bilderberg modus operandi. The Ford Foundation gave one million dollars to Rand in 1952, at a time when the president of the Ford Foundation was simultaneously the chairman of RAND."[53]

Two thirds of RAND's research involves national security issues and consequently is labeled secret. The other third of Rand Corporation research is devoted to population control studies (applied demography). One of the key areas of RAND's expertise deals with studies on how to misinform and to manipulate large groups of people. This often employs yet another tactic of deception: the Orwellian use of double talk. That is to say, peace is called war, pacifists are called terrorists, and those who try to tell the truth are denigrated for spreading hate and spewing evil.

In July 1992, influenced by the uncertainty of the dissolution of the Soviet Union and alarmed at the impending changes in Eastern Europe, RAND brought together the leading world experts to discuss the problems in the new world environment. The resulting document was "revised," that is molded to the objectives of RAND, and published as a Summer Institute Report titled, "Peacekeeping and Peacemaking after the Cold War." According to the report, the Secretary-General of the UN "defines peace building as post conflict action... The Secretary-General has linked preventive diplomacy with preventive deployments of military forces."

RAND stresses that, "the Secretary-General in his Agenda for Peace... emphasizes the need for governments to share information on political or military situations, and in so doing, he is asking for an expansion of Intelligence sharing..." Again, I emphasize that RAND's expertise in misinforming and manipulating large groups of people is one of the key attributes of this Rockefeller/CFR-funded corporation.

CHAPTER FIFTEEN

CFR AND THE MARSHALL PLAN

The Marshall Plan is so-named for the speech on June 5, 1947, by former General, and then-U.S. Secretary of State, George Marshall, at Harvard University. Marshall proposed a solution to the disintegrating economic and social conditions that faced Europeans in the aftermath of World War II. Under the program, the United States would provide aid to prevent starvation in the major war areas, repair the devastation of those areas as quickly as possible, and invite European countries to join in a cooperative plan for economic reconstruction. According to a brochure available from the Library of Congress of the United States, "America also benefited from the plan by developing valuable trading partners and reliable allies among the West European nations. Even more important were the many ties of individual and collective friendship that developed between the United States and Europe."

What is less generally acknowledged is that the "Plan" came with strings attached. America made explicit requirements for trade liberalization and increases in productivity, thus "ensuring the Americanization of Europe as European political and economic elites became wedded to their American counterparts with no significant economic or political development taking place without U.S. approval," according to English political writer Richard Greaves in his essay, "Who really runs the world?"

The Foreign Assistance Act that emerged in 1948 set up the Economic Cooperation Agency (ECA) to administer the European Recovery Program (ERP). Between the years 1948-1951, when the Marshall Plan was formally in operation, Congress appropriated $13.3 billion in aid to sixteen western European states.

In an article called "The Bilderberg Group and the project of European Unification" in *Lobster* magazine, political commentator Mike Peters writes, "This unprecedented exercise of international generosity (dubbed by Churchill the 'most sordid act in history') served direct economic purposes for the internationally oriented U.S. corporations which promoted it. William Clayton [CFR], for example, the Under-Secretary for Economic Affairs, whose tour of Europe and letters sent back to Washington played a key role in preparing the plan, and who pushed it through Congress, personally profited to the tune of $700,000 a year; and his own company, Anderson, Clayton & Co. secured $10 million of Marshall Plan orders up to the summer of 1949. General Motors similarly got $5.5 million worth of orders between July 1950 and 1951 (14.7% of the total), and the Ford Motor Company got $1 million (4.2% of the total)."

Kai Bird described the hidden aspects of the Plan in her book on the Bundy brothers. In 1949, "McGeorge Bundy, former Ford Foundation President, took on a project with the Council on Foreign Relations in New York to study Marshall Plan aid to Europe.... The Council's study group on aid to Europe included some of the foreign policy establishment's leading figures. Working with young Bundy on the project were Allen Dulles, David Lilienthal, Dwight Eisenhower, Will Clayton, George Kennan, Richard M. Bissell and Franklin A. Lindsay. Dulles, Bissell and Lindsay... would shortly become high-ranking officials of the newly formed Central Intelligence Agency... Their meetings were considered so sensitive that the usual off-the-record transcript was not distributed to Council members. There was good reason for the secrecy. These were probably the only private citizens privy to the highly classified fact that there was a covert side to the Marshall Plan. Specifically, the CIA was tapping into the $200 million a year in local currency counterpart funds contributed by the recipients of Marshall Plan aid. These unvouchered monies were being used by the CIA to finance anti-Communist electoral activities in France and Italy and to support sympathetic journalists, labor union leaders and politicians."

ORIGINS OF THE MARSHALL PLAN

The origins of the Marshall Plan are, in fact, to be found in the policy-formation networks instituted by the Council on Foreign Relations in 1939 prior to World War II. Michio Kaku and Daniel Axelrod in *To Win the Nuclear War: The Pentagon's Secret War Plans*, explain that "the minutes of the closet meetings that were held between the State Department and the CFR beginning in 1939 explicitly detail the role of the U.S. as an encroaching force and a replacement for the British Empire."[54]

Mike Peters agreed: "The plan which Marshall presented in his speech at Harvard had previously been outlined in the proposals of a CFR study group of 1946 headed by the lawyer Charles M. Spofford and David Rockefeller, entitled *Reconstruction in Western Europe*."[55]

According to G. William Domhoff in *The Powers that Be*, published by Vintage Books in 1978, another effort was made through the Committee for the Marshall Plan formed in 1947 "to combat right wing American isolationists. Chairing the committee was Henry L. Stimson, a former Secretary of War and Secretary of State, who had been a CFR member since the 1920s." He noted that five of the seven-member Committee were affiliated with the CFR.

The movement to form a united Europe was part of a larger plan to form a world government. Carroll Quigley, a professor of History at the Foreign Service School of Georgetown University, traced the evolution of the Establishment, aka future New World Order, in the 20th Century in *Tragedy and Hope*, noting that "the integration of Western Europe begun in 1948 was motivated by the Marshall Plan.... The United States had offered Marshall Plan aid with the provision that the European recovery be constructed on a cooperative basis. This led to the Convention for European Economic Cooperation... signed in April 1948 and the Hague Congress for European Union held the following month."

The Hague Congress called for a United Europe and issued seven resolutions on aspects of political union. Number seven stated, "The creation of a United Europe must be regarded as an essential step towards the creation of a United World," according to Dennis Behreandt in an article in *The New American* magazine.[56]

Behreandt further explains that "the Marshall Plan, aside from helping to put Europe back on its feet, led to the Schuman Plan in

1950, when the French Foreign Minister Robert Schuman proposed that the entire coal and steel production of both France and Germany be placed under the authority of one supranational body," which in turn led to the Coal and Iron Community, then to Euratom (the European Atomic Energy Community), and ultimately to the Common Market.

Professor Quigley noted that the Coal and Steel Community "was a truly revolutionary organization since it had sovereign powers, including the authority to raise funds outside any existing state's power ... control prices, channel investment,... allocate coal and steel during shortages, and fix production in times of surplus."

In short, "the European Coal and Steel Community (ECSC) was a rudimentary government." Coming into force during 1952, the arrangement pooled the coal and steel resources of six nations (France, West Germany, Italy, Belgium, Luxembourg and the Netherlands) under a single authority, lifting restrictions on imports and exports, creating a unified labor market, adopting a joint economic policy and harmonizing the standard of living in the member states to help prevent another war.

Hidden by General Marshall and the CFR crowd was the fact that the ECSC was the first concrete step toward political unification, the first block of the Empire building, the Empire being the One World Government. With the signing of the Treaty of Rome, paving the way for the European Economic Community in 1957, the next step towards a future world government was taken. The Treaty of Rome came into effect on January 1, 1958.

CHAPTER SIXTEEN

VISIBLE PATTERNS

Europe has been forced into a union of states. Not as Napoleon dreamed it would be, under the French flag, and not as Hitler planned to subjugate it under the Swastika. But, by a stroke of irony, as both Napoleon and Hitler sought to unify Europe under the Eagle standard, so does the Eagle emblem represent the United States, and high-powered Americans have worked in secret and in public to dismantle independent sovereignties to create today's European Union.

Ambrose Evans-Pritchard tracks this American push to European unification in an article in *The Telegraph* of London from September of 2000: "The U.S. Intelligence community ran a campaign in the Fifties and Sixties to build momentum for a united Europe. It funded and directed the European federalist movement."

During the period mentioned, the CIA was directed by influential members of the Council on Foreign Relations: Allen Dulles, General Walter Bedell Smith and William Donovan, the former head of the OSS, precursor to the CIA. Donovan led the American Committee for a United Europe, which ran and supported the European federalist movement, as noted in Evans-Pritchard's article.

The dots leading to the unification of European nations travel from the Marshall Plan, to the European Coal and Steel Community, to the European Economic Community, and it's not far-reaching to say that America's Council on Foreign Relations paved the path for the present European government. CFR members have been involved in every step of the journey.

The State Department Publication 7277, CFR Special Groups/ Secret Teams, and its War and Peace Studies have all had a tremendous impact on world geopolitics. Yet, these events and behind-the-scenes maneuverings are still not reported. Why is the role of the Council on Foreign Relations in sponsoring and carrying out these actions and operations ignored in modern history texts? Why aren't there any universities – the hub of American liberalism – offering courses on one of America's most influential and oldest private organizations, one molding United States foreign policy to its private agenda? Why haven't Pulitzer Prize-winning investigative reporters, university professors, historians, authors, statesmen, politicians, and researchers noticed the evolution toward a one-world government?

Socrates, at least, would have been appalled. The human being investigates and thereby learns. Any topic is grist for a thinker. Is the public's lack of intellectual curiosity a symptom of the mental pacification to come?

I acknowledge that it is difficult for people to believe that the CFR is a secret organization with ulterior motives, when the Council offers a copy of its annual report containing a list of all members plus invites the public to subscribe to the Council's publication, *Foreign Affairs*, as well as browse through its Web site. There, it is explained that the CFR's International Advisory Board consists of 40-odd members chosen from Europe, North and South America, Africa, Asia, and the Middle East, and that they "are invited to comment on institutional programs and strategic directions, and on practical opportunities for collaboration between the Council and institutions abroad."

Unlike the Bilderberg Group, the CFR even has a secretary, who politely answers most of your questions. However, this is all a ruse. Their true intentions can be found within the pages of the very annual reports they so politely hand out to the public each year. When you examine the CFR's life-member list, for instance, you will find that 90% either sit on the Trilateral Commission or belong to the Bilderberg Group, and sharper scrutiny, of the CFR's 1992 Annual Report for example, reveals the Council emphatically warning in many places and in varying terms that members better not tell outsiders "who said what."[57]

If this is not a secret organization, then why would the CFR insist on members' utter discretion? At this point, it is important to remember what Title-50, Section 783, of the United States Code, "War and

National Defense of the United States," declares: "It shall be unlawful for any officer or employee of the United States or of any department or agency thereof, or of any corporation the stock of which is owned in whole or in major part by the United States or any department or agency thereof, to communicate in any manner or by any means, to any other person whom such officer or employee knows or has reason to believe to be an agent or representative of any foreign government, any information of a kind which shall have been classified by the President (or by the head of any such department, agency, or corporation with the approval of the President) as affecting the security of the United States, knowing or having reason to know that such information has been so classified, unless such officer or employee shall have been specifically authorized by the President, or by the head of the department, agency, or corporation by which this officer or employee is employed, to make such disclosure of such information."

In other words, any group or individual who knowingly works against the United States to benefit a foreign power's takeover of the country commits an act of *treason*.

Zedillo and Rockefeller

Richard Armitage and Richard Perle

L to R - Lloyd Cutler, Hedley Donavan, Walter Mondale, Zbigniew Brzezinski, Jimmy Carter, Cyrus Vance, Harold Brown, Hamilton Jordan and Jody Powell participate in a Carter White House meeting.

Richard Haass and businessman Maurice Greenberg

Canadian Prime Minister Brian Mulroney with George H.W. Bush

Trilateral Commission members, Jimmy Carter, George H.W. Bush and Bill Clinton as are all the people on this page, except the Carter election strategists Jody Powell and Hamilton Jordan, who before the 1976 election said, "If after the inauguration, you find a Cy Vance as Secretary of State and Zbigniew Brzezinski as head of National Security, then I would say we failed."

Exxon CEO Lee Raymond and Mobil CEO merge their companies into ExxonMobil, the world's largest oil company.

Mobil

EXXON

Henry Kissinger

Kiichi Miyazawa, Japanese Politician

Cyrus Vance

Jimmy Carter

Zbigniew Brzezinski

PART THREE

THE ROCKEFELLER CONSPIRACY AND THE TRILATERAL COMMISSION

Whatever the price of the Chinese Revolution, it has obviously succeeded not only in producing more efficient and dedicated administration, but also in fostering high morale and community of purpose.... The social experiment in China under Chairman Mao's leadership is one of the most important and successful in human history.

—David Rockefeller, 1973

Some even believe we are part of a secret cabal working against the best interests of the United States, characterizing my family and me as "internationalists" and of conspiring with others around the world to build a more integrated global political and economic structure — one world, if you will. If that's the charge, I stand guilty, and I am proud of it.

—David Rockefeller, *Memoirs*, page 405

CHAPTER SEVENTEEN

CONFRONTATION, 2003

A circus of maroon and gold colors played in the late evening sky over the French town of Versailles, yet the night seemed sullen. Oppressive heat and humidity hung everywhere as I walked the local streets, looking to quench my thirst. Some three hundred meters from the famous Trianon Palace Hotel, a horseshoe dangling over the doorway of a rundown tavern caught my eye. Its worn purple and green exterior needed a good paint job, and the contrast between the luxurious hotel and this pub's plainness struck my sense of irony: were we destined to return to a world with only two classes — rich and poor, rulers and workers — in a system reminiscent of feudal lords and serfs, and under one government dominating the world? It was a plan few cared to know about, and tonight I was tired of searching for evidence that would expose this threat to our freedom. I had arranged no interviews. I just wanted the comfort of humdrum activity and the din of disconnected voices. Appetizing smells from within the pub perked my craving for a café cream, and I crossed the doorstep.

Inside, only standing room was left at the bar. I found a spot, leaned against the counter top and gave the bartender my order. In front of me, myriad liquor bottles, cups and glasses lined the wall racks. A coffee machine sat on the counter. Behind me and to my right, Welsh tourists and a bearded hunchback wearing leather gloves and a traveling cap occupied a group of tables gathered together. While I wondered why he was wearing gloves on such a sultry night, a fat lady with an oversized mole on her chin explained to the tourists that he was a pianist and had to protect his hands.

To my left at another table, a boisterous bunch played cards. One myopic man drew my attention. I imagined he had just stepped out of a van Gogh painting. Elderly, bald and flabby, he wore an oversized gray suit that, rather than streamlining his body, made him look dumpier. Enormous horn-rimmed glasses amplified his pink watery eyes ogling the people about him. The permanent shadow of a thick beard spread across his jaw and chin, and above his mouth perched a gray-streaked moustache, carelessly clipped. He ordered rum, filled his pipe, and gazed at the game absent-mindedly.

It was long past the Parisians' dinner hour of eight o'clock, and I could hear a piano playing in the drawing room, loud banter and laughter to the exclamations of delighted children. As I paid for my favorite coffee, my perception of the pub changed. Maybe it was so popular that the proprietor didn't have time to give the place a facelift. The thought encouraged me.

"I would like to speak to you." I could feel the man's breath stir the hairs on the back of my neck. I instinctively turned to my right. No one was there.

"Stay seated, please," wheezed a second voice.

My nerve ends bristled. How often was I to be harassed by the CIA, or the Mossad, threatened by local police, photographed by security forces? Was this another shakedown? I swiveled around on my bar stool to confront the voices. "Slumming, are we fellas?"

A British-looking gentleman ignored my barb. "Mr. Estulin, we are sorry to intrude into your space, but we would very much like to speak to you." He extended a flaccid hand in the hope I might choose to shake it. "Needless to say, we ask your maximum discretion."

I could tell from his clumsy syntax that he had acquired his pseudo-cultured English accent from fake *literati*, who specialized in teaching posh British language and manners.

"How do you know my name? I don't remember offering it to you."

"We know quite a bit about you, Mr. Estulin," claimed the rasping voice of a yellow-haired, broad-shouldered man. He stood behind, in the first man's shadow. No doubt his bodyguard. I dubbed them "Tweedle Dee" and "Tweedle Dum."

"Indeed," I said leaning back on my bar stool, letting silence spread between us. Silence was as much my friend as their weapon.

The fake Tweedle Dee lowered his gaze, fished out a cigarette case from the breast pocket of his well-cut jacket, and began to examine it. "For example, we know you are here to cover the Bilderberg conference. You have been following us for many years. Somehow, you seem to know the exact location of every meeting, even though most of the attendees do not find out where it will be held until a week prior to the conference. I regret to admit, as much as we have tried to cover our tracks and take all necessary precautions, you seem to know what we discuss and most of our future plans."

Tweedle Dee lifted his gaze and locked on my eyes. "Your meddling, Mr. Estulin, has even influenced our choice of some of the attendees. At one point, we thought we found you out. We believed a certain member not attending to the conference was *your* inside contact. Had you been wrong in your conference predictions, the unsuspecting member could have suffered great personal consequences. Fortunately, for him, you were spot on."

While I listened, my mind finally tagged the accent he was trying to imitate: Kent.

"How do you know all this stuff?" asked Tweedle Dum.

I looked the man over and resisted an urge to smile. Finally, "they" — representatives of this highly secret group of international power brokers and financiers who formed the Bilderberg Group — were reaching out directly to me. It was a compliment, if a dangerous one. I needed to keep my wits.

"Let's say it's a professional secret," I said, silently thanking my lucky stars that I had not used this pub for meeting with my contacts at the Trianon Palace. Tweedle Dee's intervention clearly meant that anyone working at the hotel seen talking to me would likely be fired.

Tweedle Dum's straw-cropped moustache and bulbous nose twitched at my terse reply. He had huge arching eyebrows and a diminutive mouth that sliced into a cold triangular smile meant to intimidate me.

Tweedle Dee inserted his right hand into his left trouser pocket, letting the divergent coat flaps reveal the watch chain across his waistcoat, and said, "You are quite an enigma, sir." Giving Tweedle Dum a noticeable glance toward the exit, he made a suggestion in a quiet, yet firm tone: "Please follow us outside where we can talk more freely."

Curious, I agreed.

By now, a huge moon burned through the distant trees edging the hotel terrace. Ahead, streetlights blinked. I could make out faint babble coming from outdoor cafés along the way as well as barking dogs. The three of us remained silent for several minutes.

"Why do you follow us around?" asked Tweedle Dee. "You don't work for any newspaper of renown. You write articles that make our members uncomfortable. Several congressmen in America and members of Parliament in Canada were forced to cancel their presence at our annual meeting when you named them as invited guests."

"Not good," intoned Tweedle Dum.

Tweedle Dee continued: "The Bilderberg Group, Mr. Estulin, is a private forum where off-the-record friendly discussion takes place among influential members of the business community. Politicians are invited to share their personal and professional experiences with the group. All this is done with the hope that these types of forums can bridge the gap between the high-stakes politics and the greater needs of the world's peoples. In no way, do we try to influence governments' policy or decision making."

"Bullshit!" I snapped. I could feel my neck muscles bulge. My indignation vented. "Had it not been for the efforts of persistent journalists, Canada by now would have become part of the Greater United States. And why did you people kill Aldo Moro?"

"You know we can't tell you anything, Mr. Estulin. I did not come to argue with you, sir." Tweedle Dee considered me. "Would it be too much to ask of you if we spoke off the record?"

"I don't usually speak off the record, especially where the Bilderberg Group is concerned."

I realized that I was acting foolishly, but for the moment, I was enjoying the opportunity to give the "face" of my underhanded nemesis a sense of my suppressed frustration with their covert agendas. Maybe, if I could force Tweedle Dee into losing his temper, I rationalized, I might find out what this meeting was really about. Instead, he rattled on for a few more minutes about the virtues of partnerships, collaboration among nations, starving children in Africa... the usual propaganda. I tried to concentrate on listening but soon caught myself watching Tweedle Dum's face. He either smiled vacantly or licked his moustache.

"We can really make it worth your while, Mr. Estulin." My attention snapped back to Tweedle Dee. "What conditions would you wish to impose?" he asked.

I glanced again at the silent Tweedle Dum, to gauge his interest in my answer. He stood stone-faced. Tweedle Dee fiddle-fingered his cigarette, gently stroked it, bit his lower lip and pondered. His eyes did not really look at the cigarette, but into the distance as he waited for me to respond.

"As a condition for my silence, I would like all future Bilderberg meetings to be announced publicly. I want free and unimpeded access granted to any journalist who wishes to attend. All conferences are to be on-the-record, the list of attendees to be released to the public in advance of the event. No CIA, guns, dogs, private security and most of all *no secrecy!*"

"You know we can't do that, Mr. Estulin. The stakes are too high, and it is very late in the game."

"Then, sir," I replied, "you will just have to put up with me until the referee blows the final whistle."

Tweedle Dee nodded in his decorous manner. "Then it's a good evening, Mr. Estulin. I'm sorry to have wasted your time."

Tweedle Dum donned his hat and walked away in step with his boss.

Only then, did I again realize how much was at stake. This was no mere conversation between the Bilderberger's emissaries and me. It was a warning.

It may be lonely at the top.

CHAPTER EIGHTEEN

BACK TO THE FUTURE

Without a doubt, the Bilderberg Group is the premier occult forum operating in the shadows of power, but a little understood entity — the Trilateral Commission (TC) — also plays a vital role in the New World Order's scheme to use wealth, concentrated in the hands of the few, to exert world control. The powerful individuals who belong to the Trilateral Commission all share the same anti-nationalist philosophy, and try to prevent the national forces within their respective countries from exerting influence on policy.

The Trilateral Commission was established in 1973. Its founder and primary mover was international financier David Rockefeller, longtime chairman of the Rockefeller family-controlled Chase Manhattan Bank. Journalist Bill Moyers spoke about the power of David Rockefeller in a TV documentary, *The Secret Government* in 1980: "David Rockefeller is the most conspicuous representative today of the ruling class, a multinational fraternity of men who shape the global economy and manage the flow of its capital ... Private citizen David Rockefeller is accorded privileges of a head of state ... He is untouched by customs or passport offices and hardly pauses for traffic lights."

The first meeting of the Trilateral Commission was held in Tokyo between October 21 and 23, 1973. Sixty-five persons represented the North American group. Of those, 35 were also affiliated with the Council on Foreign Relations.

The Trilateral Commission is divided into three regions — American, European and Pacific Asian. American headquarters are in Washington;

European, in Paris; and Asian, in Tokyo. The 2006 annual three-day Trilateral Commission meeting was held in Tokyo, the 2007 was held held in Brussels and the 2008, from April 25 to 28 in Washington, D.C. The meetings are closed to the public, and the non-aligned media is denied access. Thomas Foley has served as the North American chairman since May 2001. The European chairman for many years has been international businessman and politician Peter Sutherland; the Pacific Asian chairman is business executive Yotaro Kobayashi.

According to the Trilateral Commission's Web site, "each regional group has a chairman and deputy chairman, who all together constitute the leadership of the Committee. The Executive Committee draws together a further 36 individuals from the wider membership" with proportional representation from the three regions. Committee members meet several times per year to coordinate their work and prepare the agenda.

Trilateral membership is chosen by the group's Executive Committee. At any given time, it has around 350 members, each serving a three-year term. Even a cursory look at the membership list establishes beyond doubt that every one of the people invited to join were, and are, members of the Establishment, the proverbial insiders, recruited with consummate skill and singleness of purpose from the political, commercial, banking and media sectors. Commission members are obliged to resign their membership in the group when they enter governement, but, according to Arlene Johnson, publisher of *True Democracy*, their loyalty and ideology "does not change just because one is elected to a government post. In fact, the loyalty given to the commission for its support in obtaining a prestigious position seems to prompt reciprocal action to perpetuate the effectiveness of the Commission. Therefore, prior to their elections or appointments, many high officials in government are active Trilateral members."[58]

Moreover, members usually rejoin once their public commitment is over.

Three hand-picked experts representing each area of operations write the Trilateral Commission's annual Task Force Reports. It can take up to a year to prepare one. In *Trilateralism: The Trilateral Commission and Elite Planning for World Management*, well-known Knight-Ridder columnist and author, Holly Sklar, explains how these Task Force Reports are developed:

The topics for projects are chosen by the chairmen, deputy chairmen, and directors, with the advice of the Executive Committee and others. Authors are then invited, sometimes from the Commission membership. The authors do not relocate to the offices of the Commission while preparing their report. They remain in their existing institutional settings, and the Commission enables them to meet with each other and various consultants along the way. The reports are *to* the Trilateral Commission, not *of* the Commission. The membership of the Commission is too diverse to achieve detailed agreement quickly on a controversial set of issues; and on a few occasions a summary of discussion in the annual meeting has been added to a report to detail the controversy it created.[59]

In addition to Task Force Reports, the Trilateral Commission produces a journal called *Trialogue*. "In earlier years, the *Trialogue* series included special numbers on particular issues in addition to the numbers on Trilateral Commission meetings."[60]

The Commission has regional head offices, a small full-time staff, telephone and fax lines, business cards, and a Web site. Its annual reports are available to the general public for a small fee, although its inner workings are secret. Its membership list is available upon request, but members, as is the case with the Bilderbergers and the CFR, are pledged to secrecy regarding its goals and operations. The Trilateral Commission is certainly no Bilderberger outfit. But what are they, exactly? And how do their policies affect us?

Antony Sutton, author of *Trilaterals over Washington,* writes that "this group of private citizens is precisely organized in a manner that ensures its collective views have significant impact on public policy. They meet, they review, they discuss, they report, and, after this discussion, make their recommendations public."[61]

In its first year and a half, the Trilateral Commission released six position papers to the public. In the years that followed, producing such papers became the TC's trademark strategy, not only to gauge the mood of the public at large but also to present the Commission's agenda. These first six issued by the Commission were titled *The Triangle Papers*: two followed the Tokyo meeting in October 1973, three summarized the result of a meeting in Brussels in June 1974, and one was produced after a Washington, D.C. meeting in December 1974.

In *The Rockefeller File*, Gary Allen made a prediction concerning the Trilateral Commission, "If the *Triangle Papers* are any indication, we can look for four major thrusts toward world economic controls."

The first, he noted, would pursue a renovated world monetary system; the second would loot U.S. resources for the further radicalization of "have-not" nations; the third would step-up trade with the Communists, and the fourth would milk the energy crisis to gain greater international control.[62]

In the decades since Allen assessed the Commission's intentions in its first position papers, what has the TC actually accomplished?

> No. 1: We've seen two regional economic blocks emerge — the European Community, and the Union of the Americas with the adoption of the National Free Trade Agreement (NAFTA). The soon-to-be-created Asian monetary union is waiting in the wings.
>
> No. 2: The U.S. and western nations have heavily subsidized and carried debt for Third World countries.
>
> No. 3: The U.S. sent billions of dollars worth of technology to the Soviets and the Chinese, and established burgeoning trade following its détente with the Chinese and the Russians.
>
> No. 4: We've seen one energy crisis after another beginning with the 1973 Suez Crisis, more recently the Desert Storm action of the early '90s to restore world oil production to Kuwait following Iraq's invasion to annex the oil fields, and now the ongoing war in Iraq. U.S. justification for invading Iraq was to secure weapons of mass destruction — these threatened world stability — but they never materialized; so obviously, the Americans' true purpose was to manipulate the flow of Middle East oil, despite promises to free the Iraqi people to build their own democracy.

Holly Sklar — the first to recognize the Trilateral Commission's movement to "globalization" long before the term became a buzzword — maintains that the global interdependence between the Big Three economic world powers "allows the rich to safeguard the interests of Western capitalism in an explosive world — probably by discouraging protectionism, nationalism, or any response that would pit the elites of one against the elites of another. The anticipated economic pressures will be deflected downward rather than laterally."[63]

In *Final Warning: A History of the New World Order,* David Rivera holds the view that the Trilateral Commission's goal is "to make the world safe for interdependence by protecting the benefits, which it provides for each country against external and internal threats, which will constantly emerge from those willing to pay a price for more national autonomy. This may sometimes require slowing the pace at which interdependence proceeds, and checking some aspects of it. More frequently however, it will call for checking the intrusion of national government into the international exchange of both economic and non-economic goods."

In the late 1970s, then-Federal Reserve Chairman, Paul Volcker — a Trilateralist, who once worked for the Rockefeller's Chase Manhattan Bank — didn't mince words when he told the American people how these "economic pressures" would affect them. "The standard [of living] of the average American has to decline."

Volcker was a man of his word. Under his "fiscal austerity" program implemented during President Jimmy Carter's administration in October 1979, the Treasury bill rate increased an unfathomable six percent during a six month period. Interest rates soared from five percent in 1977 to over 18 percent in 1980, as measured by the rate paid by the government on Treasury bills. The increase added further momentum to the inflation that sent the '80s and early '90s into an economic slump that was comparable to the Great Depression in the way it restructured the global economy and eliminated industrial jobs.

When David Rockefeller read *Between Two Ages: America's Role in the Technotronic Era*, a book published in 1970 by Professor Zbigniew Brzezinski of Columbia University, he already shared the view that "people, governments and economies of all nations must serve the needs of multinational banks and corporations" with Marxist CFR founder Edward Mandell House.

In fact, Brzezinski was so bold as to dismiss the U.S. Constitution — the very document that limits government abuse of power — as "inadequate." Instead, Brzezinski claimed that "the old framework of international politics, with their spheres of influence... the fiction of sovereignty... is clearly no longer compatible with reality," and proposed "the approaching two-hundredth anniversary of the Declaration of Independence could justify the call for the national constitutional convention to re-examine the nation's formal institutional framework... [and] could serve as a suitable target date culminating a national dialogue on the relevance of existing arrangements."

That same year, Brzezinski also contributed to *Foreign Affairs*, the CFR publication, asserting that a new and broader approach was needed. He suggested the "creation of a community of the developed nations, which can effectively address itself to the larger concerns confronting mankind.... A council representing the United States, Western Europe, and Japan, with regular meetings of the heads of governments as well as some small standing machinery, would be a good start."

These words must have been the call-to-arms that set David Rockefeller in action, for in the spring of 1972, he broached the idea of a Trilateral Commission at the annual Bilderberger meeting in Knokke, Belgium. According to George S. Franklin, former Trilateral Commission coordinator, the Group responded with great enthusiasm for Rockefeller's proposal of an international alliance that would create strategies and policies to consolidate the four pillars of power – "political, monetary, intellectual and ecclesiastical" – under a central world government. "The next eight speakers said that this was a marvellous idea; by all means, somebody get it launched."[64]

Two months after the Bilderberg meeting, in July 1972, David Rockefeller lent his famous Pocantico Hills estate in New York's Hudson Valley to be the headquarters for the first organizational meetings of the Trilateral Commission. Two-hundred-and-fifty financiers and industrialists, with interlocking memberships in the Bilderberg Group and the CFR, attended that first get-together.

With the formation of the Trilateral Commission, did David Rockefeller sow the seeds of a revolution for this century within the political institutions of our modern republics? It is certainly the one step that took Brzezinski's vision off the page, making a "movement toward a larger community by the developing nations ... through a variety of indirect ties and already developing limitations on national sovereignty" into a living reality.

But, even in the very best scenario, there is something very disturbing about a power coalition of this magnitude being put together from behind the scenes. Even the Establishment-owned *Washington Post* of January 16, 1977, found unsettling features about the Trilateral Commission: "Trilateralists are not three-sided people. They are members of a private, though not secret, international organization put together by the wealthy banker, David Rockefeller, to stimulate the [E]stablishment dialogue between Western Europe, Japan and the United States. But here is the unsettling thing about the Trilateral Commission. The President-elect [Carter] is a member. So is the Vice President-elect Walter F. Mondale. So are the new Secretaries of State, Defense and Treasury: Cyrus R. Vance, Harold Brown and W. Michael Blumenthal. So is Zibigniew Brzezinski, who is a former Trilateral director and Carter's national security adviser, also a bunch of others who will make foreign policy for America in the next four years."

The Establishment crowd "got the message." Soon after, Katherine Graham, Chairperson of the Board of Washington Post Companies, was offered a Trilateral membership to go along with her memberships in the Bilderberg Group and Council on Foreign Relations. From then on, that leading newspaper no longer felt it necessary to shine the light of truth on the newest of "private" organizations.

From its inception, the Commission aimed to fashion an enduring partnership among the ruling elites of North America, Western Europe, and Japan, and its coordination among the three spheres of power constitutes the reason for dubbing itself the Trilateral Commission. The TC first needed to educate the public and leaders of most countries to switch from their concept of a world split into separate nations to thinking in terms of global perspectives.

Long after the Trilateral Commission's inauguration, its official Web site claimed credit for the realization of the global marketplace: "The 'growing interdependence' that so impressed the founders of the Trilateral Commission in the early 1970s is deepening into 'globalization.' The need for shared thinking and leadership by the Trilateral countries, who (along with the principal international organizations) remain the primary anchors of the wider international system, has not diminished but, if anything, intensified. At the same time, their leadership must change to take into account the dramatic transformation of the international system. As relations with other countries become more mature — and power more diffuse — the leadership tasks of the original Trilateral countries need to be carried out with others to an increasing extent."

So what's next? Brzezinski foresaw this international interdependent community being funded by "a global taxation system." How curious! This is exactly what the Bilderbergers have been pushing for the United Nations since the early 1990s.

CURRENT COMMISSION MEMBERSHIP

The August 2007 roster of the Trilateral Commission includes members from every European nation. While in the past, the Asian group was made up of Japanese commissioners, today's Trilateral Commission has added new members from emerging Asian economies such as Indonesia, Malaysia, the Philippines and Thailand, as well as seasoned capitalist centers such as Australia, New Zealand, South Korea and Singapore.

Furthermore, David Rockefeller and Zbigniew Brzezinski, the Commission founders and members of the Executive Committee from North America, have truly made the Trilateral Commission into a globalist organization. New Trilateralists from such exotic locations as Kuwait, Morocco, Jordan and the Ukraine have joined Domingo F. Cavallo, former Economy Minister of Argentina, and a man, according to many, responsible for destroying the Argentine economy. Carefully screened candidates from Taiwan, Turkey, Israel, Hong Kong, South Africa, Uruguay, China, Russia and Brazil have also been admitted. Excluding only equatorial Africa and the Indian sub-continent the Trilateral Commission has truly expanded into a global powerhouse.

Who are the people that form part of this "private" organization called the Trilateral Commission? Most are unknown, even to their countrymen, but inconsequential they are certainly not. They are present and past presidents, ambassadors, secretaries of state, Wall Street investors, international bankers, foundation executives, think tank executives, lobbyist lawyers, NATO and Pentagon military leaders, wealthy industrialists, union bosses, media magnates, university presidents and key professors, select senators and congressmen, as well as wealthy entrepreneurs. The largest proportion of TC membership comes from global corporations: United States, 34%; Western Europe, 39%; Japan, 65%.

Holly Sklar has explained why unions are included in the TC's membership: "A labor component helps control popular isolationism and reduces the distance separating Trilats from the masses of ordinary folk."[65]

Originally, the difference between the Bilderbergers and the TC was that the much older Bilderberg Group was limited in participation to NATO members from Western Europe, the U.S.A. and Canada. Today, the Group has expanded its qualifications in step with the European Community and NATO and admits citizens of ex-Warsaw Pact nations into the Group.

Although the Trilateral Commission paints itself as a harmless debating society of private citizens who do not influence public policy, should we believe them? Why would Commission members give so much of their time to a mere academic exercise with so little significance?

Journalist and researcher Robert Eringer notes in *The Global Manipulators* (Pentacle Books, 1980), that "many of the original members of the Trilateral Commission are now in positions of power where they are able to implement policy recommendations of the Commission; recommendations that they, themselves, prepared on behalf of the Commission."

Could the Commission's real objectives be to collaborate with the Bilderbergers and the Council of Foreign Relations in "establishing public policy objectives to be implemented by governments worldwide"? That was Antony Sutton's conclusion in *Trilaterals Over America*.

After all, as Brzezinski noted in *Between Two Ages,* "Though the objective of shaping a community of developed nations is less ambitious than the goal of world government, it is more attainable."

Debating society, indeed.

At the Trilateral Commission's 25th anniversary dinner in 1998, Henry Kissinger revealed how the proposed establishment of the TC had been initially presented to him:

> In 1973, when I served as Secretary of State, David Rockefeller showed up in my office one day to tell me that *he thought I needed a little help. I must confess, the thought was not self-evident to me at the moment.* He proposed to form a group of Americans, Europeans

and Japanese to look ahead into the future.

And I asked him, "Who's going to run this for you, David?"

He said, "Zbig Brzezinski."

I knew that Rockefeller meant it. He picked something that was important. *When I thought about it, there actually was a need.*[66] [emphases added]

This "need" Kissinger refers to, but does not mention, related to his loss of control over the members of the Council of Foreign Relations as they grew ever more divided over the Viet Nam War. He suddenly "saw" the advantage in creating a new global body that could supersede the CFR. Rockefeller's selection of Professor Zbigniew Brzezinski of Columbia University as the director of the new organization made further sense to Kissinger, because Brzezinski's ideas to create a vast alliance between North America, Western Europe and Japan not only mirrored Rockefeller's thinking, but also paralleled his own and that of CFR founder Edward Mandell House.

However, according to an article by Will Banyon in *Nexus* magazine, in David Rockefeller's autobiography, *Memoirs*, Rockefeller fails to acknowledge his goals in forming the Trilateral Commission. Evidently, Rockefeller was enraged with Nixon's New Economic Policy (NEP) of 1971, which tried to impose government management over the most basic elements of the market through wage and price controls and increased tariffs. For 90 days, Nixon succeeded in freezing wages and prices to check inflation. Nixon's position conflicted with Rockefeller's, and Banyon captures the fervor with which Rockefeller was determined to rein in the Nixon Administration, "which had taken advantage of Establishment divisions to reject the liberal internationalist program."[67]

Daniel Yergin and Joseph Stanislaw, writing in *The Commanding Heights*, agreed: "the Establishment, represented by the TC, CFR and Bilderberg elite were incensed that government officials were now in the business of setting prices and wages."

Setting up the Trilateral Commission became Rockefeller's plan to encourage "unity among the industrialized powers as a temporary alternative to a United Nations increasingly dominated by radicalized Third World states, so that together they could achieve his goal of a *more integrated global political and economic structure.*"[68]

Meanwhile, Rockefeller's attempt to set the "erring" Nixon back on course via a private meeting to discuss the "international monetary and trade picture," was rebuffed by Nixon's Chief of Staff, H. R. Haldeman. After finally securing the meeting with the President, Rockefeller's views were dismissed by one of the officials at the meeting as "not especially innovative."[69]

But what happened after that meeting is now history. Most of the NEP system was abolished in April 1974, well into Nixon's ill-fated second term. Four months later, Nixon resigned as President.

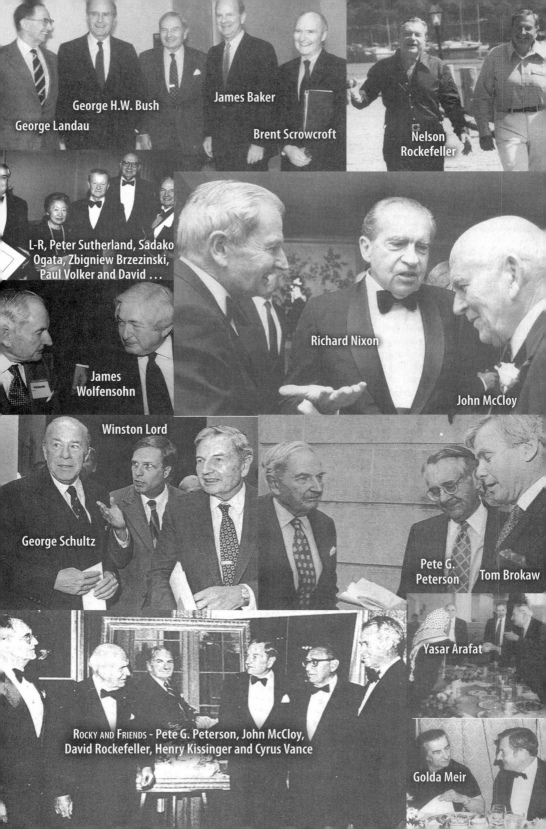

George Landau

George H.W. Bush

James Baker

Brent Scrowcroft

Nelson Rockefeller

L-R, Peter Sutherland, Sadako Ogata, Zbigniew Brzezinski, Paul Volker and David ...

James Wolfensohn

Richard Nixon

John McCloy

Winston Lord

George Schultz

Pete G. Peterson

Tom Brokaw

Yasar Arafat

ROCKY AND FRIENDS - Pete G. Peterson, John McCloy, David Rockefeller, Henry Kissinger and Cyrus Vance

Golda Meir

CHAPTER NINETEEN

SOPHISTICATED SUBVERSION

"How does one explain the subtle interdependence of the industrial north with the Third World?" asks Knight-Ridder columnist, Holly Sklar, in *The Trilateral Commission and Elite Planning for World Management.*

In 1991, an economist, and *The Nation's* Contributing Editor Doug Henwood posted his answer in the *Left Business Observer*, a newsletter he had founded in 1986: "...each member of the Triad has gathered under itself a handful of poor countries to act as sweatshops, plantations, and mines: the U.S. has Latin America; the EC, Eastern and Southern Europe and Africa; and Japan, Southeast Asia. In a few cases, two Triad members share a country — Taiwan and Singapore are split between Japan and the U.S.; Argentina, between the U.S. and the EC; Malaysia, between the EC and Japan; and India is shared by all three."

"Rockefeller's strategy," writes Will Banyon "also reveals something fundamental about wealth and power: it does not matter how much money one has; unless it is employed to capture and control those organizations that produce the ideas and the policies that guide governments and the people who eventually serve in them, the real power of a great fortune will never be realized."[70]

Writing in a Letter to the Editor of the *New York Times* on August 20, 1980, David Rockefeller, chairman of the Chase Manhattan Bank, defended the purpose of the Trilateral Commission in an unprecedented public statement. "The Trilateral Commission is, in reality, a group of concerned citizens interested in fostering greater understanding, and cooperation among international allies."

This was not the impression held by U.S. Senator Barry Goldwater, however. He put his view less mercifully. In his book, *With No Apologies*, he termed the Trilateral Commission, "David Rockefeller's newest international cabal," and said, "It is intended to be the vehicle for multinational consolidation of the commercial and banking interests by seizing control of the political government of the United States."

Senator Jesse Helms, speaking from the Senate floor on December 15, 1987, went even further in his assessment of the interlocking *private* societies:

> This campaign against the American people — against traditional American culture and values — is systematic psychological warfare. It is orchestrated by a vast array of interests comprising not only the Eastern establishment but also the radical left. Among this group, we find the Department of State, the Department of Commerce, the money center banks and multinational corporations, the media, the educational establishment, the entertainment industry, and the large tax-exempt foundations.
>
> Mr. President, a careful examination of what is happening behind the scenes reveals that all of these interests are working to create what some refer to as a New World Order. Private organizations such as the Council on Foreign Relations, the Royal Institute of International Affairs, the Trilateral Commission, the Dartmouth Conference, the Aspen Institute for Humanistic Studies, the Atlantic Institute, and the Bilderberger Group serve to disseminate and to coordinate the plans for this so-called New World Order in powerful business, financial, academic, and official circles....
>
> The influence of establishment insiders over our foreign policy has become a fact of life in our time. This pervasive influence runs contrary to the real long-term national security of our Nation. It is an influence which, if unchecked, could ultimately subvert our constitutional order.[71]

Isn't that interesting! That's exactly the conclusion that Antony Sutton reaches in the *Trilateral Observer*. "The Trilateralists have rejected the U.S. Constitution and the democratic political process."

Goldwater concludes *With No Apologies* with the following insight: "What the Trilaterals truly intend is the creation of worldwide economic power superior to the political governments of the nation-states involved.... As managers and creators of the system, they will rule the future."

What these critics warn was happening in the '70s and '80s mirrors the very imperial policies George Ball, the U.S. Undersecretary of State for Economic Affairs under JFK and Lyndon Johnson, proposed at the 1968 Bilderberg meeting at Mont Tremblant in Canada.

As noted earlier, Ball framed the issue with a question: "Where does one find a legitimate base for the power of corporate managements to make decisions that can profoundly affect the economic life of nations to whose governments they have only limited responsibility?"

The only answer that comes to mind is to orchestrate a crisis, one that binds "free" nations in common purpose against a world threat, whether economic, political or terrorist in nature. And this is the direction the Trilateralists publicly take.

Their methods were outlined in a candid 1974 report: *The Crisis of Democracy,* co-written by Harvard political scientist Samuel Huntington, Michel Crozier (a French sociologist and member of the *Académie des sciences morales et politiques)* and Japanese Trilateralist Joji Watanuki. Their report suggested "the need for a dialectic game between the Department of State and multinationals; the first one will have to exert pressure upon developing countries for them to adopt liberal legislations and to quit nationalizations, while multinationals should transfer to the Department of State their knowledge on the countries where they work."

The report further asserts that a democratic republic "is only one way of constituting authority, and it is not necessarily a universally applicable one... there are potentially desirable limits to the indefinite extension of political democracy... A government will have little ability, short of cataclysmic crisis to impose on its people the sacrifice which may be necessary... In many situations, the claims of expertise, seniority, experience and special talents may override the claims of democracy as a way of constituting authority.... The arenas where democratic procedures are appropriate are, in short, limited."

Sounds repressive, doesn't it?

The report also expressed anxiety at "the increased popular participation in and control over established social, political, and economic institutions and especially a reaction against the concentration of power of Congress and of state and local government."

In other words, the Trilateralists are worried that people in a democratic society might rebel against the way they want to run things. So, to prevent such resistance from happening, the Trilateralists recommend introducing powers of decree, says Gary Allen, to restore "a more equitable relationship between governmental authority and popular control" through "centralized economic and social planning ... centralization of power within Congress ... a program to lower the job expectations of those who receive a college education."[72]

Of course, none of these initiatives can become truly effective without first subjugating the press and then putting it on a short leash. Therefore, the Trilateral Commission proposes limitations on freedom of the press such as "prior restraint of what newspapers may publish in unspecified unusual circumstances, the assurance to the government [of] the right and the ability to withhold information at the source... moving promptly to reinstate the law of libel as a necessary and appropriate check upon the abuses of power by the press, and press councils enforcing 'standards of professionalism,' the alternative [to which] could well be regulation by the government."[73]

Make no mistake. The passages quoted here are not those published by critics of the Trilateral Commission. The wording comes directly from formal Trilateral Commission proposals.

The idea of a "media control" and "media monopoly" that obfuscates the truth may seem preposterous to many a Western person. Nevertheless, as early as 1983, Ben Bagdikian, the former editor of the *Saturday Evening Post,* in a book simply titled *The Media Monopoly*, revealed the interlocking directorates among the fifty corporations that control what Americans see, hear and read. You may recall the earlier discussion of Bilderberg influence over U.S. media? Bagdikian's most recent update the *The New Media Monoploy* (2004) puts the number at *five* corporations controlling America's Fourth Estate.

Take the Corporation for Public Broadcasting, for example. PBS, supposedly, is a public institution. According to its Web site, "PBS, is a non-profit media enterprise owned and operated by the nation's ... public television stations. A trusted community resource, PBS uses the power of noncommercial television, the Internet and other media to enrich the lives of all Americans through quality programs and education services that inform, inspire and delight. Available to 99 percent of American homes with televisions and to an increasing number of digital multimedia households, PBS serves nearly 90 million people each week."[74]

The cornerstone of PBS's programming is the evening television news program, *The NewsHour with Jim Lehrer*. Jim Lehrer, however, is a member of the Council on Foreign Relations. For most of PBS' history, funding was provided by AT&T [a CFR company]; Archer Daniels Midland, whose Chairman Dwayne Andreas was a member of the Trilateral Commission; PepsiCo [a CFR company], whose newly promoted Chief Executive Officer, Indra Krishnamurthy Nooyi, is a Bilderberger and a Trilateral Commission Executive Committee member; and Smith Barney [a CFR company], one of the world's leading financial institutions. Furthermore, Smith Barney is interlocked with Citigroup Inc., a global financial services company that is a member of the Bilderberg Group, the CFR and the Trilateral Commission.

Journalists who participate in *The NewsHour with Jim Lehrer* are some of the best-known political pundits in the United States, such as Paul Gigot, David Gergen, William Kristol and William Safire. All of them belong to the Bilderberg Group, the CFR or the Trilateral Commission.

Would it be reasonable for us to suspect that PBS might not be quite as impartial in certain delicate matters of public interest, such as the U.S. Constitutional crisis envisioned by Brzezinski, the future of nation-states, and of national sovereignty?

Three years after publishing *The Crisis of Democracy*, Samuel Huntington, a member of the CFR and TC, was promoted to the post of coordinator of national security planning for Jimmy Carter's National Security Council. As the Council's coordinator, Huntington drafted Presidential Review Memorandum 32 [PRM 32], which led to Carter's presidential order creating the Federal Emergency Management Agency on June 19, 1979. FEMA, the crisis command center, does not operate under the orders of the President, but under the National Security Council whose members belong to the Bilderberg/CFR/TC combines and interlocked leadership. One of FEMA's past directors is the ubiquitous Zbigniew Brzezinski, the prognosticator of one-world idealism.

Craig S. Karpel wrote "Cartergate: The Death of Democracy" for *Penthouse*'s November 1977 edition. "The presidency of the United States and key cabinet departments of the federal government," he asserted, "have been taken over by a private organization dedicated to the subordination of the domestic interests of the United States to the international interests of the multi-national banks and corporations. It would be unfair to say that the Trilateral Commission dominates the Carter Administration; the Trilateral Commission *is* the Carter Administration."

Karpel's words may seem like a gross exaggeration until we note Henry Kissinger's declaration to the head of state of Canada, a neighboring country and a staunch ally of the United States: "Jimmy Carter is not the President of the United States," said Kissinger. "The Trilateral Commission is the President of the United States; I represent the Trilateral Commission." This was reported to me by persons within earshot of the conversation.

Are you still not convinced we are facing a grave threat to our individual freedoms and democratic way of life? Here are a few more examples.

Richard Cooper, a Maurits C. Boas Professor of International Economics at Harvard, headed the Trilateral Commission's task force on monetary policy, which recommended selling official gold reserves to private markets. When Cooper was named the U.S. Undersecretary of State for Economic Affairs, the International Monetary Fund sold a portion of its gold.

In 1976, C. Fred Bergsten along with Georges Berthoin and Kinhide Mushakoji prepared Commission Task Force Report #11 called *The Reform of International Institutions*. They stated their "overriding goal": making the world "safe for interdependence." This was to be achieved by "checking of the intrusion of national governments into the international exchange of both economic and non-economic goods" (p. 90). Bergsten went on to become Assistant Secretary for International Affairs of the U.S. Treasury during 1977–81.

Trilateralist John C. Sawhill, along with Keichi Oshima and Hanns W. Maull, authored the Commission's 1978 Task Force Report #17— *Energy: Managing the Transition.* It made recommendations about how to manage a movement to higher-cost energy. On September 12, 1979, Carter appointed John Sawhill to be Deputy Secretary of Energy.

With what we have noted so far, it isn't too difficult to see that the Trilateral Commission's approach is strictly economic. "Interlocking directorates and world market shares provide the greatest political power because individual transnational corporations participate not as individual or autonomous companies but as parts of a whole network or integrated systems. The Trilateral Commission is the further extension of this network."[75]

Political conditions, such as the ideals of nation-states, common law, and social welfare are anathemas to their materialist plans. Freedom — spiritual, political and economic — is frowned upon, and its necessity denied any importance in the Trilateralist vision of global financial partnership and interdependence. All these criteria are best summed up in the infamous words of Richard Gardner, one of Carter's mentors, in the July 1974 issue of the CFR's magazine, *Foreign Affairs*. In it, Gardner called for "an end run around national sovereignty, eroding it piece by piece."

The Trilateral/Bilderberg/CFR model is composed of top financial managers and Establishment insiders. The key, however, to achieving the centralized power the TC covets is finding "a way to get us to surrender our liberties in the name of some common threat or crisis. The foundations, educational institutions, and research think tanks supported by members of the Trilateral Commission and Council on Foreign Relations oblige by financing so-called 'studies' which are then used to justify their every excess. The excuses vary, but the target is always individual liberty. Our liberty."[76]

And despite the primarily financial nature of both their motives and methods, they are not without political goals: "Although the Commission's primary concern is economic, the Trilateralists have pinpointed a vital political objective: to gain control of the American Presidency."[77]

Best Wishes
to David Rockefeller   Jimmy Carter 4/80

CHAPTER TWENTY

PACKAGING A PRESIDENT

In the spring of 1972, a high profile group of men gathered for dinner with W. Averell Harriman, the grand old man of the Democratic Party, a Bilderberger and member of the CFR. Also present were Milton Katz, a CFR member and Director of International Studies at Harvard, Robert Bowie, who would later become Deputy Director of the CIA, George Franklin, David Rockefeller's coordinator for the Trilateral Commission, and Gerald Smith, U.S. Ambassador-at-Large for Non-Proliferation Matters. The focus of their discussion was the not-too-distant 1976 U.S. Presidential elections. Harriman suggested that if the Democrats wanted to recapture the White House, "we had better get off our high horses and look at some of those southern governors." Several names cropped up. Among them were James Earl Carter, governor of Georgia, Reubin Askew, governor of Florida, and Terry Sanford, former governor of North Carolina and, at the time, President of Duke University.

Katz is reported to have promptly informed David Rockefeller that Carter was a viable candidate and could be sold politically to the American public. In the fall of 1973, Rockefeller invited Carter for dinner in London, in order to better acquaint himself with Georgia's governor. As he listened to the southern gentleman, he became convinced that Carter was ideally suited to become the next U.S. president.

The Times of London gave an account of the developing Rockefeller-Carter relationship: "Governor Jimmy Carter, 1976 Democratic

Presidential candidate, has for reasons known only to himself professed to be an innocent abroad, but the record is somewhat different. As Governor of Georgia, a state aspiring to be the centre of the New South, he led the state trade missions abroad. While in London in the autumn of 1973 he dined with another American visitor, but by no means an innocent, Mr. David Rockefeller of Chase Manhattan Bank. Mr. Rockefeller was then establishing, with the help of Professor Brzezinski of Columbia University, an international group now known as the Trilateral Commission. He was looking for American members... was impressed by the Governor, if only because he had ventured abroad, and invited him to join. Governor Carter, perhaps because he was already eyeing the White House from afar, was only too happy to accept."

Rockefeller felt that Carter "could project an image of a Southern Governor that could be used to fool many voters by appearing 'conservative' or 'moderate,' while in fact favoring the most left-wing of agendas. The idea was to use Carter to court both White and Black voters who could be delivered by the Democrat Party's big urban political machines."[78]

In fact, before moving forward, we should backtrack to the "screening" process and to 1973. That year, Carter and Askew were invited to David Rockefeller's Tarrytown, New York estate. Also present was Zbigniew Brzezinski, who was helping Rockefeller screen prospects for the Trilateral Commission. Carter's southern gentility charmed both men, but what impressed them more was that Carter had already opened up trade offices for the state of Georgia in Brussels and Tokyo. This seemed to fit perfectly with the aspirations of the Trilateral Commission.

However, what truly impressed them wasn't Carter's independence. Rather, what endeared Carter to the Establishment crowd was his ruthlessness and ambition. As Gary Allen writes in his controversial 1976 book, *Jimmy Carter, Jimmy Carter*: "Carter's overwhelming ambition and corruptibility made him vulnerable. It included conniving with his own personal banker, Bert Lance, to funnel bank depositors' money into Carter's peanut business and into the bank accounts of Lance associates and family members to finance Carter's campaign, while waiting for federal matching funds. The illegalities involved were enough to send the whole gang to jail. And the key to exposure was in the hands of David Rockefeller and his fellow banking insiders."

Thus, a peanut farmer was plucked out of the peanut field by the CFR/Bilderberg and soon-to-be Trilateral Commission organizations and "discovered" as a potential presidential candidate.

In Carter's acceptance speech after winning the nomination at the Democratic National Convention, he attacked the "unholy, self-perpetuating alliances [that] have been formed between money and politics... a political and economic elite who have shaped decisions and never had to account for mistakes nor to suffer from injustice. When unemployment prevails, they never stand in line for a job. When deprivation results from a confused welfare system, they never do without food, or clothing or a place to sleep. When public schools are inferior or torn by strife, their children go to exclusive private schools. And when bureaucracy is bloated and confused, the powerful always manage to discover and occupy niches of special influence and privilege."

On the basis of the last paragraph, one may actually feel inclined to believe that Jimmy Carter truly was an outsider. But, was he really? Let's see. Twelve individuals belonging to the CFR/TC combines, according to a June 1976 article in the *Los Angeles Times*, helped Carter prepare his first major speech on foreign policy: Zbigniew Brzezinski, Richard Cooper, Richard Gardner, Henry Owen, Edwin O. Reischauer, Averell Harriman, Anthony Lake, Robert Bowie, Milton Katz, Abram Chayes, George Ball and Cyrus Vance. With a writing team like this, how could Carter come up with a bad political speech? But each of these men was an insider heavyweight with an agenda. Most belonged to the Bilderberg Group. All were members of the Council on Foreign Relations and the Trilateral Commission. In the speech they created for Carter, they created what the American people craved to hear from a prospective leader.

Carter's early support group from Atlanta, in his pre-candidate days, featured several people "with very close ties to the Rockefeller family, such as Gambrell, Kirbo and Austin."[79] The "outsider" Gambrell family was a major shareholder in Eastern Airlines, where David's brother Laurence Rockefeller was the biggest individual shareholder.

However, Carter played the role of an outsider to perfection. And, immediately upon entering the White House, he filled many of the administrative positions with CFR and Trilateralist insiders. An astounding 40% of the American Trilateral members joined the Carter

Administration. In all, 291 members of either the CFR or TC or both formed part of the Carter presidency; among them, of course, both President Carter and Vice President Mondale.

The December 2, 1976 edition of the *Wall Street Journal* covered the screening of sixteen prospects in Plains, Georgia, and reported that Cyrus Vance, Trilateralist, was to be given the post of Secretary of State. At the time, he was a director of IBM, Pan-Am Airways, and a member of the Foreign Policy Task Force, vice-chairman of the CFR as well as a former Deputy Director of Defense. With such an associate, Carter could hardly be called an outsider. Michael Blumenthal, a Trilateralist and a member of the CFR, was given the post of Secretary of Treasury. This appointment was quickly followed by that of Harold Brown, TC/CFR, to the post of Secretary of Defense. Zbigniew Brzezinski, Bilderberg, CFR/TC, was chosen to become Carter's National Security Advisor. Andrew Young, CFR, TC, became U.S. Ambassador to the United Nations, and Paul A. Volcker became Chairman of the Federal Reserve Board.[80]

U.S. News and World Report took note of the unmistakable influence of Trilateralists on Jimmy Carter: "The Trilateralists have taken charge of foreign policy-making in the Carter Administration, and already the immense power they wield is sparking some controversy. Active or former members of the Trilateral Commission now head every key agency involved in mapping U.S. strategy for dealing with the rest of the world."

In fact, if we are to compare Carter's words in 1976 to what Ronald Reagan said during his campaign against Carter in 1980, as quoted in *Time's* issue of October 20, we may be shocked at the similarity of language and ideas. These are Reagan's words: "I think there is an elite in this country, and they are the very ones who run an elitist government. They want a government by a handful of people because they don't believe the people themselves can run their lives... Are we going to have an elitist government that makes decisions for people's lives, or are we going to believe as we have for so many decades, that the people can make these decisions for themselves?"

Was Reagan an anti-Trilateralist? Hardly. Reagan's campaign was managed by William J. Casey, former Chairman of the Securities and Exchange Commission and Reagan's future Director of the CIA. Casey was a full-fledged Trilateralist. Active CFR and Trilateralist members such as Caspar Weinberger, Anne Armstrong, David Packard, George

H. Weyerhauser, Bill Brock and William A. Hewitt helped manage Reagan's campaign.

Additionally, Reagan's 59-member transition team responsible for selection and screening of candidates for major governmental posts consisted of 28 CFR members, 10 Bilderbergers and 10 Trilateralists. Amongst them figured such "outsiders" as Henry Kissinger, Alexander Haig, George Shultz (former Secretary of Treasury under Nixon), Donald Rumsfeld and Alan Greenspan.

Yet, this maneuvering would never have become nearly as effective or even possible had it not been for the close cooperation between the media and people under the control of the Bilderberger/CFR/TC apparatus. When in December 1975, seven months before the Democratic National Convention, the Gallup Poll indicated that only 5% of registered Democrats wanted Carter as President, alarms went off in the plush offices of David Rockefeller. For Carter to win the nomination, they needed to create the most elaborate media campaign in history — just like the media circus we have come to expect today from any top name in the entertainment industry — all in the effort to convince the electorate that James Earl Carter was indeed America's only hope for a better future.

But, former Georgia Governor Lester Maddox spoke out against Carter's candidacy: "Based on false, misleading and deceiving statements and actions... Jimmy Carter, in my opinion, neither deserves or should expect one vote from the American people."

Nevertheless, the American people, with the help of incessant bombardment from the media, convinced themselves that Carter was indeed their first choice.

Cyrus Vance (CFR), then on the board of the *New York Times*, and Hedley Donovan, then editor-in-chief of *Time* magazine, (a CFR/TC member as well as director of the Carnegie Endowment for International Peace) used *Time's* elaborate range of resources to aid Carter's campaign. First, *Time* painted Carter as an "outsider with no connections to the corrupt politics of Washington."[81]

But of course *Time* had been pushing Carter for sometime: "After *Time* devoted a flattering 1971 cover photo to him as a progressive Southern governor, it used that cover photo in all of *Time's* ads in other magazines through 1975. The *Time* reports on the Carter campaign were so adulatory that they could scarcely be differentiated from the campaign's own literature."[82]

Senator Barry Goldwater was definitely not a Carter fan. In his book *With No Apologies*, he wrote, "David Rockefeller and Zbigniew Brzezinski found Jimmy Carter to be their ideal candidate. They helped him win the nomination, and the presidency."

Candidate Carter went from five percent support among Democrats to becoming almost overnight the candidate of choice. "To accomplish this purpose," explained Goldwater, "they mobilized the money power of the Wall Street bankers, the intellectual influence of the academic community — which is subservient to the wealth of the great tax-free foundations — and the media controllers represented in the membership of the CFR and the Trilateral."

In his ensuing 1976 presidential campaign and stump speeches, Carter's repeated themes became twin mantras: "The time has come to replace balance-of-power politics with world order politics" and to "seek a partnership between North America, Western Europe and Japan."[83]

Where have we heard this before? Doesn't it sound as if Jimmy Carter was parroting the TC's mission statements? His emphasis on world order and trading partners definitely indicated Trilateralist views.

In campaigning against Carter's presidential candidacy, the publisher of the *Manchester Union Leader*, William Loeb, made the Trilateral Commission an issue during the New Hampshire primary: "It is quite clear that this group of extremely powerful men is out to control the world."

The selection of Jimmy Carter for the office of the President is one of the best illustrations of the market value of political contact — who you know, not who you are, wins the most votes. At the same time, it also demonstrates how easily the lack of market value can crush the presidential aspirations of a non-favorite like Senator Barry Goldwater.

Both John Kerry and George W. Bush have also been financed by the same elite combines — the Bilderberg Group, the Council on Foreign Relations and the Trilateral Commission. But, it really doesn't matter who wins. The epicenter of power always seems to remain in the hands of the people with a One World Government–One World Company agenda.

CHAPTER TWENTY-ONE

GAME OF MONOPOLY

"Nowhere," writes Gary Allen in Chapter Nine of *The Rockefeller File*, "do we find any policy determinations [of the Trilateral Commission] in favor of individual free enterprise and individual freedoms."

This complete rejection of free enterprise and individual freedom is puzzling. How can Marxism, and its resulting system of social and economic equalization, fascinate David Rockefeller, or the Trilateral Commission? Rockefeller is not only rich; he is well-educated. He knows the failure of Marxism in the form of Communism under ruthless dictators like Stalin in the twentieth century, in which an estimated 100 million citizens were slaughtered under the Communist regime, over a billion more enslaved.

How do we reconcile the mental image of a Capitalist embracing a Marxist, or any Communist/Socialist? The reason for the apparent incongruity is in our learned definitions of these words.

In school, we are taught Capitalism is based on free enterprise. Capitalists are wealthy entrepreneurs, people who go into business for themselves to make money, and you can't make money unless you produce profits. This is the cornerstone of free enterprise. Worldwide, free enterprise becomes free trade in a global marketplace. Everyone works to make money, which produces profits to invest in more businesses and industries that make money to create more jobs that spread wealth and build a higher standard of life for all. The goods and services produced are the collaborative result of individual imagination and innovation. "Whatever the mind can conceive, it can achieve." The individual "owns" his job, his business, his property. Whatever he earns for himself, he keeps and can spend in any way he chooses. Individual wealth generates state wealth through the application of taxes.

Not so for a Marxist, as we understand Marxism. Everything is for the state; nothing is for the individual. Under Marxist, Communist or socialist systems, private ownership is banned. A one-party political structure controls the state's economic planning, in which the people receive an equal distribution of goods and property. There is no incentive to excel at a job or to implement improvements to the state's methods of working, because there is no recognition of individual effort.

So, why should anyone seriously believe the apparent contradiction that bankers of the magnitude of Rockefeller, Morgan and the Rothschilds, the mainstays of our Free Enterprise system, would voluntarily support and finance an "anti-capitalist, Godless" revolution for Communists? How would the West, the paragon of capitalism and freedom, benefit from such a program?

The magic word is *monopoly*, "an all-encompassing monopoly" that not only controls the government, the monetary system and all property, but is also a "monopoly which, like the corporations it emulates, is self-perpetuating and eternal."[84]

We've seen monopoly power under state control in the Soviet Union and China. Under their Communist regimes, rather than create an economic system of equal distribution, some people were treated *more* equal than others, depending on their rank and stature in the state hierarchy. Those enjoying the most perks headed the state. However, following Mikhail Gorbachev's *glasnost*, which opened up the state to public inquiry, the Soviet Union's Communist system dissolved.

Ironically, the inequality of economic wealth hasn't improved since Russia's move to a free market, nor have the former provinces experienced a better standard of living after regaining their independence. Instead, the Russian Mafia has taken advantage of the new capitalism to exercise a corrupt power over a land further victimized. Meanwhile the merger of Communism with capitalism is seeing phenomenal success and economic growth in China. In fact, China is emerging as the next super power, all because it is practising what the West's financial elite and Bilderbergers covet for their one-world order: state-planned capitalism.

The fact is that members of the Establishment operating through "private" organizations such as the Bilderbergers, the CFR and the

Trilateral Commission understand socialism as the ultim
system for control, and understand its psychology bette,
Marxists do. This is why their members push through Congress s,
anti-capitalist programs as Welfare Reform and Regulation. Socialism
to them, again, is not a system to redistribute wealth from the rich
to the poor. Rather it's a mechanism for gaining a greater and greater
concentration of power and control.

For example, by giving generous loans to Third World nations to
help them develop their economies, the national banks actually make
more profit and flex greater power internationally. How do they manage
to do this? Let's go back to 1976. Then, the Big Five New York banks (all
run by members of the Trilateral Commission and Council on Foreign
Relations) loaned over $52 billion to several Third World and Communist
countries, "many of which were already having a hard time paying just the
interest, let alone the principal. So, the Trilateralists demanded, and got,
an 'overhauled' International Monetary Fund, subsidized for the most
part by the American taxpayer, which loaned money to these deadbeat
Third World countries to allow them to meet their obligations to the
big banks. And, of course, the money injected into the International
Monetary Fund to do this is paid for by still more and more domestic
inflation," explains Gary Allen in *The Rockefeller File*.

In *Confessions of a Monopolist* published in 1906, Frederick C.
Howe talked about how the strategy works in practice: "The rules of
big business: Get a monopoly; let Society work for you. So long as
we see all international revolutionaries and all international capitalists
as implacable enemies of one another, then we miss a crucial point
... a partnership between international monopoly capitalism and
international revolutionary socialism is for their mutual benefit."

Gary Allen in his underground bestseller, *None Dare Call it
Conspiracy*, describes how, through absolute control, the wealthy
can create and perpetuate a monopoly. "Control necessitates a static
society. A growing, competitive, and free society gives new people a
chance to make their fortune and replace some of those already at
the top. So, legislation is promoted to restrict entrepreneurial effort
and tax away capital accumulations not protected in the tax-free
foundations of the Establishment insiders. Every effort is made to press
a medium-size business to the wall and allow it to be swallowed up by
the Establishment giants."

The insiders' drive to stifle competition is no different from the way American railroad owners between 1877 and 1916 used the Interstate Commerce Commission to retain state control of railroads, which effectively gave them monopoly power.[85]

In *The Rockefeller File*, Allen notes the subversive manner of imposing monopolies: "By the late nineteenth century, the inner sanctums of Wall Street understood that the most efficient way to gain an unchallenged monopoly was to say it was for the 'public good' and the 'public interest.'"

Brzezinski too recognized the value of a monopoly under Marxism, as did David Rockefeller. David learned it at the feet of his father, John D., Jr. "Junior," as he was known, hated competition, and his children were taught that the only competition worth having is the one where you control both sides of the equation.

"To the Rockefellers," reports Gary Allen, "socialism is not a system for redistributing wealth — especially not for redistributing their wealth — but a system to control people and competitors. Socialism puts power in the hands of the government. And since the Rockefellers control the government, government control means Rockefeller control. You may not have known this, but you can be sure they do!"[86]

This reality is the optimum benefit of monopoly power. Thus, we shouldn't be surprised that what international financiers favor in the formation of a "World Company" of cartels is their ability to control world finance, markets, natural resources and, ultimately, people.

At the beginning of the 1900s, however, Marxism was still a new economic theory, and American power brokers and financiers gleaned from it another way to go after "markets that could be exploited monopolistically without fear of competition," states Antony Sutton in his book, *Wall Street and the Bolshevik Revolution*.[87]

CHAPTER TWENTY-TWO

BOLSHEVIKS' BENEFACTORS

Had the Bolshevik Revolution failed, Russia's industrial development would surely have rivaled that of the United States, Great Britain and Europe, and we would have been living in a very different world today. But, by supporting the Bolshevik Revolution, American financiers slowed down Russian industrial growth to a snail's pace in the lead-up to World War II. They prevented Russia from emerging as a super power, while the Soviet industry that did develop was controlled by Wall Street bankers and investors behind the scenes.

From the outset, a key player in the financial support of the Russian Revolution was Scottish-born Andrew Carnegie, an American steel magnate who in 1892 owned the largest steel company in the world. Carnegie also evolved into the richest philanthropist of his time and supported what he considered worthy causes. He believed a "man who dies rich dies disgraced." By his death in 1919, he had given away $350 million dollars, and one of the organizations he created to disperse his wealth was the Carnegie Corporation of New York. Because Carnegie had witnessed the horrors of the Civil War as a young man, he donated $10 million to establish the Endowment for International Peace, whose mandate was to prevent future wars from happening. Under this direction, the Endowment's board of trustees formulated the Marburg Plan.

The objective of this Plan, writes Jennings C. Wise in *Woodrow Wilson: Disciple of Revolution,* was to weld "international financiers and the socialists into a movement to compel the formation of a league [the League of Nations, the precursor of the United Nations] to enforce peace... and to control its councils... [and so] provide a specific for all the political ills of mankind."[88]

This Plan was formed on the heels of World War I, the most dreadful of wars based on loss of life for both the Allies (which included Russia) and the Central Powers. "To enforce peace" was a politically correct motive then, and an ideal Carnegie was proud to strive for. There is a hidden assumption, however. To "enforce" peace also implies that war must be created as a necessary prerequisite, and Carnegie may not have been aware of the secret intent buried in the Marburg blueprint that his board of trustees prepared for the future.

Antony Sutton provides us with the background preceding the Marburg Plan to coordinate international governments under the "ultimate power" of financial controllers. "Russia was then – and is today – the largest untapped market in the world. Moreover, Russia, then and now, constituted the greatest potential competitive threat to American industrial and financial supremacy."[89]

Thus, Sutton further explains, the creators of the Marburg Plan needed to develop a monopoly that encircled the globe, not just their own backyard. "What the Interstate Commerce Commission and the Federal Trade Commission under the thumb of American industry could achieve for that industry at home, a planned socialist government could achieve for it abroad – given suitable support and inducements from Wall Street and Washington, D.C."[90]

SEEDBED FOR DISCONTENT

At the turn of the twentieth century, Tsar Nicholas II ruled Russia. He was the last Romanov to reign, in a dynasty that lasted from 1613 to 1917. Before World War I, his empire covered 8,500,000 square miles, and bordered Turkey, Persia, Afghanistan, Mongolia and China, while Poland, the Baltic States and Finland were Russian territories. According to Major-General Sir John Hanbury Williams, a British officer stationed in Russia during the War, the loyalty of the tsar "to the Allied cause was only equalled by his determination to fight out the war to the bitter end."

The Romanovs had been westernizing Russia since the reign of Peter the Great, and Nicholas II intended to modernize Russian industry to equal the standard of European technology. Unfortunately, he was taking advantage of his labor force to do it. Many were working 12-

hour shifts for minimal wages, and this set the stage for the organized workers' protest in St. Petersburg on "Bloody Sunday" in 1905. The tsar's troops, however, squashed this first attempt at a revolt. The old order maintained precarious power through the first years of the War, until an opportunity rose again in 1918 to achieve the overthrow of the monarchy, and the eventual execution of Nicholas II and his family.

So, it is interesting to learn in Gyeorgos C. Hatonn's book, *Rape of the Constitution; Death of Freedom,* that John D. Rockefeller's personal emissary, George Kennan, spent twenty years promoting revolutionary activity against the Tsar in Russia. His presence and influence made it easy for American capitalists to exploit the "captive" Russian market under the guise of well-meaning aid to downtrodden rebels.

Why were Rockefeller and his band of bankers so anxious to overthrow the Russian monarchy? Was there another, more relevant reason to advance the Russian Revolution?

In one word: Yes. The answer is as meaningful today as it was one hundred years ago. *Oil!* Before the Bolshevik revolt, Russia had surpassed the U.S. as the world's number one oil producer.[91] In 1900, the oil-saturated Baku fields in Russia *were producing more crude oil than the United States* and, in 1902, produced more than half of the total world output.

The chaos and destruction of the Revolution destroyed the Russian oil industry. In *Wall Street and the Bolshevik Revolution,* Sutton writes: "By 1922, half the wells were idle," and the other half barely functioning, because they lacked the technology to make them operational.[92]

In *The Rockefeller File,* Gary Allen also notes that the revolution crushed America's competition. "The Revolution effectively eliminated Standard Oil's competition from Russia for several years until Standard could move in and get a piece of the Russian oil business."

But, for the Wall Street bankers to wipe out their competition and condemn the Russian people to poverty and corruption for decades, they had to have leaders who could deliver a successful revolution. Enter Vladimir Ulyanov Lenin and Leon Trotsky.

MAIN ACTORS ON STAGE

Sounding rather like Brzezinski more than 50 years later, Lenin outlined his ideas in *The Threatening Catastrophe,* in September, 1917:

Nationalization of the banks. Ownership of capital, which is manipulated by the banks is not lost or changed when the banks are nationalized and fused into one state bank, so that it is possible to reach a stage where the state knows whither and how, from where and at what time millions and billions are flowing. Only control over bank operations, providing they are merged into one state bank, will allow, simultaneously with other measures, which can easily be put into effect the actual levying of income tax without concealment of property and income. The state for the first time would be in a position to survey all the monetary operations, then to control them, then to regulate economic life; finally, to obtain millions and billions for large state operations, without paying the capitalist gentlemen sky-high commissions for their services. It would facilitate the nationalization of syndicates, abolition of commercial secrets, and the nationalization of the insurance business; facilitate the control of and the compulsory organization of labor into unions, and the regulation of consumption. The nationalization of banks would make circulation of checks compulsory by law for all the rich, and introduce the confiscation of property for concealing incomes. The five points [sic] of the desired program then, are nationalization of the banks, nationalization of the syndicates, the abolition of commercial secrets, and the compulsory organization of the population into consumer associations.[93]

It is no coincidence that one of the first orders issued by the new Bolshevik regime was, "The banking business is declared a state monopoly." One of the names signed on the order was Lenin's.

Trotsky published a book in 1918, *The Bolsheviks and World Peace*. In it, Trotsky parrots Lenin but proclaims himself an "internationalist" — not a Russian — who is for *world* revolution and for *world* dictatorship. Immediately, we see what bonds American bankers to these two Bolshevik leaders: their concept of "internationalism" matches their own.

MONEY LAUNDERING BRETHREN

Does anyone still think that the Bolshevik revolution was a spontaneous uprising? This is what John Reed would have us believe in his best-known work, *Ten Days that Shook the World*. Reed, who died of typhus in Russia in 1920, was not only a popular author in the World War I era; he also contributed to the J.P.Morgan-controlled journal, *Metropolitan*. Is this mere coincidence?

Even though channels linking the Rockefellers and the Soviets have been largely censored, Antony Sutton's detailed document, *Wall Street and the Bolshevik Revolution,* exposes how John D. Rockefeller and American super capitalists financed the Bolshevik Revolution in Russia. At the outset of his investigation, he found "virtually nothing written on the close relationship over the past century that the Rockefellers have had with its supposed arch-enemies, the Communists. [Nevertheless,] there has been a continuing, albeit concealed, alliance between international political capitalists and international revolutionary socialists to their mutual benefit."[94]

For example, Simpson, Thacher and Bartlett, the leading Wall Street law firm specializing in reorganizations and mergers was firmly behind the Bolshevik regime in Russia. "As one indication of their support," writes Sutton, "partner Thomas D. Thacher wrote a report which became decisive in gaining British cabinet support for the Bolsheviks... This memorandum not only made explicit suggestions about Russian policy that supported the pro-Bolshevik position of William Boyce Thompson, the then director of Chase, now Chase Manhattan Bank, but even stated that 'the fullest assistance should be given to the Soviet government in its efforts to organize a volunteer revolutionary army.'"

It is worth noting that one of Simpson, Thacher and Bartlett's alumni was the young Cyrus Vance, who would later become President Carter's Secretary of State and, following that, a senior director of the Rockefeller Foundation. Small world, indeed.

One of the Wall Street firms involved with the Bolsheviks was J.P. Morgan, as was revealed in Harold Nicholson's biography of Morgan partner Dwight Morrow, the father-in-law of Charles Lindbergh, Jr.:

> [Morrow's] interest in Russia dated from March 1917 when Thomas D. Thacher, his law partner, had been a member of the American Red Cross Mission during the revolution. It was strengthened by his friendship with Alex Gumberg, who had come to New York as representative of the All-Russian Textile Syndicate. 'I have felt,' he wrote in May 1927, 'that the time would come when something would have to be done for Russia.' He was himself active in furthering official relations between Soviet emissaries and the State Dept., and he provided M. Litvinov with a warm letter of recommendation to Sir Arthur Salter in Geneva. Nor was this all. When in Paris, he gave a dinner party at Foyot's, to which he invited M. Rakovsky and other Soviet representatives.

Another mega-organization supporting the Bolshevik cause was the Federal Reserve Bank of New York, controlled by the five principal New York banks. In *The Unknown War with Russia*, Robert J. Maddox noted in 1977, "William Laurence Sanders, chairman of Ingersoll Rand, and deputy chairman of the Federal Reserve Bank of New York, wrote to President Wilson, on October 17, 1918, 'I am in sympathy with the Soviet form of government as the best suited for the Russian people.' George Foster Peabody, also deputy chairman of the Federal Reserve Bank of New York since 1914, and noted philanthropist, who organized the General Education Board for the Rockefellers, stated that he supported the Bolshevik form of state monopoly."

The scam boggles the mind when we consider that three of the top officers of the Federal Reserve Bank of New York publicly supported Bolshevism — Sanders, Peabody and William Boyce Thompson.

Current knowledge makes clear that Wall Street bankers reacted with help as early as 1905, when Lenin and Trotsky's initial rebellion had failed. They arranged safe passage for Lenin to Switzerland, where he remained out of harm's way.

Trotsky after 1905 had lived in exile, notes Antony Sutton in *Wall Street and the Bolshevik Revolution*, first in France. But after writing rabble-rousing articles for a Russian-language newspaper in Paris in September 1916, the French police escorted him across the Spanish border.

A few days later, Madrid police arrested him and lodged him in a 'first-class cell' at a charge of one-and-one-half pesetas per day. Subsequently, Trotsky was taken to Cadiz, then to Barcelona and finally placed on board the Spanish Transatlantic Company steamer *Monserrat*. Trotsky and family crossed the Atlantic Ocean and landed in New York on January 13, 1917.

How did Trotsky, who knew only German and Russian, survive in capitalist America? According to his autobiography, *My Life* [Scribner's, 1930], "My only profession in New York was that of a revolutionary socialist." In other words, Trotsky wrote occasional articles for *Novy Mir*, the New York Russian socialist journal. Yet we know that the Trotsky family apartment in New York had a refrigerator and a telephone, and, according to Trotsky, that the family occasionally traveled in a chauffeured limousine. This mode of living puzzled the two young Trotsky boys. When they went into a tearoom, the boys would anxiously demand of their mother, "Why doesn't the chauffeur come in?" The stylish living standard is also at odds with Trotsky's reported income. The only funds that Trotsky admits receiving in 1916 and 1917 are $310, and, said Trotsky, "I distributed the $310 among five emigrants who were returning to Russia." Yet Trotsky had paid for a first-class cell in Spain, the Trotsky family had traveled across Europe to the United States, they had acquired an excellent apartment in New York — paying rent three months in advance — and they had use of a chauffeured limousine. All this on the earnings of an impoverished revolutionary for a few articles for the low-circulation Russian-language newspaper *Nashe Slovo* in Paris and *Novy Mir* in New York!

By then, the American International Corporation had already been founded in New York in 1915. Its principal responsibility was to coordinate financial assistance to the Bolsheviks. J.P. Morgan, the Rockefellers, and the National City Bank provided the funding, while the new corporation's Chairman of the Board was Frank Vanderlip, former president of National City Bank, and member of the Jekyll Island group, which had written the Federal Reserve Act in 1910.

According to Eustace Mullins in *The World Order*, the Bolsheviks sought more funds shortly after their return to Russia:

> To whom should Lenin turn but his powerful friend in the White House? Wilson promptly sent Elihu Root, Kuhn Loeb lawyer and former Secretary of State, to Russia with $20 million from his Special War Fund, to be given to the Bolsheviks. This was revealed in Congressional Hearings on Russian Bonds, HJ 8714.U5, which shows the financial statement of Woodrow Wilson's expenditure of the $100 million voted him by Congress as a Special War Fund. The statement, showing the expenditure of $20 million in Russia by Root's Special War Mission to Russia, is also recorded in the Congressional Record, Sept. 2, 1919, as given by Wilson's secretary, Joseph Tumulty.

Wilson's assistance was but the tip of the iceberg. Using Colonel Raymond Robins, head of a Red Cross Mission to Russia, as its emissary, J.P. Morgan & Co. sent several million dollars in cash to the Russians through Henry P. Davison, Morgan's right-hand man.

Now Wall Street's financial manipulation takes on a larger meaning. Although the Japanese had appeared to make the most of the internal strife within Russia during 1905, it was U.S. President Theodore Roosevelt who mediated a peace treaty that forced Russia to give up its Eastern and Baltic fleets and cede the southern half of Sakhalin Island to Japan. The Russian monarchy further agreed to hand over Manchuria to Japan and to abandon protection of Korea, which Japan then annexed in 1910, to little international objection.

What American bankers backed with one hand, they took away with the other. Clearly, they wanted to reduce Russia's sea power and trading ability, and influenced Roosevelt's intercession in the negotiated settlement between Japan and Russia, but the outcome was staggering. This action by the Russian monarchy had the effect of weakening Soviet naval strength in the Far East until well after World War II.

Other avenues also provided secret funding on a supra-national level. One of the key men involved was Dr. Parvus Helphand. In his 1931 book, *Lenin: Red Dictator,* Yale Professor George Vernadsky wrote, "In the autumn of 1915, the German Russian Social Democrat Parvus [Helphand], who had formerly been active in the Revolution of 1905, announced in the paper published by him in Berlin, *Die Glocke* [The Bell], his mission to serve as an intellectual link between the armed German and the revolutionary Russian proletariat.... During the war, Parvus was engaged in furnishing supplies to the German army and in huge speculations, and so considerable amounts of money passed through his hands."

German Imperial records that only came to light after World War II document the important role of this "Marxist millionaire" in funneling German funds to revolutionaries in Russia. In December of 1915, for example, the German State Secretary telegraphed the Minister in Copenhagen: "Your Excellency is authorized to pay one million rubles to Helphand."[95] The following month the Minister submitted a report: "Dr. Helphand, who has returned to Copenhagen after spending three weeks in Stockholm, where he conferred with Russian revolutionaries, has told me the following, in confidence: The sum of a million rubles which was put at his disposal, was immediately sent on, and has already reached Petrograd and been devoted to the purposes for which it was intended."[96]

Now almost forgotten, the Russian Alexander Israel Helphand was an enigmatic character whose career was as strange as anything served up in fiction. His active role in the abortive Revolution of 1905, when he became a close associate of Trotsky, led to a Siberian exile, so necessary for the resume of any true Russian revolutionary. He had taken the alias "Parvus" as a Socialist pamphleteer in Germany in 1894, having received in 1891 a doctorate in philosophy from the University of Basel in Switzerland, where he had deepened his Marxist convictions. Later, as Maxim Gorky's German publisher, he became involved in a scandal over royalties, the result of a long-running dispute that led to a secret conviction and expulsion by the German Socialists.

After a brief stay in Vienna, he traveled in 1910 to Istanbul, which became his base of operations. There he somehow made a large fortune. In January of 1915 he advised the German Ambassador to the Ottoman Empire, for three months the allies of Germany: "The interests of the German government were ... identical with those of the Russian revolutionaries, who were already at work."[97] This led to his role as intermediary.

Helphand had a part in arranging the notorious "sealed train," which in April of 1917 delivered Lenin and other Bolsheviks from exile in Switzerland through Germany to a steamer bound for Sweden, whence they made their way through Finland to Russia. As Vernadsky noted, Germany's interest lay in both providing safe passage and maintaining its secrecy: "To afford Lenin and his comrades an opportunity of passage to Russia was in the nature of introducing disease germs into the organism of the Russian state."[98]

By the time the wily Lenin had reached Stockholm, however, he refused a meeting with Parvus, who was awaiting him, and began to distance himself from this entire episode. It clearly did not suit the Bolshevik program to be linked to Russia's enemy while Russian soldiers were being slaughtered at the front. Helphand received his own entry in the first official Soviet Encyclopedia; by the second he had vanished.[99]

Meanwhile, in New York Trotsky received word to return to Russia immediately. Conditions were now ripe for a Revolution. With $10,000 for "traveling expenses," he left New York on March 26, 1917, on the S.S. *Kristianiafjord*, along with 275 Communist revolutionaries under the watchful eye of Lincoln Steffens, an American Communist and John D. Rockefeller's emissary, to make sure Trotsky was returned safely to Russia.

Where did Trotsky get his passport? How was it arranged and why? It appears that John D. Rockefeller himself obtained a special passport for Trotsky through Woodrow Wilson, the President of the United States. Why would the President of the United States arrange for passage of a known revolutionary merely at the request of a private, albeit wealthy, citizen?

According to de-classified Canadian government archives, when the *Kristianiafjord* stopped in Halifax on April 13, 1917, Canadian Secret Service officers and British naval personnel immediately boarded the ship and removed Trotsky (under official instructions received from London via cablegram on March 29, 1917) and interned him for questioning in Amherst, Nova Scotia.

The cablegram described Trotsky as a German prisoner of war, and warned that he was "on his way to take Russia out of the war, which would free many German divisions to attack the Canadian troops on the Western Front," explains Eustace Mullins in *The World Order*. A previous Canadian government memo stated that Trotsky was carrying "10,000 dollars subscribed by socialists and Germans."[100]

Immediately, Prime Minister Lloyd George cabled orders from London to the Canadian Secret Service to set Trotsky free. His order was ignored. Finally, Mackenzie King — at this stage of his career he was a labor expert for John D. Rockefeller, Jr. — intervened, and obtained Trotsky's release. As soon as he was freed, King sent Trotsky on his way to Russia to share leadership of the Bolshevik Revolution with Lenin.

For his efforts, King was rewarded with a $30,000-a-year salary as head of the Rockefeller Foundation department of Industrial Research, at a time when the average wage in the United States was $500 per year. On the other hand, the agents who had arrested Trotsky were dismissed from the Canadian service.

King, destined to become Prime Minister of Canada, has remained an enigma to his countrymen. Was he a fool, a genius, or a self-absorbed opportunist? His admiration for Rockefeller was clearly, if not naïvely, stated in a note he sent at the time to his friend, Violet Markham. "John D. Rockefeller Jr., the truest follower of Christ, has one purpose — to serve his fellow man."

While historians J.L. Granatstein and Norman Hillmer in 1999 ranked King as the greatest of Canada's Prime Ministers,[101] this is the same man who "was exposed as a principal in the $30 million Beauharnais-Power Co. swindle during the building of the St. Lawrence Seaway. [He] had accepted $700,000 from Beauharnais for the Liberal Party, and among other enticements had received a trip to Bermuda."[102]

Once Lenin and Trotsky were back in Russia, and the revolution succeeded in overthrowing the monarchy in 1918, a world headquarters for providing Bolshevik aid was consolidated at 120 Broadway on Wall Street:

> During the early 1920s, 120 Broadway not only housed Equitable Life, but also the Federal Reserve Bank of New York, whose directors were enthusiastically supporting the Bolsheviks; the American International Corporation, which had been organized to aid the Soviet Union; Weinberg and Posner, which received a $3 million order for machinery from the Soviet Union in 1919, and whose vice president was Ludwig Martens, first Soviet Ambassador to the U.S.; John McGregor Grant, whose operations were financed by Olaf Aschberg of Nya Banken, Stockholm, who had transmitted large sums furnished by the Warburgs for the Bolshevik Revolution; the London agent of Nya Banken was the British Bank of North Commerce, whose chairman was Earl Grey, a close associate of Cecil Rhodes – Grant had been blacklisted by the U.S. Government for his support of Germany during World War I; and on the top floor of 120 Broadway was the exclusive Bankers Club. These were the organizers of the World Order.[103]

To add another ring to this dazzling mesh of intrigue, it is tempting to see a link from 120 Broadway through Nya Banken to the German support of the Bolsheviks. Nya was the bank in Stockholm used by Parvus Helphand to funnel rubles and marks (often in gold) to Russian revolutionaries. As Helphand apparently destroyed all his personal records shortly before his death in 1924 (in a Berlin mansion destined twelve years later to become the residence of Josef Goebbels!), this nexus is likely to remain speculative.

John Sr., famously handing out a dime.

L-R, John Jr., Abby Aldrich, Laurence, John Sr., Winthrop, Abby "Babs" and David Rockefeller

David Rockefeller

Grandpa John D. and Great Uncle William with little David Rockefeller

J.P. "Jack" Morgan Jr. and sons Junius S. (I) and Henry S.

J.P. Morgan around town.

CHAPTER TWENTY-THREE

TREASON FOR PROFIT

F rom the 1920s, Morgan-Rockefeller interests played a leading role in numerous pro-Soviet commercial arrangements. They controlled the principal firms doing business with Soviet Russia: Vacuum Oil, International Harvester, Guaranty Trust and New York Life. In 1926, the Vacuum Oil Company, owned by Rockefeller, closed an agreement with the Soviet Naptha Syndicate to market Soviet oil in European countries through the Chase National Bank (also Rockefeller-owned).

At the time, it was reported that John D. Rockefeller agreed on a $75,000,000 loan to the Bolsheviks as "part of the price for the arrangement." As a result of this deal, Rockefeller's Standard Oil built an oil refinery in Russia in 1927, after they were promised 50% of the Caucasus oil production.

But, as early as 1911, John Moody had already nicknamed the Standard Oil Co. the Standard Oil Bank because, as he observed, the "Standard Oil Co. was really a bank of the most gigantic character – a bank within an industry ... lending vast sums of money to needy borrowers just as other great banks were doing."[104]

Again, the Rockefellers played a key role in founding the American-Russian Chamber of Commerce in 1922 to promote trade with Russia under the direction of its chairman, Reeve Schley, who was vice president of Chase National Bank as well.

As a prerequisite to opening up the Russian market to the Establishment, in 1925 John D. Rockefeller added pressure to the

Chamber's lobbying for the U.S. government to change its foreign policy, through a private campaign under his press agent, Ivy Lee, "to sparkplug a public relations drive" and promote Communism in the U.S. This combined effort culminated in 1933 with the U.S. government's recognition of Soviet Russia.

In 1935, Stalin quietly repaid Rockefeller when he seized a sizable chunk of assets owned by foreign companies investing in Russia, but did not touch Standard Oil properties.

Through the 1920s and '30s, lone U.S. Congressman Louis McFadden tracked the secret financial manipulations of the Federal Reserve System for the benefit of the Soviet Union. By June 10, 1932, he was fed up with the deliberate drainage of U.S. funds to Russia and harangued the House: "Open up the books of Amtorg, the trading organization of the Soviet government in New York, and of Gostorg, the general office of the Soviet Trade Organization, and of the State Bank of the Union of Soviet Socialist Republics, and you will be staggered to see how much American money has been taken from the United States Treasury for the benefit of Russia. Find out what business has been transacted for the State Bank of Soviet Russia by its correspondent, the Chase Bank of New York."

Years later, during World War II, Amtorg's bank of choice to handle the billions of dollars of Lend Lease transactions for Soviet Russia was, of course, the Chase National Bank.

Unfortunately, funneling U.S. taxpayers' money to the Soviet Union was not a profitable enough operation for the Wall Street gang of profiteers. They finally engaged in treason for profit when they secretly began transferring the most sophisticated and expensive American technology to the Soviets in 1943.[105] Then, the Soviet Purchasing Commission requested from the U.S. government 200 pounds of uranium oxide, 220 pounds of uranium nitrate, and 25 pounds of uranium metal, commodities virtually unknown at that time, for their war efforts. On April 29, 1943, the Board of Economic Warfare granted a special license to Chematar Corp. of New York to fill this order.

This provided the Soviets with the resources to build their own atomic bomb (if they had the formula), while at the same time, Winston Churchill demanded from President Roosevelt that Stalin be barred from sharing scientific intelligence leading to the development of nuclear weapons before Britain or the U.S. had produced an atom bomb first. It was enough that the Allies were in a race with Hitler to beat him at building atomic capabilities without worrying about another "madman" launching a nuclear threat on the world.

While the rich became richer, Americans were told that a détente was necessary, because without bilateral agreements the enemy would attack. For the illusion of a partnership among equals to become a reality, there must at least be the "semblance of parity among the senior member states before you can justify a merger."[106]

Is this why, according to hundreds of U.S. State Department documents, the Soviet industrial and military capabilities such as trucking, aircraft, oil, steel, petrochemicals, aluminum, and computers were constructed at the U.S. taxpayers' expense in the Soviet Union? For the sake of parity?

As Sutton pointed out in 1972, "There was no such thing as Soviet technology."[107]

Of the technology that did exist, almost 90 to 95% came directly or indirectly from the United States and its Allies. "Even stranger," commented Sutton in testimony he gave to the Subcommittee of the Platform Committee of the Republican Party, "the U.S. apparently wants to make sure this enemy remains in the business of being an enemy."

The Soviets' merchant marine, for example, was the largest in the world, containing nearly 6,000 vessels. But, Sutton further testified, "About two-thirds of the vessels were built outside the Soviet Union. About four-fifths of the engines for these ships were also built outside the Soviet Union."[108]

"All Soviet automobile, truck, [guns, tanks, aircraft] and engine technology come from the West. The Gorki organization, built by the Ford and Austin companies, produced most of the trucks that once carried Soviet-supplied military equipment down the Ho Chi Minh Trail [during the Viet Nam War]. Automobile factories can also be used to build tanks. The same Gorki organization under the guise of 'peaceful trade,' produced in 1964 the first Soviet wire-guided anti-tank system. The Soviets have the largest iron and steel plant in the world. It was built by McKee Corporation. It is a copy of the U.S. steel plant in Indiana."[109]

How many billions did the United States spend on defense against a phantom enemy it created, nurtured, supported and built up? Do the costs justify the means? Of course, they do! Remember, the Great Merger will be controlled by the same Bilderberg-CFR-TC combines that are orchestrating behind-the-scenes regional blocks and "temporary" monetary unions.

CHAPTER TWENTY-FOUR

SACRIFICING A NATION

While many biographies, including David Rockefeller's autobiography, *Memoirs*, describe the Rockefellers' unlimited economic and political power, and the family's fabulous wealth, as spent on feeding the starving in Third World countries, educating the poor through myriad benevolent foundations and societies, and building the infrastructure of underdeveloped and war-ravaged nations, few have dealt with what many believe to be the most remarkable aspect of the family — *its single-minded intent to destroy the United States* as an independent nation, to establish, for the greater good, a New World Order.

Without a justifiable and a visible *enemy*, no nation will voluntarily give up its individual rights and freedoms. The Bilderberg, CFR and Trilateral brethren know they have to produce a reason for people to "buy into" their One World Plan. Every day their rhetoric grows louder.

The Web site of the Trilateral Commission, for instance, speaks boldly of "sharing leadership responsibilities," and advocates "closer cooperation" and "mutual understanding." How they understand these terms, however, varies greatly from how the greater part of the population understands them.

By the time Brzezinski, Cyrus Vance, Defense Secretary Harold Brown and Undersecretary of the Treasury Anthony Solomon came together to help found the Trilateral Commission, they were already actively participating in a parallel initiative promoted by the CFR called the "1980s Project": "the largest single effort in CFR's history." The aim of the project was to see "how world trends might be steered toward a particular desirable future outcome."

This desirable future outcome dealt with the utter disintegration of the economy. In *Alternatives to Monetary Disorder*, Fred Hirsch, at the time editor of the London *Economist*, explained how this would be done:

> A degree of controlled disintegration in the world economy is a legitimate objective for the 1980s and may be the most realistic one for a moderate international economic order. A central normative problem for the international economic order in the years ahead is how to ensure that the disintegration indeed occurs in a controlled way and does not rather spiral into damaging restrictionism. The problem therefore is not to minimize politicization in the process sense of political intervention in market outcomes; it is rather to create a framework capable of containing the increased level of such politicization that emerges naturally from the changed balance in both domestic economies and the international system.

Translation: the key political commitment is to impede at all costs the reemergence of economic nationalism in all of its manifestations — industrial, technological and scientific.

Why would Rockefeller and other U.S. Trilateralists, Bilderbergers and the CFR members want to dismantle the industrial might of the United States? To understand the reasons, we must briefly review the economic history of the twentieth century.

The British Empire began to lose its grip on industrial superiority in the last two decades of the nineteenth century. As the British power began to wane, the United States, Japan, France and Germany overtook it in industrial production. How was it that a nation such as France, almost ruined under the reign of Napoleon III, could build itself up in such a short period of time? It was simple. Their economic policies were based upon a "decidedly anti-liberal economic theory, the theory of dirigisme, identified with the theoretical works of Alexander Hamilton, and also with the works of the great American economists Henry and Mathew Carey."[110]

Japan's economic miracle was due to its adherence to the principles of the January 3, 1868 Meiji Revolution, which brought about significant reforms to the Japanese society in terms of compulsory universal education, mass modernization and the encouragement of capitalism and markets in the tradition of American economists. The reforms of the Meiji Revolution shaped the basis of the modernization of pre-World War II Japanese industry, and also the makings and experience for the post-WWII "Japanese miracle."

Germany too was built up into a leading world industrial power because it followed the policies of the great German economist Friedrich List, who was largely influenced by Hamilton's economic principles and the American school of political economy. In the nineteenth century, List was very much against the British model of free trade: buying cheap and selling expensive.

The British oligarchy was well aware that, to survive, it needed to destroy Hamilton's "American System" of developmental economic nationalism, which was intended to allow the United States to become economically independent and nationally self-sufficient by imposing industry protection through (a) selective high tariffs to keep out British manufactured goods, (b) government investments in infrastructure to create targeted internal improvements, and (c) a national bank with policies to promote the growth of productive enterprises.

In the early 1950s, Anglo-American leadership faced their first real challenge from the then-Western Alliance partners, as the post-WWII liberal economic system was discernibly going to pieces. France, the Federal Republic of Germany, as well as American nationalist forces were proposing a new orientation in favor of a commitment for renewed industrial development worldwide. "Such a policy would have meant industrialization of key sectors of the Third World and thus the eventual emergence of new, sound, and strong nations – a repeat of the British nightmare at the turn of the 20th century. Such a policy would also have meant that France, the Federal Republic of Germany, and Japan, with their special relations with Third World nations, would experience an industrial boom, as their economies mobilized to provide the capital goods needed by the new nations. In the beginning of 1973, the West German deutschmark had already smashed the British pound and by July-August was on its way to gaining hegemony over the ailing U.S. dollar."[111]

Economic development would have also meant future competition from up-and-coming nations: competition, which needless to say, had to be strangled in the cradle. From the Establishment's point of view, there is a clear advantage to conducting business in this manner. "First, economic exchanges [with weaker nations] can always be used as a tool of political power through boycotts, bribery, and manipulation of trade incentives. Second, economic relationships can operate on a more fundamental level, shaping the political economic foundations of a weaker, less developed economy through the opportunity offered to it in the form of trade and finance. The weaker country in the economic relationship, like a weaker class, then becomes not just a group of assorted individuals but a particularized, isolated and dependent participant in the world economy."[112]

British surrogates were launched in the United States in an attempt to destroy Hamilton's "American System" of economic nationalism – the Ditchley Foundation and the Aspen Institute for Humanistic Studies in Colorado. The institute was founded by Lord Bullock of the Royal Institute of International Affairs [RIIA]. The RIIA is a branch of the Round Table, whose American branch is the Council on Foreign Relations.

The Aspen Institute played a leading role in the Malvinas War between Argentina and Britain, as noted in Part One. Latin America is important to the United States because it has the potential to provide a huge market for American exports of technology and heavy industrial equipment, which could galvanize many of America's faltering companies and provide thousands of new jobs. In the Bilderberg/CFR/TC "post industrial" age, this has to be prevented at all costs.

One of the stranger propositions coming out of the Ditchley Foundation was its public advocacy for dual citizenship for England and the United States, a shocker to the U.S. constitutional experts, as the English do not possess the legal status of "citizens," but that of "subjects."

Aspen and Ditchley do not represent themselves, but rather form part of a vast overlapping systemic organization with the Bilderbergers, CFR and Trilateralists, all playing a different function in their long-range objectives of shaping a community of developed nations. As David Rockefeller said in his *Memoirs*, "Some even believe we are part of a secret cabal working against the best interests of the United States, characterizing my family and me as 'internationalists' and of conspiring with others around the world to build a more integrated global political and economic structure – one world, if you will. If that's the charge, I stand guilty, and I am proud of it."

What we have witnessed from this "cabal" is the gradual collapsing of the U.S. economy that began in the 1980s.

> The corporate raiders, financed by the dirty-money junk bond networks, bought up significant chunks of corporate America, and terrified the rest. The raiders' targets, and those who feared they might become targets, turned to Wall Street's investment banks and law firms for "protection." As such, the leveraged buy-out/junk bond operation functioned as a giant protection racket, destroying some as a way of collecting tribute from the rest. At the same time, dirty money poured into the real estate market, notably through the giant Canadian developers.... These firms built the skyscrapers, which were then filled up with service workers — bankers, lawyers, accountants, clerks, and other white-collar types....
>
> The pouring of hot money into the real estate markets caused real estate prices to rise. The "wealth" created by these rising values provided more money to pump into the bubble....
>
> The speculator went from being the enemy to being the role model....
>
> The old-style productive industry became the realm of "losers," replaced by the hot new "industries" of finance and information....
>
> The effect of all this deregulation and speculation has been the decimation of the physical economy of the United States. Over the last three decades, the productive capacity of the U.S. economy has been cut in half, measured in terms of market baskets of goods on a per-capita, per-household, and per-square-kilometer basis. At the same time, the monetary claims on that declining production have risen hyperbolically.[113]

As a result, the rich have grown richer, and the poor, poorer, while the middle class has continued to shrink. This is the price the interconnected organizations of "international insiders" have exacted behind our backs. They have sacrificed our dreams, our independence and our self-sufficiency at the altar of their New World Order.

Richard N. Cooper, a Trilateralist and one of the authors of a 1977 Task Force Report entitled, *Toward a Renovated International System,* defined the Commission's objectives for world control: "The support for human rights will have to be balanced against other important goals of world order. Some Trilateral conceptions of détente with the Soviet Union and other Communist states tend to conflict with a policy of promoting human rights."

Is this the sound of dissent? One member calling for balance in the Trilateral Commission's goals, implying there is a lack of balance in the Commission's actual implementation of its plans.

As much as we may wish for dissent to develop within Rockefeller's Trilateral Commission, we will never see it implode and fall in upon its own foundation. As Eustace Mullins explains, "The Rockefellers operate under clearly defined spheres of influence. The 'charitable' organizations, the business companies, and the policy groups always meld into a working operation. No department of the Group can strike out on its own or formulate an independent policy, no matter what may be its justification, because it operates under the control of the world financial structure, which means that on any given day, all of its assets could be rendered close to worthless by adroit financial manipulation. This is the final control, which ensures that no one can quit the organization. Not only would he be stripped of all assets, but he would be under contract for immediate assassination."[114]

So, how can any one person stand up to such a mammoth machine, which, like an octopus, grows larger, bolder and more powerful as its tentacles reach out and strangle everything and everyone in its path?

Our political, military and financial leaders are still accountable for their actions. Make your vote count. Bring back Abe Lincoln's original democracy: a government of the people, by the people, and for the people. The one thing this self-appointed "cabal" of financial aristocrats is most afraid of is a public revolt, because they have been the masterminds behind one of the most devastating revolutions in history. But, not all revolutions have to be violent. There is tremendous power in everyone saying "NO" in a quiet yet firm, collective voice.

What Edwin H. Chapin said in the nineteenth century remains true today: "Not armies, not nations, have advanced the race; but here and there, in the course of ages, an individual has stood up and cast his shadow over the world."

CHAPTER TWENTY-FIVE

DETENTION, 2004

For once, my mind wasn't on the Bilderbergers. Nor was it on the sleepy resort town of Stresa in Italy, where they planned to meet this year. Instead, as I made my way through Milan's Malpensa International Airport, my thoughts were busy seeking meaning in my past. Was it a storehouse of remembered images and concealed patterns that contain the key to the mysterious designs on my life? What if I never discovered that key? What would become of me?

"*Buona sera*. Would you please come with us, sir?"

The sharp voice penetrated my ponderings. I looked up. A man, dressed in a raincoat, approached me. The raincoat struck me as odd. Through the wall of windows lining the airport terminal, I could see the Mediterranean blue sky. No cloud in sight. And then I spotted the shiny automatic weapon slung across his shoulders under his coat.

Butterflies fluttered in my stomach. Feelings of prearranged tragedy, or more precisely, the ever-present shadow I lived with, reminded me of the perilous ways in which I chose to make my living.

The man in the raincoat stopped directly in front of me, clicked his heels and tipped his index and middle fingers to his temple in salute. Flashes of Tweedle Dum and Tweedle Dee sprung to mind from the prior year's experience in Versailles.

He introduced himself as a detective. "Would you please come with us?" he asked again.

Flanked by two local guards and a narcotics officer with a Doberman, the detective and I passed into a detention room where small-time hoodlums and big-time criminals were usually questioned and searched. The room was so tiny it scarcely accommodated the wide desk dominating the space. Adding to this impression of absurd imbalance was the low table standing next to it. A small desk lamp sat on top. Once we were all crowded inside, including the Doberman, the detective closed the door.

In the eerie quiet, I could hear the wind outside brush the window glass, while inside, through the room's thin walls, I could make out someone weeping next door followed by rhythmic whimpering. And then, my attention was caught by heavy footsteps across the hallway.

"You may take off your coat," said one of the guards, jerking his head in the direction of a tall coat rack standing in the corner.

Looking back, I am ashamed to recall the anxiety I felt as I mechanically unzipped my windbreaker. Straining to reach up, I slung my windbreaker over the top hook, but it fell short, taking down two other coats and a plaid jacket with it. The four garments swished to the floor. I debated picking them up and then decided to leave the pile on the floor. I leaned against the wall and faced my interrogators, determined to keep my cool yet aware of the sweat greasing the back of my neck.

Lei come si chiama? (What is your name?)

I gave him my name.

"What is your nationality?"

"Canadian."

Di che parte di Canada é lei? (What part of Canada are you from?) *Lei dove abita?* (Where do you live?) *Qual é il suo numero di telefono?* (What is your telephone number?) *Éla prima volta che viene in Italia?* (Is this your first visit to Italy?)

I gave them straight answers. Years of covering the Bilderberg Group taught me this was the easiest way to avoid confrontations with bullish border guards and trigger-happy policemen. I had seen other journalists turned back at the border for their impudence.

"We would like to examine your suitcase. We have reason to believe you may be transporting drugs," said the detective.

Drugs! The accusation stunned me.

"If you have drugs, you better tell us before we open up your bag," added the narcotics officer.

Being accused of carrying illegal drugs would not normally scare me — I don't use drugs, much less transport them internationally in a suitcase — but my name is known internationally by all divisions of the secret service, from Mossad to the KGB, MI6, the FBI, and the CIA. Each reporter covering an annual Bilderberg meeting is photographed, his personal details taken and the information passed through Interpol to all international protection agencies. Could someone have slipped drugs into my suitcase?

I had only brought what luggage I could carry. No check-ins so I could keep my bag with me. I wracked my brain. Was there a moment when I left it unguarded? No matter how I tried to contain my nervousness, I failed to find one crumb of hope. The best scenario I could look forward to was to be put back on the plane and sent home. "Bilderberg Paradise Lost" would be the headline in my newspaper's next issue.

One of the guards lifted my suitcase and placed it on the wide desk. He opened it with his back to me. All I could see were the sharp angles of his elbows moving to and fro as he rummaged through my things. Suddenly he looked up, gave a cry, and pulled out a thin, well-worn volume of poetry by Afanasii Fet from my bag. Fet, an impressionist Russian writer of the late nineteenth century, could write a verse using only nouns yet create a sense of restiveness that utterly amazed me. This book represented the essence of my Russian soul, and I nervously watched the guard rifle through the dog-eared pages printed in Russian. As if on cue, everyone in the room started talking at once.

The other bespectacled guard grabbed the book from him and immediately proclaimed he had been to Russia and knew some Russian words. "*Borsch* (beet soup)," he said to me proudly, followed by *raduga* (rainbow) and *privet* (hello).

With his limited vocabulary, he then tried to form a coherent sentence. I listened dutifully, with half-opened mouth: his knowledge of Russian reminded me of the vastness of a *stepa* [steppes], that island of hope amongst the enormity of emptiness. Just listening to his bastardizing my native language was difficult enough, but trying to make sense out of what he was saying became sheer torture.

The detective sat down on the bench beside me, where I was still standing against the wall. He popped a peppermint into his mouth and then took my volume of Fet from the guard. He passed his fingers across the spine before he opened the book and leafed through its pages. His head moved in rhythm with his lips as he tried to follow the words across one page. Then the book lost his interest, and he laid it on the bench beside him, forgotten. He was an embarrassing representative for any airport security: none too young, with a sharp-tipped nose, sleekly parted hair, jutting eyelids and badly bitten fingernails.

In the next room, someone roared with laughter. Across the hall, a chair violently slid across the floor. Suddenly, our door burst open. A plainsclothesman with a holster slung over his shoulder stepped inside. He carried a red folder in his left hand. Recognizing the detective, he bellowed in delight, and his right hand spread open, all five fingers dancing. The detective grabbed the other man's free hand and zealously slapped his back. The plain clothes operator whispered something to the detective, and they turned their backs to me, while they talked in hushed voices. They motioned to the two guards and the narcotics officer, and all of them huddled together. In spite of their attempts to whisper, I could make out isolated phrases in Italian: *Cosa vuol dire?* (What do you mean?), *Non capisco nulla.* (I don't understand anything!), *Che cerca?* (What is he looking for?)

Some agreement formed, for they all stopped talking at once. The detective turned, stood and walked towards me. He braced himself in front. We were eyeball to eyeball. The guards took their place at the door, the narcotics cop sat on the edge of the desk, and the plain clothes operator leaned against the opposite wall. Through all their switches of position, the Doberman remained asleep on the mat.

"Let me see, where do I know you from?"

Completely out of character, the detective had switched to using a velvet tone, but his D-grade acting performance only made him less threatening and more laughable. I resisted the urge to smile. After an hour of this endless interrogation, our routine had become rote, and I was beginning to find bizarre humor in the situation.

He began with the same questions again. *Dove siete alloggiati?* (Where are you staying?)

But, this time he asked me for my plane tickets and hotel reservation. I produced both, crumpled beyond recognition in the habitual chaos of my satchel.

"What possible reason would you have to come to Stresa at this time of the year?"

I said nothing. I bent down to retrieve my Fet volume, lying forgotten on the bench.

"Never mind the book," instructed the detective.

I obeyed mid-motion and resumed standing erect.

The detective produced a photograph out of the red folder he was now holding in his right hand. I could hardly believe it. Staring at me was a copy of my own hideous black-and-white Spanish national identity photograph.

"What business do you have to attend to in Stresa?" he repeated in perfect English.

There could be no mistake about it. Someone in the Spanish Ministry of the Interior had provided the Italian security forces with my photo. The Italians knew why I had flown into Milan and were waiting for me. What's worse, the Spanish Ministry of the Interior had to be cooperating with the Bilderbergers to stop my investigation. I stared intently at a piece of tinfoil sparkling on the floor as thoughts scrambled through my mind.

All at once, the pieces of the puzzle slid into place. I understood something I had been seeing without understanding — why airport security had stopped me, why they questioned me, why they made me lose time. They couldn't retain me, for I had done nothing; nor did they want to let me go, for they were told to keep me at bay. The simple solution leapt to mind. The next move was mine, and if I made it right, I was a free man.

"Gentlemen," I said, "you have two choices. Either you arrest me and charge me with a crime, or you let me go. The masquerade is over. You know why I am here, and I know that you know that I know your game plan."

Another brief consultation ensued amongst the five of them. I waited and focused on the shadow left by the slip of tinfoil still lying on the floor. Sick of it all, angry at them, at me, at the world, for not knowing, not wanting to know and not caring about the Bilderbergers, I saw in the insignificant shape of the shadow the orderly existence of the moment.

I also knew that, within minutes, I'd be driven by taxi to the shores of Lake Maggiori, to Stresa and to the Bilderberg Group's annual conference; to a reunion with a group of fearless journalists, my friends, all of whom against all odds made their way to this sleepy little town; people like me who put up with unimaginable hardships to expose the Bilderberger's master plan for Global Government and One World Order.

So, what is "time" — I asked myself in the taxi, once more escaping into my thoughts — if not mere brutal passage and decay? A form of awareness? A birth of consciousness? And yet, even less do I understand why Fate brings the Bilderbergers and me constantly together, why I need to write about them.

To write, I once read, *is not to be absent but to become absent; to be someone and then go away, leaving traces*. And those traces, I finally realized, add up to our past.

I tried to concentrate on what was awaiting me in Stresa. Twenty-two-hour working days, phone calls to check information from sources, continual harassment by the secret service, threats, unauthorized searches, meetings and more meetings with those few valiant souls who brave the threats of Bilderbergers to give us precious details of their diabolical plans. But, I simply couldn't get my mind around it.

Incoherent images danced in my head. Total Enslavement. Man-made famines that swept millions to their grave. Suffering, more suffering. Unspeakable, inhuman sacrifice. Why? Is it really possible that someone might want to inflict so much pain on the world for personal gain? As I struggled to hold back tears, I kept reminding myself that my quest for the truth was a vindication of decency at the expense of greed and power.

I kept mulling over happy endings to the yet-to-be-written tale about paradise lost: our damage-strewn world. What would it mean to lose happiness forever? Paradise and its loss are integral to each other. Not only that true paradises are lost paradises, but that there are also no paradises without loss — it isn't paradise if you can't lose it.

Bilderberg, of course, has become a metaphor for fear. Beneath its insanity, there is an understanding that time and space, like love and death, alter us and affirm us, cling to us and explore us. They include the irrevocable, and make us who we are.

BEHIND THE CLOSED DOOR

IN DOCUMENTS AND PICTURES

„DE BILDERBERG"
CONFERENCE

AT OOSTERBEEK

NEAR ARNHEM

29th, 30th, 31st May 1954

Top: Cover page of the program for the very first Bilderberg conference held at Oosterbeek, the Netherlands.
Bottom: Official 1954 Bilderberg badge for Bilderberg staff.

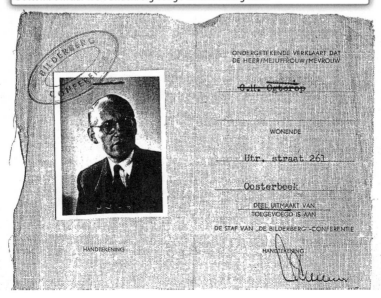

THE WHITE HOUSE
WASHINGTON

March 11, 1955.

MEMORANDUM FOR

GABRIEL HAUGE

I understand that next week Prince Bernhard
is having a meeting at Barbizon, continuing
his exploration looking toward improving
European and American relations.

If personally you can fit such a trip into
your schedule, I suggest you find the money *(govt)*
and go to France.

D.E.

D. D. E.

U.S. President Dwight Eisenhower urges his assistant Gabriel Hauge to attend the 1955 Bilderberg conference in Barbizon, France. Notice the hand-written "(govt)" meaning that Hauge should travel at U.S. government's/taxpayers' expense. Bilderbergers have for years claimed that members attend as individuals and not as representatives of the government. That, as you can see from Ike's hand-written note, is another big lie.

Op „de Bilderberg" kunn
de groten stoom afblazeı

In stilte

DE keuze was op „De Bilderberg" gevallen, omdat de ligging van dit hotel voor ons doel zo bijzonder geschikt was. Wij zochten een hotel van standing en sfeer, waar topfiguren uit de internationale diplomatie en uit de internationale zakenwereld zich thuis zouden voelen. Maar tevens moest het een beetje geïsoleerd zijn. Dus niet aan een grote weg, bij een grote stad, of aan een meer, waar tal van journalisten, fotografen of cineasten hen konden aanklampen of „plaatjes zouden kunnen schieten".

Want conditio sine qua non voor het slagen van de conferentie was: beslotenheid. En De Bilderberg bood die beslotenheid; men bereikt het hotel van de hoofdweg naar Arnhem langs een koetshuis via een lange oprijlaan. Indien wij dus het gehele hotel voor enkele dagen konden huren, en aparte doorlaatkaarten lieten drukken, dan konden een paar controleurs de gehele zaak in handen houden.

Waarom dan die beslotenheid? Wat beoogden wij, wat zou er bekokstoofd worden? Niets dat het daglicht niet kon velen, maar ook niets dat niet zou kunnen worden bedorven of tot eindeloze kettingreacties zou kunnen leiden, als het daglicht er wel bij zou kunnen komen.

Bilderbergconferentie begonnen

De Bilderbergconferentie, besloten bijeenkomst van het „steering-committee", welke dit weekeinde onder voorzitterschap van Prins Bernhard te Oosterbeek wordt gehouden, is begonnen. De namen van de deelnemers worden niet bekend gemaakt. De conferentie wordt maandagmiddag gesloten.

The first known report on the Bilderberg conference written for a Dutch daily about a Bilderberg Steering Committee meeting in 1958:

At "the Bilderberg" the great can blow off steam.

Bilderberg Conference has begun
The Bilderberg Conference, the secluded gathering of the "Steering Committee," which is held this weekend in Oosterbeek under chairmanship of Prince Bernhard, has begun. The names of the participants are not made known. The conference will end Monday afternoon.

In silence
The choice had fallen on "The Bilderberg" because the site of this hotel was particularly suitable. We were seeking a hotel of standing and atmosphere, where top figures of international diplomacy and business would feel at home. But it also had to be a bit isolated. Hence not along a main road, near a big city or at a lake, where numerous journalists, photographers or news reel personnel could intrude and take pictures.

Because the necessary condition for the success of the conference was: seclusion. And the Bilderberg offered this seclusion. One can only reach the hotel from the main road to Arnhem through an entrance gate at the start of an alley. If we could hire the entire estate for a few days and print individual entrance tickets, only a few guards could control the whole undertaking.

Why then this secrecy? What was the aim, what were they cooking?
Nothing that could not bear the light of day, but neither anything that could be spoiled or would lead to endless chain-reactions if the light of day would shine on it.

BILDERBERG GROUP

ENLARGED STEERING COMMITTEE MEETING

De Bilderberg Hotel
Oosterbeek
25th - 26th April 1958

List of Participants

H.R.H. The Prince of The Netherlands

Mr. Joseph E. Johnson

Dr. J.H. Retinger

Belgium: M. Paul van Zeeland

France: M. Antoine Pinay

Germany: Dr. Hermann Abs
                    Mr. Fritz Erler

Italy: M. Alberto Pirelli
                    M. Pietro Quaroni

Netherlands: Dr. Paul Rykens
                    Mr. Evert A. Vermeer

Norway: Mr. Jens Christian Hauge

Turkey: M. Muharem Nurri Birgi

United Kingdom: Mr. George Brown
                    Sir Colin Gubbins
                    Mr. Denis Healey
                    Lord John Hope

United States: Mr. John Ferguson
                    Prof. Michael A. Heilperin

Copies of three pages of the agenda of the 1958 Steering Committee meeting. The Steering Committee decides on the final list of attendees and the final agenda items to be discussed and debated during a Bilderberg meeting. Notice that Guy Mollet, the "father" of the European Union, is present. In fact, the work on the mechanism of the European Union was continued and finalized during the early '50s Bilderberg meetings. Other notables are David Rockefeller, Antoine Pinay of the secretive Pinay Circle and Britain's Denis Healey

BILDERBERG CONFERENCE

September 1958

United Kingdom

List of suggested participants

ium:

M. Paul van Zeeland (S)
M. P. Bonvoisin
M. Louis Camu
Baron Léon Lambert
M. Victor Larock (I)
M. Roger Motz
Baron Snoy

rk:

Mr. Ole Bjørn Kraft (S)
Mr. Hakon Christiansen
Mr. J.O. Krag
Mr. Terkel Terkelsen (I)
o o o o o o o o o o o o o o

::

M. Guy Mollet (S)
M. Antoine Pinay (S)
M. Raymond Aron
M. W. Baumgartner
M. Pierre Commin
M. Edmond Giscard d'Estaing
M. R. Marjolin
M. P. Pflimlin
M. Jean Raty

y:

Dr. Rudolf Mueller (S)
Mr. Carlo Schmid (S)
Mr. Otto Wolff von Amerongen (S)
Mr. Hermann Abs (I)
Mr. Heinrich von Brentano
Mr. Fritz Berg

Member of the Steering Committee

Already invited

Turkey: Mr. Muharrem Nuri Birgi
                           o o o o o o o o o
                           o o o o o o o o o o
                           oo o o o o o o o o

United Kingdom: Sir Colin Gubbins (S)
                           Mr. Denis Healey (S)
                           Mr. Reginald Maudling (S)
                           Mr. Aneurin Bevan
                           Mr. George Brown
                           Mr. V. Cavendish-Bentinck (I)
                           Mr. Frank Cousins
                           Sir Oliver Franks
                           Mr. Hugh Gaitskell
                           Mr. Joseph Grimmond
                           Lord Kilmuir (I)
                           Mr. D. Ormsby-Gore (I)
                           Mr. Duncan Sandys
                           Mr. J. Lincoln Steel (I)
                           Sir John Slessor (I)
                           Mr. Henry Tiarks

Canada: Mr. Paul Dupuy
                           Mr. Paul Martin
                           Mr. N.A. Robertson

United States: Mr. A. Dean (S)
(to be decided   Mr. J. Ferguson (S)
   by U.S. group)   Mr. J. Heinz (S)
                           Mr. J. Johnson (S)
                           Mr. G. Nebolsine (S)
                           Mr. D. Rockefeller (S)
                           Mr. G. Hauge
                           Mr. M. Heilperin (I)
                           Mr. Tom Finletter
                           o o o o o o o o o
                           o o o o o o o o o
                           o o o o o o o o o

202

WASHINGTON OBSERVER

NEWSLETTER

"There is no subtler, surer means of overturning the existing basis of society than to debauch the currency."
—JOHN MAYNARD KEYNES

NUMBER 119

MAY 15, 1971

CONTROLLERS CONFAB

WASHINGTON OBSERVER NEWSLETTER can exclusively reveal that a top secret meeting of the Bilderberger Group took place in the United States, April 22 through 25, 1971.

The Bilderbergers, first exposed to the light of day by the late Westbrook Pegler, is the name given to the periodical conferences of the international pro-communist big-money Establishment, the members of which control the Council on Foreign Relations and, through the CFR, all of the governments of the West, including the United States' government.

The Bilderberger Group is considered to be only two ranks removed from the apex of the secret government which rules the world. Above the Bilderbergers are two levels of International Zionism.

The secret meeting was held at the Woodstock Inn, Woodstock, Vermont. The Inn is owned by the Rockefeller family and was completely closed to outsiders during the secret conferences.

Security for the meeting of super-rich capitalists was provided by the United States taxpayers through the cooperation of the FBI, the Secret Service and state and local police. Transportation for the guests—most of whom had to be flown in

BELGIUM
JANSSEN, Daniel
    Deputy General Manager UCB, S.A.
    Lecturer Brussels University
LAMBERT, Baron
    Chairman, Banque Lambert
SIMONET, H.
    Member of Parliament
    President, Brussels University
VANISTENDAEL, August A. J.
    Secretary General, International Cooperation for Socio-Economic Development [CIDSE]

CANADA
BOURASSA, Robert
    Prime Minister of Quebec
GRIFFIN, Anthony G. S.
    President, Triarch Corporation Ltd.
LEMAN, Paul H.
    President, Aluminum Company of Canada Ltd.
MACDONALD, Donald S.
    Minister of National Defence
ROTSTEIN, Abraham
    Professor at the Department of Political Economy University of Toronto

DENMARK
SCHLEIMANN, Jorgen
    Editor, Radio Denmark
SORENSEN, Svend O.
    General Manager, Den Danske Landmandsbank
TERKELSEN, Terkel M.
    Chief Editor, "Berlingske Tidende"

FINLAND
ENCKELL, Ralph
    Head of the Finnish Delegation to OECD
von JULIN, Jacob
    Chairman of the Finnish Cellulose Association

FRANCE
AUMONIER, Andre
    Vice President of "Fondation Europeene pour l'Economie"
BAUMGARTNER, Wilfrid S.
    President, Rhone-Poulenc S.A.

Typical of the information available about the Bilderbergers, this *Washington Observer Newsletter* report includes diatribe alongside valid information.

203

ELCON
David Rockefeller/Kissinger
11:12 a.m. - 3/13/72

K: David, how are you?

R: How are you?. I want to congratulate you for carrying it off. It was absolutely fabulous. Do you feel comfortable about it?

K: Oh yes, I think we got exactly what we wanted.

R: That's wonderful. I partly wanted to speak to you about that and partly on Bilderberg. You indicated you wanted to go if you could.

K: I would like to go.

R: I am taking our plane over on Wednesday the 19th and thought you might want to go over with us.

K: I would like to do it but it may be a little early.

R: I am taking some of the Congressional members like Matt Mathias.

K: Oh yes. When are you coming back?

R: I'm coming back - well I'm staying over Monday and having a _____ group meeting in Paris so I'm not coming back until Tuesday. I had to squeeze in a few things at the same time.

K: I wouldn't dare show up in Paris or 500 pressmen will be following me wherever I go.

R: (Laughter) One other thing is this: I've just been at one of our international advisory meetings and Otto Wolf sends his best to you.

K: He is a Bilderberger too. In fact that is where I met him.

R: He has been to China on frequent occasions and may have been there almost more than any European so I was asking him as to his reactions as to whether it would be desirable for me to go in. His feeling was it might be a good idea if I did it, but not in an official way, but just through my own channels. I wanted to get your reaction as to whether it would be a good idea for me to put in motion or to wait.

A two-page 1972 declassified telephone conversation between the then-Nixon Secretary of State Henry Kissinger and David Rockefeller discussing the upcoming Bilderberg meeting and unofficial overtures with the Chinese.

K: Look, I will call you at the end of this week because I will get some answers to questions like this.

R: I'm going to Europe and leaving Friday morning.

K: I'll have an answer by Thursday.

R: His suggestion was to go through our Hong Kong office.

K: No, my advice is to do it through the Chinese Paris Ambassador.

R: Dick Watson. That makes sense to me.

K: Let me tell you one thing. I sat next to the President of American Express at dinner and he said he is going to get into China. He had written to every non-Communist embassy in the world and one was going to get him a visa. I related this to the Premier when I was in China and he said how is he going to do it and I told him. He asked me if I thought he would get it and I said not one. He said - or fifty. My point is wherever you apply it is going to wind up with Chou En-lai.

R: Well, if you feel . . .

K: No, I think it is a good idea. They are a little less hung up on the name Rockefeller than the Russians. They don't think they're running the country. But they know the name and I think they would be very interested.

R: Well, Otto Wolf seems to think this might help them to realize that we are serious.

K: I think it would be excellent from our point of view and theirs. I think you will find them pleasant to deal with.

R: The reason I mention it now is I have to be in Japan in June and. . .

K: I will tell you Thursday where to apply and if these various channels develop I may be able to drop a word about my relations to your family so I think you will be well-known.

R: Good. Well, thanks a lot. I hope you are all right otherwise.

K: I am fine. I'll call you Thursday.

TO: Mr. George W. Ball
       Mr. Emilio G. Collado
       Mr. Arthur H. Dean
   — Mr. Gabriel Hauge
       Mr. Henry J. Heinz II
       Mr. William Moyers
       Mr. Robert Murphy
       Mr. James A. Perkins
   — Mr. David Rockefeller
       Mr. Shepard Stone

DATE: January 8, 1973

Bilderberg US Steering Cttee *[handwritten]*

FROM: Joseph E. Johnson

RE: Bilderberg Steering Committee

1. This is to confirm that the meeting of the American members of the Bilderberg Steering Committee will take place at the Carnegie Endowment Building on **Thursday, January 11**, at 5:30 p.m.

2. I shall try to get in touch before or after the meeting with everyone not able to come at that time.

3. As you will know from Ernst van der Beugel's memo of 2 January, there will be a dinner at the Amstel Hotel on Saturday evening, January 20, and the meeting itself will take place at Soestdijk on Sunday, January 21, at 11 o'clock. I shall inform Ernst van der Beugel after our meeting on the 11th about those attending and their arrival times, unless the individuals have already written.

4. For your information, the American papers on the two agenda items will be written by **Walter Levy** (Energy) and John Newhouse (European Security Conference). These gentlemen, together with their European opposite numbers, M. Fernand Spaak and Stoltenberg, will also be there. (They will attend the dinner and the meeting at Soestdijk.)

5. The principal purpose of the meeting on the 11th is to discuss in a preliminary way possible American participation on the basis of the attached preliminary list.

6. There will also be a brief report on financing.

RECEIVED JAN 9 1973 [stamp]

Copies of our pages out of a report on a meeting of the American members of the 1973 Bilderberg Steering Committee that was held in January 1973, helping to set the the agenda and players for the upcoming Bilderberg Group meeting that May in Saltsjöbaden, Sweden. Part of that agenda concerned "energy," which five months after the Swedish meeting had its first "crisis," the 1973 Energy Crisis.

BILDERBERG MEETINGS

SALTSJÖBADEN CONFERENCE

11, 12 and 13 May 1973

PROVISIONAL LIST OF PARTICIPANTS

H.R.H. the Prince of the NETHERLANDS
    Chairman

Ernst H. van der BEUGEL
    Professor International Relations, Leiden University
    Honorary Secretary General for Europe

Joseph E. JOHNSON
    President Emeritus, Carnegie Endowment for
                        International Peace
    Honorary Secretary General for the United States

C. Frits KARSTEN
    Managing Director, AMRO Bank N.V.
    Honorary Treasurer

BELGIUM

HOUTHUYS, Jozef
    Chairman of the Belgian Christian Union

JANSSEN, Daniel
    Director-Deputy General Manager, UCB S.A.
    Lecturer, Brussels University

(UNITED KINGDOM)

    HEALEY, Denis
        Member of Parliament

    MAUDLING, REGINALD
        Member of Parliament

    OWEN, David
        Member of Parliament

  X ROLL, Sir Eric
        Deputy Chairman, S.G. Warburg & Co. Ltd.

    SIMON, John
        Managing Director, British Leyland

    TAVERNE, Richard
        Member of Parliament

UNITED STATES

    AKINS, James
        The White House

  X ANDERSON, Robert O.
        Chairman of the Board, Atlantic Richfield Co.

  X BALL, George W.
        Senior Managing Director, Lehman Brothers Incorporated

  X BRZEZINSKI, Zbigniew
        Director, Research Institute on Communist Affairs,
                School of International Affairs, Columbia University

    BUNDY, William P.
        Editor of "Foreign Affairs"

    COLLADO, Emilio G.
        Executive Vice-President, Exxon Corporation

    DEAN, Arthur H.
        Senior Partner, Sullivan & Cromwell

- 8 -

(UNITED STATES)

HEINZ II, Henry J.
Chairman of the Board, H.J. Heinz Company

X KISSINGER, Henry A.
Assistant to the President for National Security Affairs

LAPHAM Jr., Lewis A.
Junior Editor, Harper's Magazine

Y LEVY, Walter J.
Oil Consultant
Author working paper

Moyers, Bill D.
Mitchell, Hutchins & Co. Incorporated

MURPHY, Robert D.
Honorary Chairman of the Board, Corning Glass International

NEWHOUSE, John
Author and Consultant
Author working paper

PERKINS, James A.
Chairman, International Council for Educational Development

STONE, Shepard
President, International Association for Cultural Freedom

TOWER, John G.
U.S. Senator

WILSON, Carroll
Professor, Alfred Sloan School of Management,
Massachusetts Institute of Technology

PERSONAL AND
ꞰICTLY CONFIDENTIAL

NOT FOR PUBLICATION
EITHER IN WHOLE OR IN PART

BILDERBERG MEETINGS

SALTSJÖBADEN
CONFERENCE

11-13 May 1973

Part of a 1973 Bilderberg "for eyes only" report handed out to Bilderberg attendees. Some things in this report are certainly worth mentioning. For example, the report shows that the Bilderbergers were well aware back in 1973 of the near-future oil crisis. On page 55, there is talk of manipulating energy markets for personal gain. During Bilderberg 1973, Bilderbergers openly discussed (p.63 of the report) increasing oil from the May 1973 price of $3/barrel to somewhere in the range of $10-12.50/barrel. Miraculously, some 6 months later oil went up to $11.65/barrel. On page 66 of the report, it was proposed for the Group to work *toward an international federal reserve system*. Curiously, Europe is now an embodiment of this system, with North America not too far behind. And if that wasn't enough, a French speaker, on page 69 of the report, proposed *the creation of an international clearing house to channel hot money from oil revenues*. Is it any wonder the Bilderbergers would much prefer to keep their discussions secret?

The complete report is available at www.BilderbergBook.com.

CONTENTS

LIST OF PARTICIPANTS

CHAIRMAN:
H.R.H. The Prince of the Netherlands

HONORARY SECRETARY GENERAL FOR EUROPE:
Ernst H. van der Beugel

HONORARY SECRETARY GENERAL FOR THE UNITED STATES:
Joseph E. Johnson

A composite of four pages of the report, listing all persons acknowledged as attending the 1973 meeting.

HONORARY TREASURER:
C. Frits Karsten

Agnelli, Giovanni	Italy
Anderson, Robert O.	United States
Ball, George W.	United States
Baumgartner, Wilfrid S.	France
Bennett, Sir Frederic	United Kingdom
Beyazit, Selahattin	Turkey
Birgi, M. Nuri	Turkey
Bjøl, Erling	Denmark
Björgerd, Anders	Sweden
Boiteux, Marcel	France
Breuel, Birgit	Germany
Brzezinski, Zbigniew	United States
Bundy, William P.	United States
Cittadini Cesi, Il Marchese	Italy
Collado, Emilio G.	United States
Dean, Arthur H.	United States
Drake, Sir Eric	United Kingdom
Ducci, Roberto	Italy
Girotti, Raffaele	Italy
Granier de Lilliac, René	France
Greenhill, Sir Denis	United Kingdom
Griffin, Anthony G. S.	Canada
Haagerup, Niels J.	Denmark
Hallgrimsson, Geir	Iceland
Healey, Denis	United Kingdom
Heinz II, Henry J.	United States
Høegh, Leif	Norway
Houthuys, Jozef	Belgium
Janssen, Daniel E.	Belgium
Kersten, Otto	International
Kohnstamm, Max	International
Lapham Jr., Lewis H.	United States
Lehto, Sakari	Finland
Lennep, Jonkheer Emile van	International
Levy, Walter J.	United States

212

Levy, Walter J.	United States
Lied, Finn	Norway
Lombardini, Siro	Italy
Luns, Joseph M. A. H.	International
Lougheed, Peter	Canada
Macdonald, Donald S.	Canada
Maudling, Reginald	United Kingdom
Merlini, Cesare	Italy
Mettler, Erich	Switzerland
Moyers, Bill D.	United States
Newhouse, John	United States
Owen, David	United Kingdom
Palme, Olof	Sweden
Perkins, James A.	United States
Philips, Frits J.	Netherlands
Ritchie, Albert E.	Canada
Roll, Sir Eric	United Kingdom
Rothschild, Baron Edmond de	France
Rozemond, Samuel	Netherlands
Schmidt, Helmut	Germany
Seydoux de Clausonne, Roger	France
Simon, John M.	United Kingdom
Smith, Gerard C.	United States
Snoy et d'Oppuers, Baron	Belgium
Sommer, Theo	Germany
Spaak, Fernand	International
Stehlin, Paul	France
Stille, Ugo	Italy
Stoltenberg, Thorvald	Norway
Stone, Shepard	United States
Sträng, Gunnar	Sweden
Taverne, Richard	United Kingdom
Terkelsen, Terkel M.	Denmark
Tidemand, Otto G.	Norway
Udink, Berend J.	Netherlands
Umbricht, Victor H.	Switzerland
Wagner, Gerrit A.	Netherlands
Wallenberg, Marcus	Sweden
Wickman, Krister	Sweden
Wilson, Carroll L.	United States
Wischnewski, Hans-Jürgen	Germany
Wolff von Amerongen, Otto	Germany

IN ATTENDANCE:

Svensson, Nils	Sweden
Lindgren, Hugo	Sweden
Vernède, Edwin	Netherlands
Getchell Jr., Charles W.	United States

INTRODUCTION

The twenty-second Bilderberg Meeting was held at the Grand Hotel Saltsjö-baden in Saltsjöbaden, Sweden, on 11, 12 and 13 May 1973 under the chair-manship of H.R.H. The Prince of the Netherlands.

There were 80 participants, drawn from a variety of fields: government and politics, universities, journalism, diplomacy, industry, transport, trade unions the law, banking, foundation administration and military service. They came from thirteen Western European countries, the United States, Canada and various international organizations.

In accordance with the rules adopted at each Meeting, all participants spoke in a purely personal capacity without in any way committing whatever govern-ment or organization to which they might belong. To enable participants to speak with the greatest possible frankness, the discussions were confidentia with ho reporters being admitted.

The Agenda was as follows:

I. The Possibilities of the Development of a European Energy Policy, and the Consequences for European-North American Relations.

II. Conflicting Expectations Concerning the European Security Conference.

At the opening of the meeting, H.R.H. The Prince of the Netherlands read a telegram of thanks and good wishes which he had sent to H.M. Gustav VI Adolf and the reply which he had received from the latter.

His Royal Highness expressed his regret at the absence of Professor John Pesmazoglou, whose request for permission to leave Greece had been denied and of Mr. Gerhard Schröder of West Germany, whose political commitment had prevented him at the last moment from attending.

After recalling the Bilderberg rules of procedure, The Prince turned to the first item of the Agenda.

THE POSSIBILITIES OF THE DEVELOPMENT OF A EUROPEAN ENERGY POLICY, AND THE CONSEQUENCES FOR EUROPEAN-NORTH AMERICAN RELATIONS

The background for discussion of this topic consisted of two working papers - one written by an International participant, the other by an American participant - which had been distributed before the meeting. These papers, and the comments of their authors in introducing them to the meeting, are summarized below.

• •
• •

GUIDELINES FOR A EUROPEAN ENERGY POLICY AND ITS CONSEQUENCES ON RELATIONS BETWEEN EUROPE AND NORTH AMERICA

The International author of this working paper began by pointing out that there was fairly widespread agreement as to why the energy situation was alarming. The relevant figures were generally known, and diagnoses of the energy trend differed little. The problem was what treatment to apply: we needed an effort of imagination to avoid lapsing into fatalism, and a strong sense of realism to guard against a Utopian approach.

In this spirit, he proposed to examine the guidelines of a common energy policy for the European Community, and then to consider how the main energy-consuming countries might cooperate with one another.

I. *The Community energy policy.* Mapping out a Community energy policy was a long-term task. So far it had produced a limited number of specific measures, but a new impetus was called for now, inspired by an overall vision.

A. *Gradual materialization of the Community energy policy*

Since the ECSC and Euratom treaties had dealt specifically with coal and

12

Excerpts from the 1973 report:

However, the development of the oil resources of the Middle East did not reflect any extensive industrial involvement of the economies of those countries or any important contribution by their people to the huge flow of oil outward and of revenue backward. Operations were limited fundamentally to a small enclave.

These various issues added up to a political crisis, not an oil crisis, in the view of a British participant. Middle Eastern countries had taken over quantities of oil contrary to their agreements, with two importants practical consequences. First, there was no limit to the price increases, and to the resulting impact on the balance of payments of consuming countries. Second, there was no particular incentive for the producing countries to develop the additional oil wells which would be needed if the civilized world were to continue using energy at the rate predicted. With a rising value to their asset, it was in their interest to leave it in the ground, regardless of world shortages. Producing countries would thus be able to determine the standard of living of consuming countries, and to enforce their political will upon them. It was not just a question of price (as an American participant had suggested) but of quantity. A French speaker agreed with this analysis.

The announcement of Libya's price demands, which had been made just as this meeting convened, happened to furnish an excellent illustration of the sort of problem faced by the oil companies. That country was responsible for one-sixth of Europe's oil supplies, so that one's access to a daily hot bath depended very much on the attitude of Colonel Qadhafi, as the British speaker put it.

sovereign-to-sovereign negotiations. The speaker replied that, at some point, the developed world would have to "take unusual steps" to protect its supply of energy, in order to avid widespread unemployment and social unrest. Economic boycotts or shut-ins would obviously be against the interest of the world community, to which the producing countries had a definite responsibility. Whatever measures might be envisaged, sovereign governments could present a more convincing front than private entities.

A Belgian intervention emphasized the need for a "psycho-social and political" reorientation of our values, to enable an efficient network of public transport to replace our "absurd system" of urban transportation by private automobiles, with its attendant problems of parking, road congestion and air pollution. Although this reorientation would not completely solve the energy problem, even a marginal reduction in demand would be welcome in the supply crisis which lay ahead.

An American speaker pointed out that one official US estimate of the future delivered price had been as high as $5 a barrel – which was now perhaps on the low side – but that certain cost factors would reduce the net return to the producing countries by around $1. Two other American participants reported that the author of the estimate just referred to – Mr. James Akins – had subsequently said that the $5 figure would prove to be too low, and might indeed range up to $10-12.50 a barrel.

BILDERBERG MEETINGS

1, Smidswater, 2500 GK 's Gravenhage
P.O. Box 30418
Tel. 70 - 46 21 21

List of Participants

August 1978

CHAIRMAN:
Lord Home of the Hirsel, K.T.

HONORARY SECRETARY GENERAL FOR EUROPE:
Ernst H. van der Beugel

HONORARY SECRETARY GENERAL FOR THE UNITED STATES:
William P. Bundy

HONORARY TREASURER:
C. Frits Karsten

AARON, David
National Security Council
The White House
Washington D.C. 20500
U.S.A.
Tel. (202) 456 2235

ABS, Hermann J.
Junghofstrasse 5-11
6000 Frankfurt/Main
Fed. Republic of Germany
Tel. (611) 2141

ACHILLES, Theodore C.
Atlantic Council of the U.S.
1616 H Street, N.W.
Washington D.C. 20006
U.S.A.
Tel. (202) 347-9353

AGNELLI, Giovanni
FIAT S.p.A.
Corso Marconi 10/20
10100 Torino, Italy
Tel. (11) 6565

AGNELLI, Umberto
FIAT S.p.A.
Corso Marconi 10/20
10100 Torini, Italy
Tel. (11) 6565

AIRD, John B.
Aird & Berlis
1500, 145 King Street W.
Toronto, Ontario M5H 2J3
Canada
Tel. (416) 364 1241

AIREY, Sir Terence
Frittin Old Rectory
Fritton, near Norwich
Norfolk NR 152 QT, U.K.
Tel. Hempnall 214

AKBIL, Semih
Ambaixada da Turquia
SQA 119, Bloco F. Apt. 206
Brasilia, Brasil

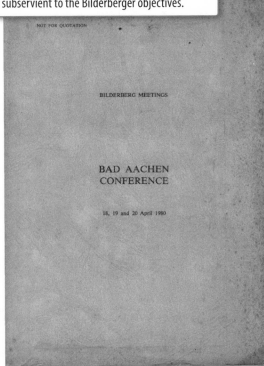

Second page from the 1978 meeting with a partial list of attendees, as well as the 1980 cover page from the Aachen conference. Bilderberg 1980 openly discussed the future Reagan presidency and ways to make it subservient to the Bilderberger objectives.

NOT FOR QUOTATION

BILDERBERG MEETINGS

BAD AACHEN
CONFERENCE

18, 19 and 20 April 1980

GOLDMAN SACHS INTERNATIONAL

REGULATED BY THE FINANCIAL SERVICES AUTHORITY

PETERBOROUGH COURT

133 FLEET STREET

LONDON EC4A 2BB

Peter D. Sutherland
Chairman
020 7774 4141

Ref: PDS/mjb

```
PE  -  COURRIER
EP  -     ENTRÉE

1 8 -11- 2002

N°  14774
```

29th October 2002

Mr Pat Cox MEP
President
European Parliament
Rue Wiertz
B 1047 Brussels
Belgium

Dear Pat.

I wonder would you accept an invitation to a Bilderberg meeting scheduled for Versailles, France from 15th to 18th May 2003. The meetings are usually most stimulating. I enclose a list of those who attended this year. Next year's group will be at least at prestigious. You are looked after fully when you arrive at the venue.

If you could let me have a preliminary response I would be grateful.

Yours ever,

Peter Sutherland, one of Bilderberg heavyweights, inviting the European Parliament President to the 2003 Bilderberg conference.

BILDERBERG MEETINGS

P.O.Box 3017   Phone +31 71 5280 521
2301 DA LEIDEN   Fax   +31 71 5280 522
The Netherlands

Mr. Pat Cox
President
European Parliament
Rue Wiertz
1047 BRUSSELS
Belgium

```
PE - COURRIER
EP - ENTREE

1 2 -03- 2003

N°  3 3 78
```

5 March 2003

Subject: Bilderberg Meeting Trianon Palace Hotel, Versailles, France from
dinner on Thursday, May 15 through lunch on Sunday, May 18, 2003

Dear Mr. Cox,

1. Thank you for confirming your participation in the forthcoming conference.
I am pleased to enclose:

- The current list of participants. If you wish to have changes made in the way your affiliation is mentioned, please let me know before May 1; the suggested corrections will then be made in the next version.

- The notice to participants, detailing various arrangements.

- A travel advisory form. **Please do follow the instructions about completing this form and return it as soon as possible by fax to the Bilderberg office in Leiden (fax nr. +31 71 528 0522).** This will assure prompt reception at points of arrival, timely transportation and smooth departure.

- Special Bilderberg labels for rapid identification at the reception points; please attach these to all your luggage.

- A copy of your biography which we have on file. Please return it to me with any changes you may wish to make (preferably by e-mail), or advise me that it may be used as it is for the 2003 Profiles of Participants which, as you know, will be distributed to all participants at the conference.

Official reply on Bilderberg stationary from Bilderberg secretary directed to Pat Cox, President of the European Parliament, thanking him for his confirmed presence at the conference in Versailles, Paris, 2003. Curiously enough, his name did not appear on the "official" Bilderberg press release listing conference attendees. It is a usual Bilderberg practice to keep sensitive names off the list.

From: The Rt. Hon. Kenneth Clarke, QC, MP

HOUSE OF COMMONS

LONDON SW1A 0AA

24th March, 2003

Dear Mr. Martin,

Thank you very much for your recent letter. This year's Bilderberg Meeting is being held at Versailles in France, but I am afraid it is not open to the public. The whole point of the meetings is that they are informal and relaxed exchanges of views between politicians and businessmen, who can talk to each other without being on the record or reported publicly. Some of the people are very well known and, if they were talking in public, they would have to speak in the language of a press release, which does inhibit the flow of argument.

Yours sincerely,

Official reply from the office of Honourable Kenneth Clarke, member of British Parliament, to a request for information from a citizen concerned about Mr. Clarke's Bilderberg attendance. The text of the letter is identical to every reply on the record from every Bilderberg attendee regarding attendance at the conference.

Mr. F. M. Martin,

Imverbervie,
Montrose,
SCOTLAND DD10 0PX

Liberté · Égalité · Fraternité
RÉPUBLIQUE FRANÇAISE

MINISTERE DE L'INTERIEUR
DE LA SECURITE INTERIEURE ET DES LIBERTES LOCALES

DIRECTION GÉNÉRALE
DE LA POLICE NATIONALE

SERVICE DE PROTECTION
DES HAUTES PERSONNALITES

SECRETARIAT DE DIRECTION
☎ 44718

SPHP 2003/N°884

PARIS, le 15 mai 2003

L'Inspecteur Général,
Chef du Service de Protection
des hautes Personnalités

à

Monsieur le Directeur Général
de la Police Nationale

O B J E T : Conférence de BILDELBERG au Trianon Palace de Versailles.

Du 15 au 18 Mai 2003, se tiendra la Conférence informelle annuelle regroupant à titre privé des hommes d'affaires et des personnalités politiques, européens et américains.

Le Service de Protection des Hautes Personnalités n'a pas été saisi au préalable pour assurer le déroulement de cette manifestation. Toutefois, des personnalités de haut rang y participant, la protection de certaines d'entre elles qui le souhaitaient a été organisée par le S.P.H.P. en accord avec le Préfet de Versailles selon le dispositif suivant :

Le S.P.H.P. assurera la protection rapprochée des Reines d'Espagne, et des Pays-Bas, du Premier ministre Danois et du Ministre de l'Intérieur Allemand, M. Schilly (saisine confirmée par le Chef de Cabinet de Monsieur le Ministre de l'Intérieur).

Par ailleurs, une escorte moto de la C.R.S. n°1 sera fournie ponctuellement en fonction des besoins au profit d'autres personnalités notamment de nationalité américaine, qui n'ont pas souhaité d'autre dispositif d'accompagnement.

Le Chef de mission en charge de la coordination des équipes de protection et des escortes motos C.R.S. n°1 sera le Lieutenant MARTIN. Les dispositions ont été portées à la connaissance de Madame la Directrice de Cabinet du Préfet des Yvelines à laquelle cet officier rendra compte du déroulement de cette conférence « Privée ».

Le Contrôleur Général Patrick BARDEY
Adjoint au Chef du Service de Protection
des Hautes Personnalités

Ashley JONES

ADRESSE POSTALE : PLACE BEAUVAU - 75800 PARIS CEDEX 08- STANDARD TEL : 49 27 49 27 - 40 07 60 60

Secret document written on official Ministry of the Interior stationary from the division of French police responsible for guarding VIPs. They are very upset that the Bilderberg Group decided to bypass them and use mercenaries for their protection.

221

More bad news for the Bilderbergers. A Swedish daily broke the news on the 2001 conference in Sweden, publishing the list of participants and the seating order. Notice that the now-deceased *Washington Post* chairwoman, Katherine Graham is present, along with the 2004 Democratic challenger, John Kerry, and the now-disgraced former media owner, Conrad Black.

Bilderberg *modus operandi*: using a small local newspaper to announce to the townspeople that a group of retired, out-of-service former government employees are coming to town to discuss international relations. This press release was published the first day of the 2005 conference in Germany. Notice the size of the release.

KINGSTON
EYE OPENER

In Search of Our Social Conscience

October 7th, 2005.

Box 2154
Kingston, Ontario, Canada
K7L 5J9

Mr. Jaun Eloy Roca
Editor Planeta
Fax Number: 00 34 93 217-7748

An independent Canadian publication, the **Kingston Eye Opener**, declares Daniel Estulin's *"La Verdadera Historia del Club Bilderberg"* its choice for the 2005 foreign non-fiction Book of the Year. Estulin's book strips the power elite to the core and reveals the shockingly callous agenda of a secretive clique known globally as the Bilderberg Club. The **Eye Opener's** panel of independent jurors agreed unanimously that this hard-hitting volume stands out amongst various publications as the closest to the truth and pulls no punches in exposing the power elites plotted, wilful subjugation of humanity at the hands of this Shadow World Power.

Cordially,

Geoffrey Matthews
Publisher & Editor
Kingston Eye Opener

> One of the best Canadian independent periodicals, the legendary *Eye Opener*, awards the 2005 foreign non-fiction book of the year award to the Spanish edition of this book.

brookstreet
work·play·getaway

June 1st, 2006

Dear Guest,

Thank you for choosing Brookstreet to work, play or getaway! We trust you will enjoy your experience with us.

Please be advised that on Thursday June 8th, 2006 we will require that you check out of your room and the hotel no later than 8:30am. Unfortunately, during this time we will not be able to extend late check outs, luggage storage or return entrance to the hotel. We apologize for any inconvenience experienced. This is an exceptional occurrence at Brookstreet and we appreciate your patience and understanding throughout this process.

Should you have any questions or concerns prior to this time, please do not hesitate to contact us by pressing '0' or the 'Guest Services' button on your telephone and asking for the Manager on Duty.

Again, thank you for experiencing Brookstreet.

I acknowledge by my signature below, I must depart Brookstreet by 8:30 AM on Thursday, June 8th, 2006.

Letter to the guests at Brookstreet 2006, informing them that they will have to vacate the premises on June 8, 2006 by 8:30 A.M. As soon as the guests left, security swoops in and goes through the hotel with a fine-tooth comb. The conference itself started on June 9.

PRESS RELEASE

BILDERBERG MEETINGS
8 June 2006

The 54th Bilderberg Meeting will be held in Ottawa, Canada, 8-11 June 2006. The Conference will deal mainly with European-American relations, Energy, Russia, Iran, the Middle East, Asia, Terrorism, and Immigration.

Approximately 130 participants will attend of whom about two-thirds come from Europe and the balance from North America. About one-third is from government and politics, and two-thirds are from finance, industry, labor, education, and communications. The meeting is private in order to encourage frank and open discussion.

Bilderberg takes its name from the hotel in Holland, where the first meeting took place in May 1954. That pioneering meeting grew out of the concern expressed by leading citizens on both sides of the Atlantic that Western Europe and North America were not working together as closely as they should on common problems of critical importance. It was felt that regular, off-the-record discussions would help create a better understanding of the complex forces and major trends affecting Western nations in the difficult post-war period.

The Cold War has now ended. But in practically all respects there are more, not fewer, common problems - from trade to jobs, from monetary policy to investment, from ecological challenges to the task of promoting international security. It is hard to think of any major issue in either Europe or North America whose unilateral solution would not have repercussions for the other.

Thus the concept of a European-American forum has not been overtaken by time. The dialogue between these two regions is still - even increasingly - critical.

What is unique about Bilderberg as a forum is the broad cross-section of leading citizens that are assembled for nearly three days of informal and off-the-record discussion about topics of current concern especially in the fields of foreign affairs and the international economy; the strong feeling among participants that in view of the differing attitudes and experiences of the Western nations, there remains a clear need to further develop an understanding in which these concerns can be accommodated; the privacy of the meetings, which has no purpose other than to allow participants to speak their minds openly and freely.

In short, Bilderberg is a small, flexible, informal and off-the-record international forum in which different viewpoints can be expressed and mutual understanding enhanced.

Bilderberg's only activity is its annual Conference. At the meetings, no resolutions are proposed, no votes taken, and no policy statements issued. Since 1954, fifty-three conferences have been held. The names of the participants are made available to the press. Participants are chosen for their experience, their knowledge, and their standing; all participants attend Bilderberg in a private and not an official capacity.

Participants have agreed not to give interviews to the press during the meeting. In contacts with the news media after the conference it is an established rule that no attribution should be made to individual participants of what was discussed during the meeting.

There will be no press conference. A list of participants is appended.

Bilderberg press release along with the complete list of 2006 attendees was faxed to us from the hotel by one of our sources.

06/09/2006 FRI 11:39 FAX 6132711850 Brookstreet Hotel ☒003/006

08/06/2006

BILDERBERG MEETINGS
Ottawa, Canada
8-11 June 2006
LIST OF PARTICIPANTS

	Honorary Chairman	
B	Davignon, Etienne	Vice Chairman, Suez-Tractebel
PNA	Abu-Amr, Ziad	Member of the Palestinian Legislative Council; President of the Palestinian Council on Foreign Relations; Professor of Political Science, Birzeit University
P	Aguiar-Branco, José Pedro	Former Minister of Justice; Member of Parliament (PSD)
CH	Aigrain, Jacques	CEO, Swiss Re
USA	Ajami, Fouad	Director, Middle East Studies Program, The Paul H. Nitze School of Advanced International Studies, The Johns Hopkins University
GR	Alogoskoufis, George	Minister of Economy and Finance
TR	Bağiş, Egemen	Member of Parliament; Foreign Policy Advisor to the Prime Minister
GB	Balls, Edward	Economic Secretary to the Treasury
P	Balsemão, Francisco Pinto	Chairman and CEO, IMPRESA, S.G.P.S.; Former Prime Minister
F	Barnier, Michel	Former Minister for Foreign Affairs; CorporateVice-President, Mérieux Alliance
A	Bartenstein, Martin	Minister of Economics and Labour
I	Bernabè, Franco	Vice Chairman, Rothschild Europe
S	Bildt, Carl	Former Prime Minister
TR	Boyner, Ümit N.	Member of the Executive Board, Boyner Holding
F	Bressand, Albert	Professor and Managing Director designate, Center for Energy, Marine Transportation and Public Policy, School of International and Public Affairs, Columbia University
A	Bronner, Oscar	Publisher and Editor, Der Standard
GB	Browne, John	Group Chief Executive, BP plc
B	Burda, Hubert	Publisher and CEO, Hubert Burda Media Holding GmbH & Co. KG
F	Castries, Henri de	Chairman of the Management Board and CEO, AXA
E	Cebrián, Juan Luis	CEO, PRISA
IRQ	Chalabi, Ahmad	Former Deputy Prime Minister
CDN	Clark, Edmund	President and CEO, TD Bank Financial Group
GB	Clarke, Kenneth	Member of Parliament
USA	Collins, Timothy C.	Senior Managing Director and CEO, Ripplewood Holdings, LLC
F	Collomb, Bertrand	Chairman, Lafarge
CDN	Comper, Tony	President and CEO, BMO Financial Group
CDN	Crawley, Phillip	Publisher and CEO, The Globe and Mail
GR	David, George A.	Chairman, Coca-Cola H.B.C. S.A.
INT	Derviş, Kemal	Administrator, UNDP
F	Descoing, Richard	Director, Institut d'Études Politiques
CDN	Desmarais, Jr., Paul	CEO, Power Corporation

227

06/09/2006 FRI 11:40 FAX 6132711850 Brookstreet Hotel ⌀004/006

08/06/2006

F	Devedjian, Patrick	Member of Parliament
USA	Donilon, Thomas E.	Partner, O'Melveny & Myers LLP
D	Döpfner, Mathias	Chairman of the Board of Management, Axel Springer AG
DK	Eldrup, Anders	President, DONG A/S
I	Elkann, John	Vice Chairman, Fiat S.p.A.
USA	Feldstein, Martin S.	President and CEO, National Bureau of Economic Research
USA	Geithner, Timothy F.	President and CEO, Federal Reserve Bank of New York
USA	Gigot, Paul A.	Editor of the Editorial Page, The Wall Street Journal
ISR	Gilady, Eival	Head of Coordination and Strategy at the Office of the Prime Minister
IRL	Gleeson, Dermot	Chairman, AIB Group
B	Goldschmidt, Pierre	Former IAEA Deputy Director General and Former Head of the Department of Safeguards; Visiting Scholar, Carnegie Endowment for International Peace
A	Gusenbauer, Alfred	Parliamentary Leader SPÖ
NL	Halberstadt, Victor	Professor of Economics, Leiden University; Former Honorary Secretary General of Bilderberg Meetings
B	Hansen, Jean-Pierre	CEO, Suez-Tractebel S.A.
FIN	Heinäluoma, Eero	Minister of Finance
USA	Holbrooke, Richard C.	Vice Chairman, Perseus, LLC
USA	Hubbard, Allan B.	Assistant to the President for Economic Policy, Director National Economic Council
N	Jensen, Siv	Member of Parliament
D	Joffe, Josef	Publisher-Editor, Die Zeit
USA	Johnson, James A.	Vice Chairman, Perseus, LLC
USA	Jordan, Jr., Vernon E.	Senior Managing Director, Lazard Frères & Co. LLC
GB	Kaletsky, Anatole	Editor at Large, The Times
F	Kerdrel, Yves de	Editor, Le Figaro
GB	Kerr of Kinlochard, John	Deputy Chairman, Royal Dutch Shell plc
USA	Kimsey, James V.	Founding CEO and Chairman Emeritus, America Online, Inc.
USA	Kissinger, Henry A.	Chairman, Kissinger Associates
NL	Kleisterlee, Gerard J.	President and CEO, Royal Philips Electronics
TR	Koç, Mustafa V.	Chairman, Koç Holding A.S.
TR	Köprülü, Kemal	Founding Chairman, ARI Movement
FIN	Korkman, Sixten	Managing Director, The Research Institute of the Finnish Economy ETLA and Finnish Business and Policy Forum EVA
TR	Koru, Fehmi	Senior Writer, Yeni Safak
CDN	Koss, Johann O.	President and CEO, Right To Play
USA	Kravis, Henry R.	Founding Partner, Kohlberg Kravis Roberts & Co.
USA	Kravis, Marie-Josée	Senior Fellow, Hudson Institute, Inc.
INT	Kroes, Neelie	Commissioner, European Commission
INT	Kronenburg, Ed	Director of the Private Office, NATO Headquarters
CH	Kudelski, André	Chairman of the Board and CEO, Kudelski Group
F	Lauvergeon, Anne	Chairman of the Executive Board, AREVA
E	León Gross, Bernardino	Secretary of State, Ministry of Foreign Affairs

2

228

08/06/2006

USA	Sant, Roger	Co-Founder and Chairman Emeritus, The AES Corporation The Summit Foundation
IRN	Sariolghalam, Mahmood	Associate Professor of International Relations, School of Economic and Political Sciences, National University of Iran (Shahid Beheshti)
I	Scaroni, Paolo	CEO, Eni S.p.A.
D	Schily, Otto	Former Minister of Interior Affairs; Member of Parliament; Member of the Committee on Foreign Affairs
A	Scholten, Rudolf	Member of the Board of Executive Directors, Oesterreichische Kontrollbank AG
D	Schrempp, Jürgen E.	Former Chairman of the Board of Management, DaimlerChrysler AG
D	Schulz, Ekkehard D.	Chairman, ThyssenKrupp AG
DK	Seidenfaden, Tøger	Executive Editor-in-Chief, Politiken
P	Silva, Augusto Santos	Minister for Parliamentary Affairs
USA	Steinberg, James B.	Dean, Lyndon B. Johnson School of Public Affairs, University of Texas
S	Stråberg, Hans	President and CEO, AB Electrolux
IRL	Sutherland, Peter D.	Chairman, BP plc and Chairman, Goldman Sachs International
I	Tremonti, Giulio	Vice President of the Chamber of Deputies
GR	Tsoukalis, Loukas	President, Hellenic Foundation for European and Foreign Policy (ELIAMEP)
NL	Verhagen, Maxime J.M.	Parliamentary Leader, Christian Democratic Appeal (CDA)
USA	Vinocur, John	Senior Correspondent, International Herald Tribune
S	Wallenberg, Jacob	Chairman, Investor AB
CDN	Waugh, Richard E.	President and CEO, Bank of Nova Scotia
NL	Wellink, A.H.E.M.	President, De Nederlandsche Bank
GB	Wolf, Martin H.	Associate Editor and Economics Commentator, The Financial Times
USA	Wolfensohn, James D.	Special Envoy for the Gaza Disengagement
USA	Zelikow, Philip D.	Counselor of the Department, US Department of State
CHN	Zhang, Yi	Deputy Secretary General, China Society for Strategy and Management Research
USA	Zoellick, Robert B.	Deputy Secretary of State
D	Zumwinkel, Klaus	Chairman of the Board of Management, Deutsche Post AG

Rapporteurs

GB	Bredow, Vendeline von	Paris Correspondent, The Economist
GB	Wooldridge, Adrian D.	Foreign Correspondent, The Economist

OTTAWA CITIZEN

FRIDAY, JUNE 9, 2006 — ESTABLISHED IN 1845 — 93 CENTS

WORLD CUP: GAME ON!
Despite the scandals, the fans are ready. SPORTS, B1
Why Germany won't win. BUSINESS, E1

How to cu
graffiti:
Don't sell
spray pai
to teens.
CITY, F1

WORLD'S ELITE SLIP INTO TOWN FOR SECRET MEETING

The Bilderberg members began arriving yesterday for their meeting at the Brookstreet Hotel over the next few days. They include, clockwise from top left: U.S. banker David Rockefeller, of the famous Rockefeller family and chairman of the Trilateral Commission; Frank McKenna, former New Brunswick premier and ambassador to the U.S.; Jorma Ollila, chairman of Royal Dutch Shell, one of the world's largest energy companies; Queen Beatrix of the Netherlands; former U.S. defence policy adviser Richard Perle and World Bank President James Wolfenson.

VIPs' arrivals marked by a discreet 'B'

The limo drivers had them, so did the luggage tags – signs with a single B – and they were the ticket to get into the Bilderberg meeting at the Brookstreet, write **ANDREW MAYEDA** and **GLEN MCGREGOR**.

Greeted at the airport by limousine drivers holding single-letter "B" signs, global luminaries such as Henry Kissinger, David Rockefeller and Queen Beatrix of the Netherlands began quietly slipping into Ottawa yesterday for the annual gathering of the ultra-secretive Bilderberg Group.

Over the next three days at the

cal and business leaders from North America and Europe are expected to discuss issues such as the security threat posed by Iran and the direction of oil markets.

The group's discreet approach was evident as attendees arrived yesterday at the Ottawa Airport.

Outside the airport, a phalanx of limousines lined up to ferry

kept watch over the barricaded entrance to the hotel parking lot.

Limos were also dispatched to the nearby Shell Aerocentre to retrieve participants arriving on private aircraft. Some attendees had the single-letter "B" on their luggage tags.

Approached by a Citizen reporter upon his arrival, former U.S. defence policy adviser Richard Perle shot down criticism about the secrecy of the group's meetings. "It's a private organization," he said. He denied the charge, advanced by Bilderberg critics, that the organization crafts public policy behind closed doors. "It discusses

Mr. Perle also dismissed suggestions that the group's heavy representation from the oil industry gives it influence over energy prices. "If it did, I'd be trading on oil futures," he said.

A former assistant secretary of defence to president Ronald Reagan, Mr. Perle is still considered an influential adviser in U.S. conservative circles. He advised President George W. Bush and is said to be a close friend of Defence Secretary Donald Rumsfeld.

See BILDERBERG on PAGE A4

MCKENNA: OPPORTUNITIES, BUT NO

U.S. hails 'severe blov to al-Qaeda

Death of terror chief al-Zarq a political win for Bush, but admits the war is far from w

BY SHELDON ALBERTS AND STEVEN EDWARDS

WASHINGTON - President George W. Bush hailed yesterday's death of terror leader Abu Musab al-Zarqawi as a "severe blow to al-Qaeda," but tempered his jubilation by warning that it was unlikely to stop the violence in Iraq.

Touting the killing of Mr. al-Zarqawi as a chance to "turn the tide" against insurgents, Mr. Bush said he would assemble his war cabinet at Camp David, Maryland, next week to plot strategy with members of Iraq's new unity government.

"Zarqawi has met his end, and this violent man will never murder again," Mr. Bush said in a statement delivered from the White House Rose Garden.

"We can expect the terrorists and insurgents to carry on without him. We can expect the sectarian violence to continue. Yet the ideology of terror has lost one of its most visible and aggressive leaders. Zarqawi's death is a severe blow to al-Qaeda ... and it is an opportunity for Iraq's new government to turn the tide of this struggle."

Mr. al-Zarqawi, his spiritual adviser Sheik Abdul Rahman, and four other people died after U.S. forces, acting on intelligence provided by Iraqis, dropped two 227-kilogram bombs on a remote safe house located in a palm grove near Baquba, 65 kilometres north of Baghdad. One woman and a child were among the dead, the U.S. military said.

At a packed news conference in the Iraqi capital, U.S. military commanders displayed a framed photograph of Mr. al-Zarqawi with his eyes closed and his bearded face surrounded by a circle of stained blood.

Iraqi reporters in attendance erupted in applause when Iraqi

FROM THUG, TO MASTERM

Jordanian-born Abu Mu Zarqawi started out as town street thug, but qu found his calling as lea the murderous al-Qaed terror group. In the end his own supporters fou methods too brutal. Ri Beeston has the story.

SUCCESSOR: Egyptian maker 'logical' choice,
REACTION: Some clan the streets, others mou al-Zarqawi as a martyr,
HOPE: Iraqi governmer up security chiefs, A7
EDITORIAL: A monster has been slain, A14

announced: "Al-Zarq eliminated."

The 39-year-old Jord tremist, whom Osama once called the "prii Qaeda in Iraq," had wa ly campaign of bombin sassinations against U and Iraqis since the fi dam Hussein's regime i

☐☐☐ TERRORIST

The Bilderberg Group's efforts to keep their confab secret were in vain, as leading Canadian media outlets answered our calls and fully covered the 2006 conference in Kanata, Ottawa, Canada.

BILDERBERG CONFERENCE

MIKE CARROCCETTO, OTTAWA CITIZEN

RZEJ OLECHOWSKI
former minister of
gn affairs and finance in
native Poland, where he
frequently been involved
olitics since the 1990s.
an unsuccessfully in the
0 presidential election
Warsaw's 2002 mayoral
. Mr. Olechowski was a
ding member of the
rist Civic Platform party,
is currently a member of
supervisory boards of
ndi Universal, Citibank
dlowy and PKN Orlen.

MIKE CARROCCETTO, OTTAWA CITIZEN

EGIL MYKLEBUST
served as president and CEO of Norsk Hydro, a Norwegian oil and gas group that is one of that countries biggest companies, between 1991 and 2001. He then served as Norsk's chairman until 2004 and was also a member of the World Business Council for Sustainable Development. While he is a well-known face in the world's oil and gas industry, Mr. Myklebust is currently chairman of Scandinavian Airlines.

MIKE CARROCCETTO, OTTAWA CITIZEN

ROBERT ZOELLICK
now reports to Condoleezza Rice as the U.S. deputy secretary of state, after serving as the U.S. trade representative from 2001 to 2005. A lawyer, Mr. Zoellick has worked in economic and diplomatic policy development in different Republican administrations for more than two decades. He has a strong reputation for hammering out international trade deals; he played a key role in sealing NAFTA and has been an important player in World Trade Organization talks.

MIKE CARROCCETTO, OTTAWA CITIZEN

JAMES B. STEINBERG
is best known for his work as deputy national-security adviser to U.S. president Bill Clinton from 1996 to 2000. After working in government, Mr. Steinberg went on to direct foreign policy studies at the Brookings Institution in Washington and is now the dean of the Lyndon B. Johnson School of Public Affairs at the University of Texas at Austin. He is a frequent media commentator on U.S. foreign policy and has written several books on national security topics.

MIKE CARROCCETTO, OTTAWA CITIZEN

JUAN LUIS CEBRIAN
is the CEO of the Spanish media conglomerate Grupa Prisa, which owns *El Pais*, a centre-left daily that is the country's leading newspaper. Mr. Cebrian is a former editor at *El Pais* and has also served as chairman of the International Press Institute. He is also an acclaimed author of books such as *Red Doll* and the essay collection, *The Press and Main Street*.

MIKE CARROCCETTO, OTTAWA CITIZEN

MARIO MONTI
dubbed "Super Mario" by the press, is an Italian economist, president of Bocconi University in Milan and chairman of the European think-tank Bruegel. He has most notably served on the European Commission, where he was sometimes called an antitrust czar. Mr. Monti fought against a proposed merger between General Electric and Honeywell in 2001. The European Union eventually blocked that merger, earning criticism from U.S. regulators.

MIKE CARROCCETTO, OTTAWA CITIZEN

JEAN-PIERRE HANSEN
is CEO of energy giants Electrabel, Belgium's top power producer, and Suez-Tractebel, Belgium's top utility holding company and one of the world's biggest independent power producers. Mr. Hansen holds advanced degrees in engineering and economics and has worked in the electricity and gas sectors since the 1970s.

MIKE CARROCCETTO, OTTAWA CITIZEN

ELIE KROES
veteran Dutch politician
businesswoman who has
ved as European
nmissioner for
npetition since 2004. Ms.
es' appointment to the
ition was met with some
troversy, due to her
ensive business contacts.
ce assuming her post, Ms.
es has been in the middle
Microsoft's on-going
pute with the EU over a
04 antitrust ruling against

JEAN LEVAC, OTTAWA CITIZEN

FRANCO BERNABE
is vice-chairman of the European investment bank Rothschild Europe, former CEO of the Italian energy giant ENI and a board member of Petro-China. Mr. Bernabé headed ENI's privatization process in the early 90s and was recently quoted as saying the world oil industry remains "uneasy" with the feverish development of Alberta's oilsands near Fort McMurray

JEAN LEVAC, OTTAWA CITIZEN

DAVID ROCKEFELLER
is founder of the Trilateral Commission, formed in 1973 by citizens of Japan, European Union countries, the U.S. and Canada with the goal of fostering closer co-operation among those regions. Mr. Rockefeller, who has a PhD from the University of Chicago, spent 35 years as an officer of the Chase Manhattan Bank and was chairman and CEO from 1969 to 1980. He serves as

FRANK GUNN, THE CANADIAN PRESS

FRANK MCKENNA
served as Canada's ambassador to the U.S. under prime minister Paul Martin. When Mr. Martin lost the election, Mr. McKenna returned to private life, quickly quelling rumours he would run for the Liberal party leadership. Before his U.S. stint, Mr. McKenna practised law and served on numerous corporate boards. He became New Brunswick's premier in 1987, winning

MIKE CARROCCETTO, OTTAWA CITIZEN

JORMA OLLILA
served as chairman and CEO of Nokia Corporation for 14 years, from 1992 until this month when he became non-executive chairman of Royal Dutch Shell while hanging on to his Nokia association, also as non-executive chairman. He is the first non-Dutch, non-Briton to head Shell. He took Nokia from a cellphone company on the brink of takeover to the world's most successful. The

JEAN LEVAC, OTTAWA CITIZEN

QUEEN BEATRIX
of the Netherlands became queen in 1980 when her mother, Juliana, abdicated. Ottawa is not new to the queen, who moved to the capital in the 1940s, and lived in Stornoway. She went to Rockcliffe Park Public School and her sister, Princess Margriet, was born in Canada. Queen Beatrix, who has a degree in law, married Claus von Amsberg, a German diplomat, in 1966.

MIKE CARROCCETTO, OTTAWA CITIZEN

RICHARD PERLE
was assistant secretary of defence to U.S. president Ronald Reagan and is still considered influential in the U.S., having advised President George W. Bush. Mr. Perle served as chairman of the Defence Policy Board from 2001-2003 and was assistant secretary of defence for international security policy from 1981 to 1987. His opinions appear regularly in

JEAN LEVAC, OTTAWA CITIZEN

MES WOLFENSOHN
president of the World
nk, walks the fine line
ween being a banker and
advocate for the world's
or. Born in Australia, he
ded up on Wall Street via
ndon, eventually founding
anking firm with former
ad of the U.S. Federal
serve, Paul Volker. Today,
is credited with working to
urn the World Bank to its
ginal mandate of relieving
verty.

JEAN LEVAC, OTTAWA CITIZEN

ETIENNE DAVIGNON
is a former Belgian politician and president of the annual Bilderberg conference. Mr. Davignon was born in Hungary and quickly established a name for himself in business and politics. He was the first president of the International Energy Agency from 1974-77 and at the age of 32, he became head of cabinet. Between 1977 and 1985, he was an influential member of the European Commission. In 1989, he joined the board of the Société Générale de Belgique.

JEAN LEVAC, OTTAWA CITIZEN

JOHN VINOCUR
is a senior correspondent for the *International Herald Tribune* and reports on everything from politics to sports. He went to the *Tribune* from the *New York Times*, where he was metropolitan editor. He served as the *Times* bureau chief in France and Germany. He went to the *Tribune* as executive editor and served as the newspaper's vice-president from 1986-96. He writes for *Foreign Affairs* and the *New York Times Magazine*.

CHRIS MIKULA, OTTAWA CITIZEN

ADRIAN WOOLDRIDGE
is the *Economist's* Washington bureau chief. Prior to this, he was the magazine's west coast correspondent, and also held positions as its management correspondent and its correspondent in Britain. He co-wrote *The Company: A Short History of a Revolutionary Idea*, and *A Future Perfect: The Challenge and Hidden Promise of Globalisation*, *Witch Doctors*, and *The Right Nation*, a look at American conservatism.

RICK WILKING, REUTERS

VERNON JORDAN
A Washington insider, Mr. Jordan chaired the Clinton transition team in 1992. He started his public life through the civil rights movement in the 1960s, working for the NAACP, and served as executive director of the United Negro College Fund and National Urban League in the 1970s. The lawyer is a managing director with the investment banking firm Lazard Frères & Co. LLC and is on several boards, including American Express and Dow Jones & Company.

JEAN LEVAC, OTTAWA CITIZEN

TONY COMPER
has been chief executive officer of BMO Financial Group since 1999. In his three decades with BMO, he served as chairman from 1999 to 2004, when the company moved to a non-executive chairman model. He first signed on with the bank in 1967, after completing a BA in English. Mr. Comper is a member of the board of directors of the International Monetary Conference and vice-chairman of the C.D. Howe Institute.

MIKE CARROCCETTO, OTTAWA CITIZEN

DERMOT GLEESON
chairman of Allied Irish Banks, is a lawyer. He is a member of the Royal Irish Academy and chairman of the Irish Council for Bioethics and is the former attorney general of Ireland. He also served as a member of the Council of State for Ireland and as then-Irish prime minister John Bruton's chief legal adviser from 1994-97. He joined the board of Allied Irish Banks in 2000 and was appointed chairman in 2003.

metr🌐

WEEKEND, JUNE 9-11, 2006   OTTAWA

Marty York's

CFL REPORT

Check it out at
www.metronews.ca

METRO SCOOP   P. 26
J.Lo shopping spree sparks
pregnancy rumours.

OTTAWA   P. 3
Youngsters honoured at
9-1-1 awards presentation.

SPORTS   P. 12
Henin-Hardenne to play
Kuznetsova for Open title.

WORLD   P. 6
Top al Qaeda leader killed
in air strike: Iraqi PM.

BUSINESS   P. 7
Gas sales fell last year
over high prices: StatsCan.

HI 17	LOW 7

WEATHER P. 28

A private security guard and two Ottawa police officers keep watch outside a Kanata hotel yesterday where members of the Bilderberg Group, a collection of the world's richest and most influential people, will be meeting until Sunday.

Kanata hosts world's elite

Bilderberg meet causes conspiracy theory buzz

It's like Woodstock for conspiracy theorists.

The serene suburban setting of Kanata has been transformed into a four-day festival of black suits, black limousines, burly security guards — and suspicions of world domination.

On the outskirts of the nation's capital, the tony Brookstreet Hotel is hosting the annual meeting for one of the world's most secretive and powerful societies.

It's not the Freemasons.

Forget those fairytales about the Elders of Zion.

These guys, you've probably never even heard of, and if you believe the camera-toting followers who attend all their meetings, they control the world.

They're called the Bilderberg group.

They include European royalty, national leaders, political power-brokers and heads of the world's biggest companies.

Those who follow the Bilderberg group say it got Europe to adopt a common currency, got Bill Clinton to support NAFTA, and is spending this week deciding what to do about high oil prices and that pesky fundamentalist president of Iran,

who's who in Kanata

▶ An unsigned press release, sent by fax, confirmed this year's attendees in the nation's capital include David Rockefeller, Henry Kissinger, Queen Beatrix of Holland, New York Gov. George Pataki, the heads of Coca-Cola, Credit Suisse, the Royal Bank of Canada, a number of media moguls, and cabinet ministers from Spain and Greece.

Mahmoud Ahmadinejad.

"Some people say that I advocate a conspiracy theory. That's not true. I recognize a conspiracy fact," said James P. Tucker.

The 74-year-old American journalist has been following the Bilderberg group for decades, has

written extensively about it and recently published his Bilderberg Diary. He follows the group to its annual meetings and stands outside describing to other journalists details of his privileged access to their inner workings.

Ottawa police officers are standing guard outside a dozen metal gates that serve as security checkpoints a half-kilometre from the hotel. But Ottawa's finest are clearly not in charge here.

To approach the hotel property, even these uniformed police officers are required to show their credentials to the half-dozen black-suited men working for Globe Risk, a private security firm. CANADIAN PRESS

Greenfield Newspapers Inc., operating as Metro Ottawa 116 Albert Street, Suite 402, Ottawa, Ontario K1P 5G3. Publisher: Dara Mottahed

ATERDAG 10 FEBRUARI 2007   **3**

'CIA financierde eerste Bilderbergconferenties'

AMSTERDAM – De Amerikaanse inlichtingendienst CIA financierde en organiseerde mede de eerste edities van de Bilderbergconferentie. Dat stelt Gerard Aalders van het Nederlands Instituut voor Oorlogsdocumentatie (Niod). De Bilderberg Groep is een in 1954 mede door prins Bernhard opgericht genootschap, dat bestaat uit vooraanstaande personen uit de wereld van de politiek en industrie. De groep komt jaarlijks in een luxueus hotel achter gesloten deuren bijeen om te brainstormen over de internationale politieke en economische ontwikkelingen. (ANP)

Saturday 10 February 2007

CIA FINANCED FIRST BILDERBERG CONFERENCES

Amsterdam – The American Intelligence Agency CIA co-financed and co-organized the first editions of the Bilderberg conference. This is stated by Gerard Aalders of the Netherlands Institute for War documentation (NIOD). The Bilderberg Group is a society, cofounded by Prince Bernhard in 1954, of prominent persons in politics and industry. The group gathers each year in a luxury resort to brainstorm behind closed doors about international economic and political developments.

Top: Dutch newspaper report from Algemeen Nederlands Persbureau (ANP) declaring first Bilderberg meetings were financed by the CIA.
Bottom: President Dwight Eisenhower shakes hands with C.D. Jackson. C.D. Jackson served as a Special Assistant to the President and as Chairman of the Psychological Strategy Board (later Operations Coordinating Board). Jackson was a Time-Life executive and one of the architects of the secret Bilderberg meetings. He attended the first meeting in 1954.

Top, left to right: Adrian Wooldridge of the *Economist*; Robert Kagan of Carnegie; Richard Haass, CFR President; Martin Wolf, *Financial Times*. Not a word was written in either the *Economist* or the *Financial Times* about the conclusions of the Bilderberg Group meeting.

Bottom clockwise: Dennis Ross with glasses; James D. Wolfensohn, the then-President of the World Bank.

Top, left to right: Rockwell A. Schnabel, US Ambassador to the EU with Jeroen van der Veer, Chairman of Royal Dutch Shell.
Bottom left: former European Commissioner Mario Monti with Jean-Pierre Hansen, Chairman, Suez Tractabel.
Bottom right: Heather Munroe-Blum, Principal and Vice Chancellor, McGill University with Adrian Wooldridge of the *Economist* during Bilderberg 2005.

Heir to the Belgian throne, Prince Phillip going for a leisurely walk during Bilderberg 2004. When my photographs of the Prince appeared in a Belgian magazine *Le Soir*, Belgian parliament demanded an official explanation from the Royal Family as to what exactly he was doing at the secret meeting.

Queen Beatrix of the Netherlands, one of the wealthiest people in the world, daughter of the Bilderberg founder Prince Bernhard, attending Bilderberg meetings.

A "small town affair," Bilderberg meetings are usually accompanied by an impressive display of police and security forces.

Armed Italian police were in force providing security at Bilderberg 2004.

Top: Italian secret service guarding installations at Stresa 2004.
Bottom: Italian secret service guarding Richard Perle, left, and Martin Taylor, right, International Adviser of Goldman Sachs and Bilderberger Honorary Chairman.

Top: Showtime. Mass arrival of Bilderberg guests to Rottach Egern. The first day of the conference.
Bottom: Unmarked Mercedes with an inconspicuous "B" for Bilderberg on the windshield.

Top: Bilderberg 2005, CIA guards for the US delegation.
Bottom: German security 2005, assigned to protect the less important members from smaller countries such as Greece, Denmark, Spain, Portugal, etc.

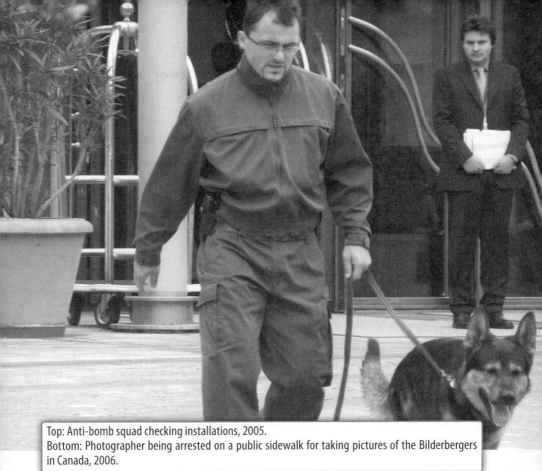

Top: Anti-bomb squad checking installations, 2005.
Bottom: Photographer being arrested on a public sidewalk for taking pictures of the Bilderbergers in Canada, 2006.

Top: CIA with Graham and Nooyi in the background.
Bottom: CIA awaiting Paul Wolfowitz. The big fat guy is Agent Smiley.

Local police and private security enforcing the law at Brookstreet 2006 in Canada.

Top: Francisco Pinto Balsemao, Former Prime Minister of Portugal and the country's "man behind the curtain."

Bottom: Break at Bilderberg 2004. In the background, Henry Kissinger is seen talking to Henry Kravis. To their right, Nicolas Beytout of *Le Figaro* newspaper. Not a word was mentioned in *Le Figaro* about the Bilderberg conference.

DIVIETO DI SOSTA CON RIMOZIONE FORZATA

DALLE ORE 7,00 DEL 2/6/04
ALLE ORE 20,00 DEL 6/6/04

Top: The sign says that cars parked in front of the "Bilderberg" hotel will be towed away by the authorities. In 2004, the Bilderberg Group meeting was held June 3-6.
Bottom: Prince Phillip and his personal bodyguard at Bilderberg 2005.

Top: NATO Secretary General Jaap G. Hoop Scheffer being helped to his vehicle.
Bottom: A rather sloppily dressed Richard Perle caught on film during Bilderberg 2004.

Top: The international press has little to say as far as Bilderberg is concerned. Martin Wolf, an award winning writer for the *Financial Times* arriving at Bilderberg 2005.
Bottom left/right: *International Herald Tribune's* John Vinocour; Adrian Wooldridge of the *Economist* with Martin Taylor.

Top: Vernon Jordan with Jessica Matthews of Carnegie Endowment.
Bottom: An impeccably dressed Henry Kravis of KKR.

In Fraganti — The now thoroughly disgraced Ahmed Chalabi attending Bilderberg 2006 in Canada. Amazingly, not a word appeared in the *Washington Post,* the *New York Times,* the *Economist,* the *Wall Street Journal* about this extremely relevant event.

STRESA 2004

Peter D. SUTHERLAND

STRESA 2004

Douglas J. FEITH

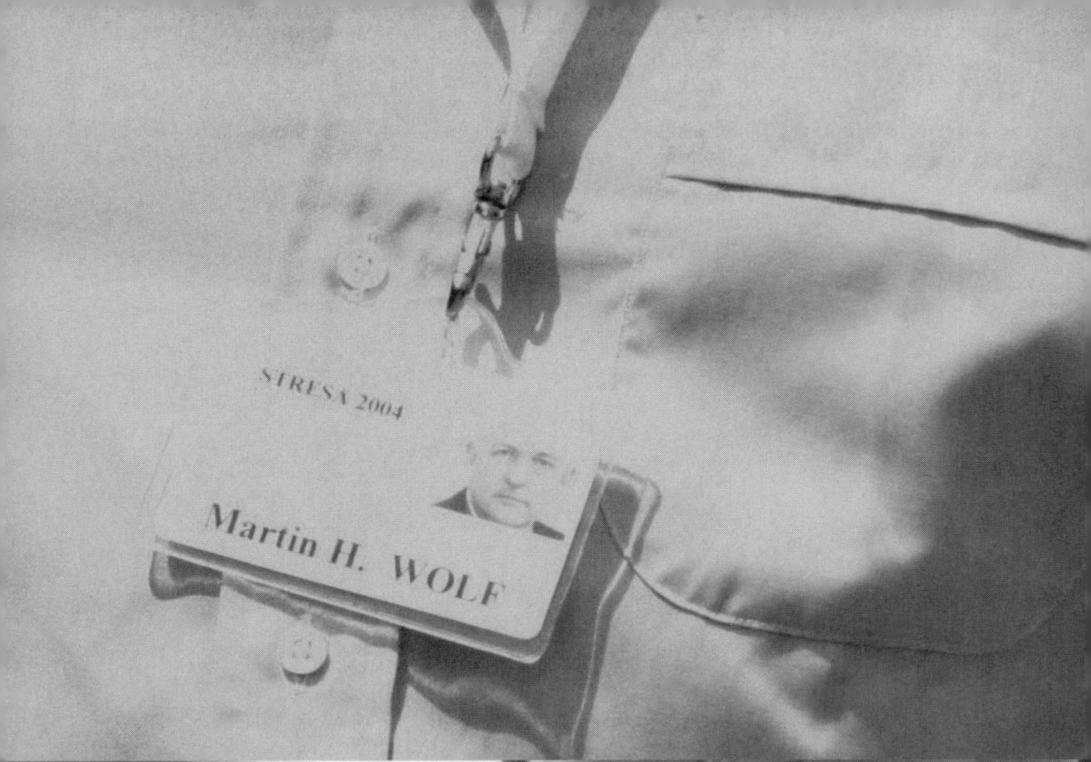
STRESA 2004
Martin H. WOLF

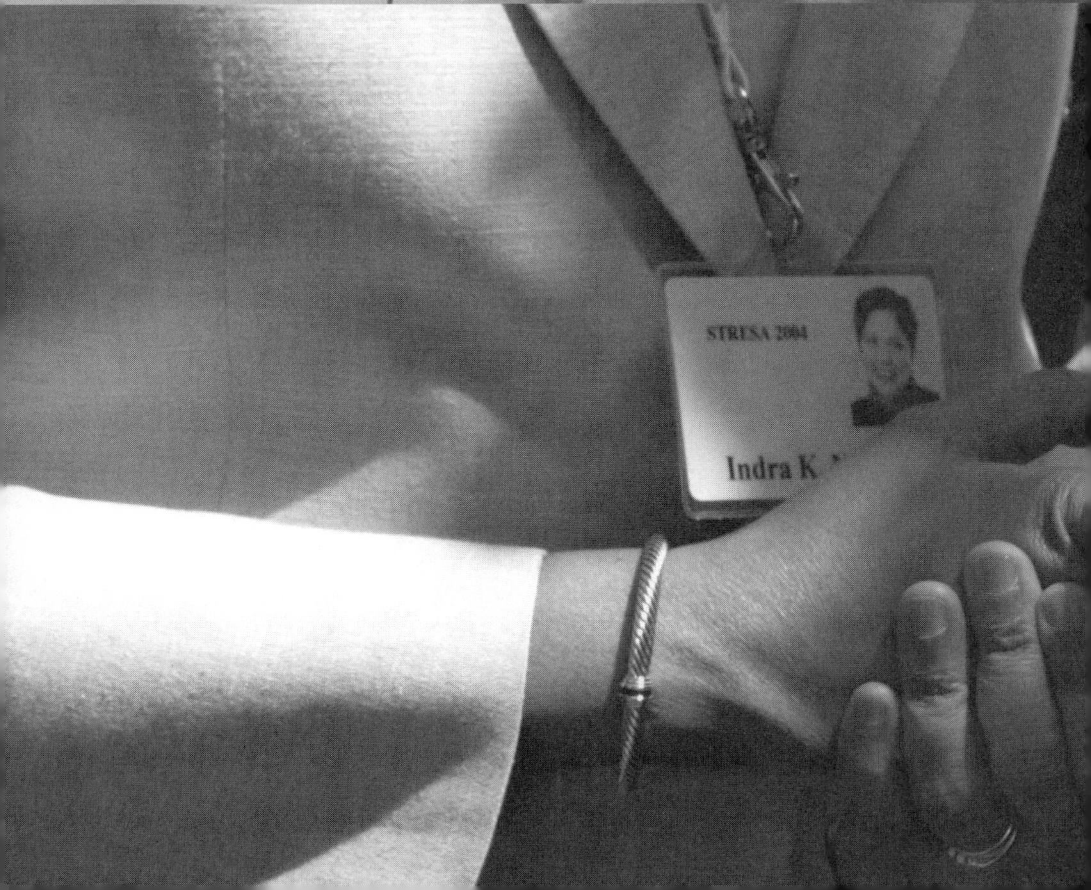
STRESA 2004
Indra K

Jordan and Matthews relaxing during a break at Bilderberg 2004.

Top: Jergén E. Schrempp, Chairman of the Board of Management, DaimlerChrysler AG greeted by Bilderberg organizer in 2004.
Bottom: from left to right: Donald Graham, *Washington Post*; Marie Josee Kravis, Hudson Institute; Indra Nooyi, PepsiCo; security guard; Henry Kissinger and Henry Kravis.

Top clockwise from left: Kravis; Bernabé, Marie Joseé Kravis; Henry Kissinger
Bottom: Kissinger, Nooyi, Graham

Tommaso Padoa-Schioppa, former Member of the Executive Board, European Central Bank and presently Minister of the Economy in the Socialist Prodi government in Italy.

Clockwise: Wolfowitz, Holbrooke, Davignon.

Top left to right: The two Irishmen, Peter Sutherland with Dermot Gleeson, Chairman, AIB Group.
Bottom: Henry Kissinger with bodyguard in tow.

Top: Fehru Koru, a polemic Turkish journalist and a former Bilderberg critic. Once he was invited to Bilderberg 2006, he suddenly changed his tune and publicly announced that he would love to be invited back.
Bottom: Jon Corzine, back to us; Allan Hubbard, Assistant to the President for Economic Policy and Director of the National Economic Council; Etienne Davignon, Vice Chairman, Suez-Tractebel and an honorary Chairman Bilderberg group.

Top: Jako Elkann, Vice Chairman Fiat.
Bottom: Craig J. Mundie, Chief Technical Officer, Advanced Strategies and Policies, Microsoft Corporation, first from right side. Martin Taylor of Goldman Sachs coming through the door and smiling.

Top: Jon Corzine with John Edwards at Bilderberg 2004, where Edwards was anointed with the VP position on the Kerry ticket.
Bottom: Edwards and Holbrooke. What could they be talking about?

Top: The only known photograph showing the presence of the then-leader of Germany, Gerhardt Schroder, at Bilderberg 2005, shown shaking hands with the Chairman of DaimlerChrysler, Jurgen E. Schrempp (right).
Bottom: Dermot Gleeson, Chairman, AIB Group.

Bernard Kouchner, founder of Doctors Without Borders. Curiously enough he has found his way into the current right-wing Sarkozy government in France.

Top: Holbrooke in Canada during Bilderberg 2006.
Bottom: Davignon flanked by Ottawa police.

Top: The two Irishmen, Gleeson and Sutherland.
Bottom: Graham between Kravis and Nooyi at Stresa 2004.

RICK SANTORUM
PENNSYLVANIA

REPUBLICAN CONFERENCE
Chairman

WASHINGTON, DC
511 Dirksen Senate Office Building
Washington, DC 20510
(202) 224-6324

COMMITTEES:
FINANCE

BANKING, HOUSING, AND URBAN AFFAIRS
AGRICULTURE, NUTRITION AND FORESTRY
RULES AND ADMINISTRATION
SPECIAL COMMITTEE ON AGING

United States Senate
http://santorum.senate.gov

September 18, 2006

Mr. Richard Haas
President
Council on Foreign Relations
1779 Massachusetts Avenue, NW
Washington, D.C. 20036

Dear Mr. Haas:

I write today to express my deep concern with your organization's reported invitation to the President of Iran, Mahmoud Ahmadinejad, to speak at a gathering of the Council on Foreign Relations in New York City this week.

By issuing an invitation to President Ahmadinejad to speak in a public forum in the United States, your organization is demonstrating that it draws no distinction between world leaders who deserve respect and those that undermine the very values of the international system the United States seeks to uphold.

President Ahmadinejad has proven to be a threatening and irresponsible leader. His denial of the Holocaust and anti-Zionist statements that Israel "must be wiped off the map" are offensive. He has routinely issued statements of hate against the United States, Israel, and Jewish peoples. Further, the government of President Ahmadinejad has funded, armed, trained, assisted, and sheltered leading terrorists, including terrorists active in Iraq using Iranian support to kill military personnel of the United States. Last but not least, he continues to defy the free world by insisting upon developing a nuclear capability -- a capability that will undoubtedly be used to develop nuclear weapons. For these reasons, it would be irresponsible to give President Ahmadinejad such a forum in the United States in which to spread his messages of hate and destruction.

President Ahmadinejad does not afford his own people the freedom of speech. By allowing him the opportunity to address a public forum in the United States, you would be sending the wrong message to the people of Iran. I strongly urge you to revoke the Council on Foreign Relations' invitation to President Ahmadinejad to speak at this event.

Thank you in advance for your consideration of this serious matter.

Sincerely,

Rick Santorum
United States Senate

THE TRILATERAL COMMISSION

February 2006
*Executive Committee

THOMAS S. FOLEY North American Chairman	**PETER SUTHERLAND** European Chairman	**YOTARO KOBAYASHI** Pacific Asia Chairman
ALLAN E. GOTLIEB North American Deputy Chairman	**HERVÉ DE CARMOY** European Deputy Chairman	**KIM KYUNG-WON** Pacific Asia Deputy Chairman
LORENZO H. ZAMBRANO North American Deputy Chairman	**ANDRZEJ OLECHOWSKI** European Deputy Chairman	**SHIJURO OGATA** Pacific Asia Deputy Chairman

DAVID ROCKEFELLER
Founder and Honorary Chairman

PAUL A. VOLCKER North American Honorary Chairman	**GEORGES BERTHOIN** European Honorary Chairman	**OTTO GRAF LAMBSDORFF** European Honorary Chairman

***

MICHAEL J. O'NEIL North American Director	**PAUL RÉVAY** European Director	**TADASHI YAMAMOTO** Pacific Asia Director

EUROPEAN GROUP

Paul Adams, Chief Executive, British American Tobacco, London
Urban Ahlin, Member of the Swedish Parliament and Chairman of the Committee on Foreign Affairs, Stockholm
Krister Ahlström, Vice Chairman, Stora Enso and Fortum; former Chairman, Finnish Employers Confederation; former Chairman, Ahlström Corp., Helsinki
Edmond Alphandéry, Chairman, Caisse Nationale de Prévoyance, Paris; former Chairman, Electricité de France (EDF); former Minister of the Economy and Finance
Bodil Nyboe Andersen, Chairperson of the Board of Governors, Danmarks Nationalbank, Copenhagen
Jacques Andréani, Ambassadeur de France; former Ambassador to the United States
*Stelios Argyros, Chairman and Managing Director, Preveza Mills, Athens; former Member of the European Parliament; former Vice President of UNICE, Brussels; former President and Chairman of the Board of the Federation of Greek Industries, Athens
Jerzy Baczynski, Editor-in-Chief, *Polityka*, Warsaw
Estela Barbot, Vice President, AGA, Porto; Vice President of the Board, AEP -- Portuguese Business Association; Consul of Guatemala, Lisbon
*Erik Belfrage, Senior Vice President, Skandinaviska Enskilda Banken; Director, Investor AB, Stockholm

Marek Belka, Executive Secretary, United Nations Economic Commission for Europe (UNECE), Geneva; former Prime Minister of Poland, Warsaw; former Ambassador-at-Large and Chairman, Council for International Coordination, Coalition Provisional Authority, Baghdad

Baron Jean-Pierre Berghmans, Chairman of the Executive Board, Lhoist Group, Limelette, Belgium

*****Georges Berthoin**, International Honorary Chairman, European Movement; Honorary Chairman, The Jean Monnet Association; Honorary European Chairman, The Trilateral Commission, Paris

Nicolas Beytout, Editor, *Le Figaro*, Paris ; former Editor, *Les Echos*, Paris

Carl Bildt, Chairman, Kreab Group of public affairs companies; Chairman, Nordic Venture Network, Stockholm; former Member of the Swedish Parliament, Chairman of the Moderate Party and Prime Minister of Sweden; former European Union High Representative in Bosnia-Herzegovina & UN Special Envoy to the Balkans

Ana Patricia Botin, Executive Chairman, Banesto; Vice Chairman, Urbis; Member of the Management Committee, Santander Group, Madrid

Jean-Louis Bourlanges, Member of the European Parliament (ALDE Group/UDF) and Chairman, Committee on Civil Liberties, Justice and Home Affairs, Brussels; former President of the European Movement in France, Paris

*****Jorge Braga de Macedo**, President, Tropical Research Institute, Lisbon; Special Advisor to the Secretary General, Organisation for Economic Co-operation and Development (OECD), Paris; Professor of Economics, Nova University at Lisbon; Chairman, Forum Portugal Global; former Minister of Finance

Lord Brittan of Spennithorne, Vice Chairman, UBS Investment Bank, London; former Vice President, European Commission

Robin Buchanan, Senior Partner, Bain & Company, London

*****François Bujon de l'Estang**, Ambassadeur de France; Chairman, Citigroup France, Paris; former Ambassador to the United States

Sven Burmester, Writer and Explorer, Denmark; former Representative, United Nations Population Fund (UNFPA), Beijing; former World Bank Deputy Secretary and Representative in Cairo

Richard Burrows, Governor, Bank of Ireland; Chairman, Irish Distillers; Non-executive Director, Pernod Ricard; former President, IBEC (The Irish Business and Employers Confederation), Dublin

*****Hervé de Carmoy**, Chairman, Almatis, Frankfurt-am-Main; former Partner, Rhône Group, New York & Paris; Honorary Chairman, Banque Industrielle et Mobilière Privée, Paris; former Chief Executive, Société Générale de Belgique

Antonio Carrapatoso, Chairman of the Board of Directors, Vodafone Portugal, Lisbon; Member of the Board of Directors, Vodafone Spain & Vodacom

Salvatore Carrubba, Culture Alderman, Municipality of Milan; former Managing Editor, Il Sole 24 Ore, Milan

Henri de Castries, Chairman of the Management Board and Chief Executive Officer, AXA, Paris

Jürgen Chrobog, Chairman, BMW Herbert Quandt Foundation, Munich; former German Deputy Foreign Minister and Ambassador to the United States

Luc Coene, Minister of State; Deputy Governor, National Bank of Belgium, Brussels

Sir Ronald Cohen, Founding partner and Executive Chairman, Apax Partners worldwide, London

Vittorio Colao, Chief Executive Officer, RCS MediaGroup, Milan; former Managing Director, Vodafone Omnitel

Bertrand Collomb, Chairman, Lafarge, Paris; Chairman, World Business Council for Sustainable Development

*****Richard Conroy**, Chairman, Conroy Diamonds & Gold, Dublin; Member of Senate, Republic of Ireland

Eckhard Cordes, former Member of the Board, DaimlerChrysler, Stuttgart

Alfonso Cortina, Chairman, Inmobiliaria Colonial; Chairman, Repsol-YPF Foundation, Madrid

Michel David-Weill, Chairman, Lazard LLC, worldwide; Managing Director and Président du Collège d'Associés-Gérants, Lazard Frères S.A.S., Paris; Deputy Chairman, Lazard Brothers & Co., Limited, London

2

Baron Paul De Keersmaeker, Chairman of the Board of Domo, Corgo, Foundation Europalia
International and the Canada Europe Round Table, Brussels; Honorary Chairman Interbrew, KBC,
Nestlé Belgilux; former Member of the Belgian and European Parliaments and of the Belgian
Government

*****Vladimir Dlouhy**, Senior Advisor, ABB; International Advisor, Goldman Sachs; former Czechoslovak
Minister of Economy; former Czech Minister of Industry & Trade, Prague

Pedro Miguel Echenique, Professor of Physics, University of the Basque Country; former Basque
Minister of Education, San Sebastian

*****Bill Emmott**, Editor, *The Economist*, London

Thomas Enders, Chief Executive Officer, EADS, Munich; Chairman, Atlantik-Brücke (Atlantic Bridge),
Berlin

Laurent Fabius, Member of the French National Assembly and of the Foreign Affairs Committee; former
Prime Minister & Minister of the Economy & Finance, Paris

Oscar Fanjul, Honorary Chairman, Repsol YPF; Vice Chairman, Omega Capital, Madrid

Grete Faremo, Former Executive Vice President, Storebrand; former Norwegian Minister of
Development Cooperation, Minister of Justice and Minister of Oil and Energy, Oslo

*****Nemesio Fernandez-Cuesta**, Executive Director of Upstream, Repsol-YPF; former Chairman, Prensa
Española, Madrid

Jürgen Fitschen, Member of the Group Executive Committee, Deutsche Bank, Frankfurt-am-Main

Klaus-Dieter Frankenberger, Foreign Editor, *Frankfurter Allgemeine Zeitung*, Frankfurt am Main

Hugh Friel, Chief Executive, Kerry Group, Dublin

Lykke Friis, Head of European Department, Federation of Danish Industries, Copenhagen

*****Michael Fuchs**, Member of the German Bundestag, Berlin; former President, National Federation of
German Wholesale & Export Traders

Lord Garel-Jones, Managing Director, UBS Investment Bank, London; Member of the House of Lords;
former Minister of State at the Foreign Office (European Affairs)

*****Antonio Garrigues Walker**, Chairman, Garrigues Abogados y Asesores Tributarios, Madrid

Wolfgang Gerhard, Member of the German Bundestag, Berlin

Lord Gilbert, Member of the House of Lords; former Minister for Defence, London

Mario Greco, Managing Director & General Manager, Assicurazioni Internazionali di Previdenza
(A.I.P.), Milan

General The Lord Guthrie, Director, N M Rothschild & Sons, London; Member of the House of Lords;
former Chief of the Defence Staff, London

Sirkka Hämäläinen, former Member of the Executive Board, European Central Bank, Frankfurt-am-
Main; former Governor, Bank of Finland

*****Toomas Hendrik Ilves**, Member of the European Parliament; former Estonian Foreign Minister and
Member of the Parliament; former Ambassador to the United States, Canada and Mexico

Alfonso Iozzo, Managing Director, San Paolo IMI Group, Turin

*****Mugur Isarescu**, Governor, National Bank of Romania, Bucharest; former Prime Minister

*****Max Jakobson**, Independent Consultant and Senior Columnist, Helsinki; former Finnish Ambassador to
the United Nations; former Chairman of the Finnish Council of Economic Organizations

*****Baron Daniel Janssen**, Chairman of the Board, Solvay, Brussels

Zsigmond Jarai, President, National Bank of Hungary, Budapest

Trinidad Jiménez, International Relations Secretary of the Socialist Party (PSOE) & Member of the
Federal Executive Committee, Madrid

*****Béla Kadar**, Member of the Hungarian Academy, Budapest; Member of the Monetary Council of the
National Bank; President of the Hungarian Economic Association; former Ambassador of Hungary to
the O.E.C.D., Paris; former Hungarian Minister of International Economic Relations and Member of
Parliament

Robert Kassai, General Vice President, The National Association of Craftmen's Corporations, Budapest

3

*Lord Kerr, Member of the House of Lords; Director of Rio Tinto, Shell, and the Scottish American Investment Trust, London; former Secretary General, European Convention, Brussels; former Permanent Under-Secretary of State and Head of the Diplomatic Service, Foreign & Commonwealth Office, London; former British Ambassador to the United States

Denis Kessler, Chairman and Chief Executive Officer, Scor, Paris; former Chairman, French Insurance Association (FFSA); former Executive Vice-Chairman, MEDEF-Mouvement des Entreprises de France (French Employers' Confederation)

Klaus Kleinfeld, Chief Executive Officer, Siemens, Munich

*Sixten Korkman, Managing Director, Finnish Business and Policy Forum EVA, Helsinki

Jiri Kunert, Chairman and Chief Executive Officer, Zivnostenska banka; President of the Czech Association of Banks, Prague

*Count Otto Lambsdorff, Partner, Wessing Lawyers, Düsseldorf; Chairman, Friedrich Naumann Foundation, Berlin; former Member of German Bundestag; Honorary Chairman, Free Democratic Party; former Federal Minister of Economy; former President of the Liberal International; Honorary European Chairman, The Trilateral Commission, Paris

Kurt Lauk, Member of the European Parliament (EPP Group-CDU); Chairman, Globe Capital Partners, Stuttgart; President, Economic Council of the CDU Party, Berlin; former Member of the Board, DaimlerChrysler, Stuttgart

Anne Lauvergeon, Chairperson of the Executive Board, Areva; Chairperson and Chief Executive Officer, Cogema, Paris

Pierre Lellouche, Member of the French National Assembly and of the Foreign Affairs Committee, Paris; President, NATO Parliamentary Assembly

Enrico Letta, Member of the European Parliament (ALDE Group), Brussels; Secretary General, AREL; Vice President, Aspen Institute; former Minister of European Affairs, Industry, and of Industry and International Trade, Rome

André Leysen, Honorary Chairman, Gevaert, Antwerp; Honorary Chairman, Agfa-Gevaert Group

Marianne Lie, Director General, Norwegian Shipowner's Association, Oslo

Count Maurice Lippens, Chairman, Fortis, Brussels

Helge Lund, Chief Executive Officer of the Norwegian Oil Company, Statoil, Oslo

*Cees Maas, Vice Chairman and Chief Financial Officer of the ING Group, Amsterdam; former Treasurer of the Dutch Government

Peter Mandelson, Member of the European Commission (Trade), Brussels; former Member of the British Parliament; former Secretary of State to Northern Ireland and for Trade and Industry

Abel Matutes, Chairman, Empresas Matutes, Ibiza; former Member of the European Commission, Brussels; former Minister of Foreign Affairs, Madrid

Francis Maude, Member of the British Parliament; Chairman of the Conservative Party; Director, Benfield Group; former Shadow Foreign Secretary, London

Vasco de Mello, Vice Chairman, José de Mello SGPS, Lisbon

Joao de Menezes Ferreira, Chairman and Chief Executive Officer, ECO-SOROS, Lisbon; former Member of the Portuguese Parliament

Peter Mitterbauer, Honorary President, The Federation of Austrian Industry, Vienna; President and Chief Executive Officer, MIBA, Laakirchen

Dominique Moïsi, Special Advisor to the Director General of the French Institute for International Relations (IFRI), Paris

Luca Cordero di Montezemolo, Chairman, Fiat, Turin; Chairman, Confindustria (Italian Confederation of Industry), Rome

Mario Monti, President and Professor Emeritus, Bocconi University, Milan; Chairman of BRUEGEL and of ECAS, Brussels; former Member of the European Commission (Competition Policy)

Sir Mark Moody-Stuart, Chairman, Anglo American; former Chairman, Royal Dutch/Shell Group, London

4

Klaus-Peter Müller, Chairman of the Board of Managing Directors, Commerzbank, Frankfurt-am-Main; President, Association of German Banks (BDB), Berlin

Heinrich Neisser, former President, Politische Akademie, Vienna; Professor of Political Sciences at Innsbruck University; former Member of Austrian Parliament and Second President of the National Assembly

Harald Norvik, Chairman and Partner, ECON Management; former President and Chief Executive, Statoil, Oslo

Arend Oetker, President, German Council on Foreign Relations (DGAP); Vice Chairman, Federation of German Industries; Managing Director, Dr. Arend Oetker Holding, Berlin

*Andrzej Olechowski, Leader, Civic Platform; former Chairman, Bank Handlowy; former Minister of Foreign Affairs and of Finance, Warsaw

Richard Olver, Chairman, BAE Systems, London

Janusz Palikot, Chairman of the Supervisory Board, Polmos Lublin; Vice President, Polish Confederation of Private Employers; Co-owner, Publishing House slowo/obraz terytoria; Member of the Board of Directors, Polish Business Council, Warsaw

Dimitry Panitza, Founding Chairman, The Free and Democratic Bulgaria Foundation; Founder and Chairman, The Bulgarian School of Politics, Sofia

Lucas Papademos, Vice President, European Central Bank, Frankfurt-am-Main; former Governor of the Bank of Greece

Schelto Patijn, Member of the Supervisory Board of the Schiphol Group and Amsterdam RAI; former Mayor of the City of Amsterdam, The Netherlands

Lord Patten of Barnes, Chancellor of the University of Oxford; Chairman, International Crisis Group, Brussels; former Member of the European Commission (External Relations), Brussels; former Governor of Hong Kong; former Member of the British Cabinet, London

Volker Perthes, Director, SWP (German Institute for International and Security Affairs), Berlin

Dieter Pfundt, Personally Liable Partner, Sal. Oppenheim Bank, Frankfurt

Josep Piqué, Chairman of the Popular Party of Catalunya, Barcelona; Member of the Parliament of Catalunya; Member of the Spanish Senate; former Minister of Foreign Affairs

Benoît Potier, Chairman of the Management Board, L'Air Liquide, Paris

Alessandro Profumo, Chief Executive Officer, UniCredito Italiano, Milan

Luigi Ramponi, Member of Parliament; Chairman of the Defence Committee of the Chamber of Deputies, Rome; former Deputy Chief of the Defence Staff (Italian Army)

Wanda Rapaczynska, President of the Management Board, Agora, Warsaw

Heinz Riesenhuber, Member of the German Bundestag; former Federal Minister of Research and Technology, Berlin; Chairman of the Supervisory Boards of Kabel Deutschland and of Evotec

Gianfelice Rocca, Chairman, Techint Group of Companies, Milan; Vice President, Confindustria

H. Onno Ruding, Chairman, Centre for European Policy Studies (CEPS), Brussels; former Vice Chairman, Citibank; former Dutch Minister of Finance

Anthony Ruys, former Chairman of the Executive Board, Heineken, Amsterdam

Ferdinando Salleo, Vice Chairman, MCC Mediocredito Centrale, Rome; former Ambassador to the United States

Jacques Santer, Honorary State Minister, Luxembourg; former Member of the European Parliament; former President of the European Commission; former Prime Minister of Luxembourg

*Silvio Scaglia, Chairman, Fastweb, Milan; former Managing Director, Omnitel

Paolo Scaroni, Chief Executive Officer, ENEL, Rome

*Guido Schmidt-Chiari, Chairman, Constantia Group; former Chairman, Creditanstalt Bankverein, Vienna

Henning Schulte-Noelle, Chairman of the Supervisory Board, Allianz, Munich

Prince Charles of Schwarzenberg, Founder and Director, Nadace Bohemiae, Prague; Member of the Czech Senate; former Chancellor to President Havel; former President of the International Helsinki Federation for Human Rights

5

*Carlo Secchi, Professor of European Economic Policy, Bocconi University, Milan; former Member of the Italian Senate and of the European Parliament

*Tøger Seidenfaden, Editor-in-Chief, *Politiken*, Copenhagen

Maurizio Sella, Chairman, Banca Sella, Biella; Chairman, Association of Italian Banks (A.B.I.), Rome; Chairman, Finanziaria Bansel

Slawomir S. Sikora, Chief Executive Officer and Citigroup Country Officer for Poland, Bank Handlowy w Warszawie, Warsaw

Stefano Silvestri, President, Institute for International Affairs (IAI), Rome; Commentator, *Il Sole 24 Ore*; former Under Secretary of State for Defence, Italy

Lord Simon of Highbury, Member of the House of Lords; Advisory Director of Unilever, Morgan Stanley Europe and LEK; former Minister for Trade & Competitiveness in Europe; former Chairman of BP, London

Nicholas Soames, Member of the British Parliament, London

Sir Martin Sorrell, Chief Executive Officer, WPP Group, London

Myles Staunton, Former Member of the Irish Senate & of the Dail; Consultant, Westport, Co. Mayo

*Thorvald Stoltenberg, President, Norwegian Red Cross, Oslo; former Co-Chairman (UN) of the Steering Committee of the International Conference on Former Yugoslavia; former Foreign Minister of Norway; former UN High Commissioner for Refugees

*Petar Stoyanov, President, Centre for Political Dialogue, Sofia; former President of Bulgaria

Peter Straarup, Chairman of the Executive Board, Danske Bank, Copenhagen; Chairman, the Danish Bankers Association

*Peter Sutherland, Chairman, BP p.l.c.; Chairman, Goldman Sachs International; Special Representative of the United Nations Secretary-General for Migrations; former Director General, GATT/WTO; former Member of the European Commission; former Attorney General of Ireland

Björn Svedberg, former Chairman and Chief Executive Officer, Ericsson, Stockholm; former President and Group Chief Executive, Skandinaviska Enskilda Banken

Péter Székely, Chairman and Chief Executive Officer, Transelektro, Budapest; President, Confederation of Hungarian Employers' Organisations for International Co-operation (CEHIC); Vice President, Confederation of Hungarian Employers and Industrialists

Pavel Telicka, Partner, BXL-Consulting, Prague

Jean-Philippe Thierry, Chairman and Chief Executive Officer, AGF (Assurances Générales de France), Paris

Marco Tronchetti Provera, Chairman, Telecom Italia; Chairman and Chief Executive Officer, Pirelli & C., Milan

Elsbeth Tronstad, Executive Vice President, ABB, Oslo

Loukas Tsoukalis, Special Adviser to the President of the European Commission; Professor at the University of Athens and the College of Europe; President of the Hellenic Foundation for European and Foreign Policy (ELIAMEP), Athens

Mario Vargas Llosa, Writer and Member of the Royal Spanish Academy, Madrid

*George Vassiliou, former Head of the Negotiating Team for the Accession of Cyprus to the European Union; former President of the Republic of Cyprus; former Member of Parliament and Leader of United Democrats, Nicosia

Franco Venturini, Foreign Correspondent, *Corriere della Sera*, Rome

Friedrich Verzetnitsch, Member of Austrian Parliament; President, Austrian Federation of Trade Unions, Vienna; President, European Trade Union Confederation (ETUC)

*Marko Voljc, General Manager of Central Europe Directorate, KBC Bank Insurance Holding, Brussels; former Chief Executive Officer, Nova Ljubljanska Banka, Ljubljana

Alexandr Vondra, Managing Director of the Prague Office, Dutko Group Companies; former Czech Deputy Minister of Foreign Affairs

Joris Voorhoeve, Member of the Council of State; former Member of the Dutch Parliament; former Minister of Defence, The Hague

6

Panagis Vourloumis, Chairman and Chief Executive Officer, Hellenic Telecommunications Organization (O.T.E.), Athens

Marcus Wallenberg, Chairman of the Board, Skandinaviska Enskilda Banken (SEB), Stockholm

*****Serge Weinberg**, Member and Chairman-designate of the Supervisory Board, Accor; Chairman, Weinberg Capital Partners; former Chairman of the Management Board, Pinault-Printemps-Redoute; former President, Institute of International and Strategic Studies (IRIS), Paris

Heinrich Weiss, Chairman, SMS, Düsseldorf; former President, Federation of German Industries, Berlin

Nout Wellink, President, Dutch Central Bank, Amsterdam

Arne Wessberg, Director General, YLE (Finnish Broadcasting Company) and Director General, YLE Group (YLE and Digits Oy), Helsinki; President, European Broadcasting Union (EBU)

*****Norbert Wieczorek**, former Member of the German Bundestag & Deputy Chairman of the SPD Parliamentary Group, Berlin

Hans Wijers, Chairman and Chief Executive Officer, Akzo Nobel, Arnhem

Otto Wolff von Amerongen, Honorary Chairman, East Committee of the German Industry; Chairman and Chief Executive Officer, Otto Wolff Industrieberatung und Beteiligung, Cologne

Emilio Ybarra, former Chairman, Banco Bilbao-Vizcaya, Madrid

Former Members in Public Service

John Bruton, European Union Ambassador & Head, Delegation of the European Commission to the United States

Lene Espersen, Minister of Justice, Denmark

Pedro Solbes, Deputy Prime Minister and Minister of the Economy and Finances, Spain

Harri Tiido, Ambassador of Estonia and Head of the Estonian Mission to NATO, Brussels

Karsten D. Voigt, Coordinator of German-American Cooperation, Federal Foreign Ministry, Germany

NORTH AMERICAN GROUP

Madeleine K. Albright, Principal, The Albright Group LLC, Washington, DC; former U.S. Secretary of State

Graham Allison, Director, Belfer Center for Science and International Affairs, Harvard University, Cambridge, MA

G. Allen Andreas, Chairman and Chief Executive, Archer Daniels Midland Company, Decatur, IL

Michael H. Armacost, Shorenstein Distinguished Fellow, Asia/Pacific Research Center, Stanford University, Hillsborough, CA; former President, The Brookings Institution; former U.S. Ambassador to Japan; former U.S. Under Secretary of State for Political Affairs

Charlene Barshefsky, Senior International Partner, Wilmer, Cutler & Pickering, Washington, DC; former U.S. Trade Representative

Alan R. Batkin, Vice Chairman, Kissinger Associates, New York, NY

Doug Bereuter, President, The Asia Foundation, San Francisco, CA; former Member, U.S. House of Representatives

*****C. Fred Bergsten**, Director, Institute for International Economics, Washington, DC; former U.S. Assistant Secretary of the Treasury for International Affairs

Catherine Bertini, Professor of Public Administration, Maxwell School of Citizenship and Public Affairs, Syracuse University, Syracuse, NY; former Under-Secretary-General for Management, United Nations

7

Dennis C. Blair, USN (Ret.), President and Chief Executive Officer, Institute for Defense Analyses, Alexandria, VA; former Commander in Chief, U.S. Pacific Command

Herminio Blanco Mendoza, Private Office of Herminio Blanco, Mexico City, NL; former Mexican Secretary of Commerce and Industrial Development

Geoffrey T. Boisi, Chairman & Senior Partner, Roundtable Investment Partners LLC, New York, NY; former Vice Chairman, JPMorgan Chase, New York, NY

Stephen W. Bosworth, Dean, Fletcher School of Law and Diplomacy, Tufts University, Medford, MA; former U.S. Ambassador to the Republic of Korea

David G. Bradley, Chairman, Atlantic Media Company, Washington, DC

Harold Brown, Counselor, Center for Strategic and International Studies, Washington, DC; General Partner, Warburg Pincus & Company, New York, NY; former U.S. Secretary of Defense

*Zbigniew Brzezinski, Counselor, Center for Strategic and International Studies, Washington, DC; Robert Osgood Professor of American Foreign Affairs, Paul Nitze School of Advanced International Studies, Johns Hopkins University; former U.S. Assistant to the President for National Security Affairs

Louis C. Camilleri, Chairman and Chief Executive Officer, Altria Group, Inc., New York, NY

Raymond Chrétien, Strategic Advisor, Fasken Martineau DuMoulin LLP, Montreal, QC; Chairman of the Board of Directors of the Center for International Studies of the University of Montreal; former Associate Under-Secretary of State of External Affairs; former Ambassador of Canada to the Congo, Belgium, Mexico, the United States and France

William T. Coleman III, Founder, Chairman, and Chief Executive Officer, Cassatt Corporation; Founder, former Chairman and CEO and Member, Board of Directors, BEA Systems, Inc., San Jose, CA

William T. Coleman, Jr., Senior Partner and the Senior Counselor, O'Melveny & Myers, Washington, DC; former U.S. Secretary of Transportation

Timothy C. Collins, Senior Managing Director and Chief Executive Officer, Ripplewood Holdings, New York, NY

Richard N. Cooper, Maurits C. Boas Professor of International Economics, Harvard University, Cambridge, MA; former Chairman, U.S. National Intelligence Council; former U.S. Under Secretary of State for Economic Affairs

E. Gerald Corrigan, Managing Director, Goldman, Sachs & Co., New York, NY; former President, Federal Reserve Bank of New York

Michael J. Critelli, Chairman and Chief Executive Officer, Pitney Bowes Inc., Stamford, CT

Lee Brooks Cullum, Columnist, *Dallas Morning News*, Dallas, TX

Gerald L. Curtis, Burgess Professor of Political Science, Columbia University, New York, NY; Visiting Professor, Graduate Research Institute for Policy Studies, Tokyo

Douglas Daft, former Chairman and Chief Executive Officer, The Coca Cola Company, Atlanta, GA

Lynn Davis, Senior Political Scientist, The RAND Corporation, Arlington, VA; former U.S. Under Secretary of State for Arms Control and International Security

Lodewijk J. R. de Vink, Chairman, Global Health Care Partners, Peapack, NJ; former Chairman, President, and Chief Executive Officer, Warner-Lambert Company

Arthur A. DeFehr, President and Chief Executive Officer, Palliser Furniture, Winnipeg, MB

André Desmarais, President and Co-Chief Executive Officer, Power Corporation of Canada, Montréal, QC; Deputy Chairman, Power Financial Corporation

John M. Deutch, Institute Professor, Massachusetts Institute of Technology, Cambridge, MA; former Director of Central Intelligence; former U.S. Deputy Secretary of Defense

Jamie Dimon, President and Chief Operating Officer, JPMorgan Chase, New York, NY

Peter C. Dobell, Founding Director, Parliamentary Centre, Ottawa, ON

Wendy K. Dobson, Professor and Director, Institute for International Business, Rotman School of Management, University of Toronto, Toronto, ON; former Canadian Associate Deputy Minister of Finance

8

Kenneth M. Duberstein, Chairman and Chief Executive Officer, The Duberstein Group, Washington, DC

Robert Eckert, Chairman and Chief Executive Officer, Mattel, Inc., El Segundo, CA

Jeffrey Epstein, President, J. Epstein & Company, Inc., New York, NY; President, N.A. Property, Inc.

Dianne Feinstein, Member (D-CA), U.S. Senate

Martin S. Feldstein, George F. Baker Professor of Economics, Harvard University, Cambridge, MA; President and Chief Executive Officer, National Bureau of Economic Research; former U.S.Chairman, President's Council of Economic Advisors

Roger W. Ferguson, Jr., Vice Chairman, Board of Governors, Federal Reserve System, Washington, DC

Stanley Fischer, Governor of the Bank of Israel, Jerusalem; former President, Citigroup International and Vice Chairman, Citgroup, New York, NY; former First Deputy Managing Director, International Monetary Fund

Richard W. Fisher, President and Chief Executive Officer, Federal Reserve Bank of Dallas, Dallas, TX; former U.S. Deputy Trade Representative

*Thomas S. Foley, Partner, Akin Gump Strauss Hauer & Feld, Washington, DC; former U.S. Ambassador to Japan; former Speaker of the U.S. House of Representatives; North American Chairman, Trilateral Commission

Michael B.G. Froman, Managing Director, Citigroup Alternative Investments, Citigroup Inc., New York, NY

Francis Fukuyama, Bernard L. Schwartz Professor International Political Economy, Paul H. Nitze School of Advanced International Studies, The Johns Hopkins University, Washington, DC

Dionisio Garza Medina, Chairman of the Board and Chief Executive Officer, ALFA, Garza Garcia, NL

Richard A. Gephardt, former Member (D-MO), U.S. House of Representatives

David Gergen, Professor of Public Service, John F. Kennedy School of Government, Harvard University, Cambridge, MA; Editor-at-Large, *U.S. News and World Report*

Peter C. Godsoe, Chairman of Fairmont Hotels & Resorts; Retired Chairman and Chief Executive Officer of Scotiabank, Toronto, ON

*Allan E. Gotlieb, Senior Advisor, Stikeman Elliott, Toronto, ON; Chairman, Sotheby's, Canada; former Canadian Ambassador to the United States; North American Deputy Chairman, Trilateral Commission

Donald E. Graham, Chairman and Chief Executive Officer, The Washington Post Company, Washington, DC

Jeffrey W. Greenberg, Private Investor, New York, NY; former Chairman and Chief Executive Officer, Marsh & McLennan Companies

Maurice R. Greenberg, Chairman and Chief Executive Officer, C. V. Starr & Company, New York; former Chairman, American International Group, Inc.

Richard N. Haass, President, Council on Foreign Relations, New York, NY; former Director, Policy Planning, U. S. Department of State; former Director of Foreign Policy Studies, The Brookings Institution

John J. Hamre, President, Center for Strategic and International Studies, Washington, DC; former U.S. Deputy Secretary of Defense and Under Secretary of Defense (Comptroller)

William A. Haseltine, Chairman and Chief Executive Officer, Haseltine Associates, Washington, DC; President, William A. Haseltine Foundation for Medical Sciences and the Arts; former Chairman and Chief Executive Officer, Human Genome Sciences, Inc., Rockville, MD

Charles B. Heck, Senior Adviser and former North American Director, Trilateral Commission, New Canaan, CT

*Carla A. Hills, Chairman and Chief Executive Officer, Hills & Company, International Consultants, Washington, DC; former U.S. Trade Representative; former U.S. Secretary of Housing and Urban Development

Richard Holbrooke, Vice Chairman, Perseus LLC, New York, NY; Counselor, Council on Foreign Relations; former U.S. Ambassador to the United Nations; former Vice Chairman of Credit Suisse

First Boston Corporation; former U.S. Assistant Secretary of State for European and Canadian Affairs; former U.S. Assistant Secretary of State for East Asian and Pacific Affairs; and former U.S. Ambassador to Germany

Karen Elliott House, Senior Vice President, Dow Jones & Company, and Publisher, *The Wall Street Journal*, New York, NY

Alejandro Junco de la Vega, President and Director, Grupo Reforma, Monterrey, NL

Robert Kagan, Senior Associate, Carnegie Endowment for International Peace, Washington, DC

Arnold Kanter, Principal and Founding Member, The Scowcroft Group, Washington, DC; former U.S. Under Secretary of State

Charles R. Kaye, Co-President, Warburg Pincus LLC, New York, NY

Henry A. Kissinger, Chairman, Kissinger Associates, Inc., New York, NY; former U.S. Secretary of State; former U.S. Assistant to the President for National Security Affairs

Michael Klein, Chief Executive Officer, Global Banking, Citigroup Inc.; Vice Chairman, Citibank International PLC; New York, NY

Steven E. Koonin, Chief Scientist, BP, London, UK

Enrique Krauze, General Director, Editorial Clio Libros y Videos, S.A. de C.V., Mexico City, DF

Robert Lane, Chief Executive Officer, Deere & Co., Moline, IL

Jim Leach, Member (R-IA), U.S. House of Representatives

Gerald M. Levin, Chief Executive Officer Emeritus, AOL Time Warner, Inc., New York, NY

Winston Lord, Co-Chairman of Overseeers and former Co-Chairman of the Board, International Rescue Committee, New York, NY; former U.S. Assistant Secretary of State for East Asian and Pacific Affairs; former U.S. Ambassador to China

E. Peter Lougheed, Senior Partner, Bennett Jones, Barristers & Solicitors, Calgary, AB; former Premier of Alberta

*Roy MacLaren, former Canadian High Commissioner to the United Kingdom; former Canadian Minister of International Trade; Toronto, ON

John A. MacNaughton, former President and Chief Executive Officer, Canada Pension Plan Investment Board, Toronto, ON

Antonio Madero, Chairman of the Board and Chief Executive Officer, San Luis Corporacion, S.A. de C.V., Mexico City, DF

*Sir Deryck C. Maughan, Managing Director and Chairman, KKR Asia, Kohlberg Kravis Roberts & Co., New York, NY; former Vice Chairman, Citigroup

Jay Mazur, President Emeritus, UNITE (Union of Needletrades, Industrial and Textile Employees); Vice Chairman, Amalgamated Bank of New York; and President, ILGWU's 21st Century Heritage Foundation, New York, NY

Hugh L. McColl, Jr., Chairman, McColl Brothers Lockwood, Charlotte, NC; former Chairman and Chief Executive Officer, Bank of America Corporation

Marc H. Morial, President and Chief Executive Officer, National Urban League, New York, NY; former Mayor, New Orleans, LA

Anne M. Mulcahy, Chairman and CEO, Xerox Corporation, Stamford, CT

*Indra K. Nooyi, President and Chief Financial Officer, PepsiCo, Inc., Purchase, NY

*Joseph S. Nye, Jr., Distinguished Service Professor at Harvard University, John F. Kennedy School of Government, Harvard University, Cambridge, MA; former Dean, John F. Kennedy School of Government; former U.S. Assistant Secretary of Defense for International Security Affairs

David J. O'Reilly, Chairman and Chief Executive Officer, Chevron Corporation, San Ramon, CA

Richard N. Perle, Resident Fellow, American Enterprise Institute, Washington, DC; member and former Chairman, Defense Policy Board, U.S. Department of Defense; former U.S. Assistant Secretary of Defense for International Security Policy

Thomas R. Pickering, Senior Vice President, International Relations, The Boeing Company, Arlington, VA; former U.S. Under Secretary of State for Political Affairs; former U.S. Ambassador to the

Russian Federation, India, Israel, El Salvador, Nigeria, the Hashemite Kingdom of Jordan, and the United Nations

Joseph W. Ralston, USAF (Ret)., Vice Chairman, The Cohen Group, Washington, DC; former Commander, U.S. European Command, and Supreme Allied Commander NATO; former Vice Chairman, Joint Chiefs of Staff, U.S. Department of Defense

Charles B. Rangel, Member (D-NY), U.S. House of Representatives

Susan Rice, Senior Fellow, Brookings Institution, Washington, DC; former Assistant Secretary of State for African Affairs; former Special Assistant to the President and Senior Director for African Affairs, National Security Council

Hartley Richardson, President and Chief Executive Officer, James Richardson & Sons, Ltd., Winnipeg, MB

Joseph E. Robert, Jr., Chairman and Chief Executive Office, J.E. Robert Companies, McLean, VA

John D. Rockefeller IV, Member (D-WV), U.S. Senate

Kenneth Rogoff, Professor of Economics and Director, Center for International Development, Harvard University, Cambridge, MA; former Chief Economist and Director, Research Department, International Monetary Fund, Washington, DC

Charles Rose, Host of the Charlie Rose Show and Charlie Rose Special Edition, PBS, New York, NY

David M. Rubenstein, Co-founder and Managing Director, The Carlyle Group, Washington, DC

Luis Rubio, President, Center of Research for Development (CIDAC), Mexico City, DF

Jaime Serra, Chairman, SAI Consulting, Mexico City, DF; former Mexican Minister of Trade and Industry

Dinakar Singh, Founder and Chief Executive Officer, TPG-Axon Capital, New York, NY; former Co-head, Principal Strategies Department, Goldman Sachs

Anne-Marie Slaughter, Dean, Woodrow Wilson School of Public and International Affairs, Princeton University, Princeton, NJ

Gordon Smith, Director, Centre for Global Studies, University of Victoria, Victoria, BC; Chairman, Board of Governors, International Development Research Centre; former Canadian Deputy Minister of Foreign Affairs and Personal Representative of the Prime Minister to the Economic Summit

Donald R. Sobey, Chairman Emeritus, Empire Company Ltd., Halifax, NS

Ronald D. Southern, Chairman, ATCO Group, Calgary, AB

James B. Steinberg, Dean, LBJ School of Public Affairs, University of Texas, Austin, TX; former Vice President and Director of the Foreign Policy Studies Program, The Brookings Institution, Washington, DC; former U.S. Deputy National Security Advisor

Jessica Stern, Lecturer in Public Policy, Belfer Center for Science and International Affairs, Harvard University, Cambridge, MA

Barbara Stymiest, Chief Operating Officer, RBC Financial Group, Toronto, ON

Lawrence H. Summers, President, Harvard University, Cambridge, MA; former U.S. Secretary of the Treasury

John J. Sweeney, President, AFL-CIO, Washington, DC

Strobe Talbott, President, The Brookings Institution, Washington, DC; former U.S. Deputy Secretary of State

Luis Tellez, Managing Director, The Carlyle Group, Mexico City, DF; former Executive Vice President, Sociedad de Fomento Industrial (DESC); former Mexican Minister of Energy

George J. Tenet, Distinguished Professor, Edmund A. Walsh School of Foreign Service, Georgetown University, Washington, DC; former U.S. Director of Central Intelligence

John Thain, Chief Executive Officer, New York Stock Exchange, Inc.; former President and Co-Chief Operating Officer, Goldman Sachs & Co., New York, NY

G. Richard Thoman, Managing Partner, Corporate Perspectives and Adjunct Professor, Columbia University, New York, NY; formerly President and CEO, Xerox Corporation; formerly CFO and N° 2 officer, IBM Corporation

11

*Paul A. Volcker, former Chairman, Wolfensohn & Co., Inc., New York; Frederick H. Schultz Professor Emeritus, International Economic Policy, Princeton University; former Chairman, Board of Governors, U.S. Federal Reserve System; Honorary North American Chairman and former North American Chairman, Trilateral Commission

William H. Webster, Senior Partner, Milbank, Tweed, Hadley & McCloy LLP, Washington, DC; former U.S. Director of Central Intelligence; former Director, U.S. Federal Bureau of Investigation; former Judge of the U.S. Court of Appeals for the Eighth Circuit

Fareed Zakaria, Editor, Newsweek International, New York, NY

*Lorenzo H. Zambrano, Chairman of the Board and Chief Executive Officer, CEMEX, Monterrey, NL; North American Deputy Chairman, Trilateral Commission

Ernesto Zedillo, Director, Yale Center for the Study of Globalization, Yale University, New Haven, CT; former President of Mexico

Mortimer B. Zuckerman, Chairman and Editor-in-Chief, *U.S. News & World Report*, New York, NY

Robert S. McNamara, Lifetime Trustee, Trilateral Commission, Washington, DC; former President, World Bank; former U.S. Secretary of Defense; former President, Ford Motor Company.

David Rockefeller, Founder, Honorary Chairman, and Lifetime Trustee, Trilateral Commission, New York, NY

Former Members In Public Service

Rona Ambrose, Canadian Minister of the Environment
Richard B. Cheney, Vice President of the United States
Paula J. Dobriansky, U.S. Under Secretary of State for Global Affairs
Bill Graham, Leader of the Opposition, Canadian House of Commons
Paul Wolfowitz, President, World Bank
Robert B. Zoellick, U.S. Deputy Secretary of State

PACIFIC ASIAN GROUP

Narongchai Akrasanee, Chairman, Seranee Holdings Co., Ltd., Bangkok

Ali Alatas, Advisor and Special Envoy of the President of the Republic of Indonesia; former Indonesian Minister for Foreign Affairs; Jakarta

Philip Burdon, former Chairman, Asia 2000 Foundation; New Zealand Chairman, APEC; former New Zealand Minister of Trade Negotiations; Wellington

Fujio Cho, President, Toyota Motor Corporation

Cho Suck-Rai, Chairman, Hyosung Corporation, Seoul

Chung Mong-Joon, Member, Korean National Assembly; Vice President, Federation Internationale de Football Association (FIFA); Seoul

Barry Desker, Director, Institute of Defence and Strategic Studies, Nanyang Techonological University, Singapore

Takashi Ejiri, Attorney at Law, Asahi Koma Law Office

Jesus P. Estanislao, President and Chief Executive Officer, Institute of Corporate Directors/Institute of Solidarity in Asia, Manila; former Philippine Minister of Finance

Hugh Fletcher, Director, Fletcher Building, Ltd., Auckland; former Chief Executive Officer, Fletcher Challenge

Hiroaki Fujii, Advisor, The Japan Foundation; former Japanese Ambassador to the United Kingdom

Shinji Fukukawa, Executive Advisor, Dentsu Inc.

12

Yoichi Funabashi, Chief Diplomatic Correspondent and Columnist, *The Asahi Shimbun*
Carrillo Gantner, Vice President, The Myer Foundation; Melbourne
Ross Garnaut, Professor of Economics, Research School of Pacific and Asian Studies, Australian National University, Canberra
*****Toyoo Gyohten**, President, Institute for International Monetary Affairs; Senior Advisor, The Bank of Tokyo-Mitsubishi, Ltd.
Han Sung-Joo, President, Seoul Forum for International Affairs; Professor, International Relations, Ilmin International Relations Institute, Korea University, Seoul; former Korean Minister of Foreign Affairs; former Korean Ambassador to the United States;
*****Stuart Harris**, Professor of International Relations, Research School of Pacific and Asian Studies, Australian National University, Canberra; former Australian Vice Minister of Foreign Affairs
Azman Hashim, Chairman, AmBank Group, Kuala Lumpur
John R. Hewson, Member, Advisory Council, ABN AMRO Australia, Sydney
Ernest M. Higa, President and CEO, Higa Industries
Shintaro Hori, Managing Partner, Bain & Company Japan, Inc.
Murray Horn, Managing Director, Institutional Banking, ANZ (NZ) Ltd., Sydney; Chairman, ANZ Investment Bank; former Parliament Secretary, New Zealand Treasury
Hyun Hong-Choo, Senior Partner, Kim & Chang, Seoul; former Korean Ambassador to the United Nations and to the United States; Seoul
Hyun Jae-Hyun, Chairman, Tong Yang Group, Seoul
Shin'ichi Ichimura, Counselor, International Centre for the Study of East Asian Development, Kitakyushu
Nobuyuki Idei, Chief Corporate Advisor, Sony Corporation
Takeo Inokuchi, Chairman and Chief Executive Officer, Mitsui Sumitomo Insurance Company, Ltd.
Noriyuki Inoue, Chairman and CEO, Daikin Industries, Ltd.
Rokuro Ishikawa, Honorary Chairman, Kajima Corporation
Motoo Kaji, Professor Emeritus, University of Tokyo
Kasem Kasemsri, Honorary Chairman, Thailand-U.S. Business Council, Bangkok; Chairman, Advisory Board, Chart Thai Party; Chairman, Thai-Malaysian Association; former Deputy Prime Minister of Thailand
Koichi Kato, Member, Japanese House of Representatives; former Secretary-General, Liberal Democratic Party
Trevor Kennedy, Chairman, Oil Search, Ltd.; Chairman, Cypress Lakes Group, Ltd.; Sydney
K. Kesavapany, Director, Institute of Southeast Asian Studies, Singapore
Kim Kihwan, International Advisor, Goldman Sachs, Seoul; former Korean Ambassador-at-Large for Economic Affairs
*****Kim Kyung-Won**, President Emeritus, Seoul Forum for International Affairs, Seoul; former Korean Ambassador to the United States and the United Nations; Advisor, Kim & Chang Law Office; Pacific Asia Deputy Chairman, Trilateral Commission
Kakutaro Kitashiro, Chairman of the Board, IBM Japan, Ltd.
Shoichiro Kobayashi, Senior Advisor, Kansai Electric Power Company, Ltd.
*****Yotaro Kobayashi**, Chairman of the Board, Fuji Xerox Co., Ltd.; Pacific Asia Chairman, Trilateral Commission
Akira Kojima, Chairman, Japan Center for Economic Research (JCER)
Koo John, Chairman, LS Cable Ltd.; Chairman, LS Industrial Systems Co.; Seoul
Kenji Kosaka, Member, Japanese House of Representatives
*****Lee Hong-Koo**, Chairman, Seoul Forum for International Affairs, Seoul; former Korean Prime Minister; former Korean Ambassador to the United Kingdom and the United States
Lee In-ho, University Professor, Myongji University, Seoul; former President, Korea Foundation; former Korean Ambassador to Finland and Russia
Lee Jay Y., Vice President, Samsung Electronics Co. Ltd., Seoul

13

Lee Kyungsook Choi, President, Sookmyung Women's University, Seoul
Adrianto Machribie, Chairman, PT Freeport Indonesia, Jakarta
*****Minoru Makihara**, Senior Corporate Advisor, Mitsubishi Corporation
Hiroshi Mikitani, Chairman, President and Chief Executive Officer, Rakuten, Inc.
Yoshihiko Miyauchi, Chairman and Chief Executive Officer, ORIX Corporation
Isamu Miyazaki, Special Advisor, Daiwa Institute of Research, Ltd.; former Director-General of the
    Japanese Economic Planning Agency
*****Kiichi Miyazawa**, former Prime Minister of Japan; former Finance Minister; former Member, House of
    Representatives
Yuzaburo Mogi, President and Chief Executive Officer, Kikkoman Corporation
Mike Moore, former Director-General, World Trade Organization, Geneva; Member, New Zealand Privy
    Council, Auckland; former Prime Minister of New Zealand
Moriyuki Motono, President, Foreign Affairs Society; former Japanese Ambassador to France
Jiro Murase, Managing Partner, Bingham McCutchen Murase, New York
*****Minoru Murofushi**, Counselor, ITOCHU Corporation
Masao Nakamura, President and Chief Executive Officer, NTT Docomo Inc.
Masashi Nishihara, President, National Defense Academy
Taizo Nishimuro, Advisor, former Chairman and Chief Executive Officer, Toshiba Corporation
Roberto F. de Ocampo, President, Asian Institute of Management; former Secretary of Finance, Manila
Toshiaki Ogasawara, Chairman and Publisher, The Japan Times Ltd.; Chairman, Nifco Inc.
Sadako Ogata, President, Japan International Cooperation Agency (JICA); former United Nations High
    Commissioner for Refugees
*****Shijuro Ogata**, former Deputy Governor, Japan Development Bank; former Deputy Governor for
    International Relations, Bank of Japan; Pacific Asia Deputy Chairman, Trilateral Commission
Sozaburo Okamatsu, Chairman, Research Institute of Economy, Trade & Industry (RIETI)
*****Yoshio Okawara**, President, Institute for International Policy Studies; former Japanese Ambassador to
    the United States
Yoichi Okita, Professor, National Graduate Institute for Policy Studies
Ariyoshi Okumura, Chairman, Lotus Corporate Advisory, Inc.
Anand Panyarachun, Chairman, Thai Industrial Federation; Chairman, Saha-Union Public Company,
    Ltd.; former Prime Minister of Thailand; Bangkok
Ryu Jin Roy, Chairman and Chief Executive Officer, Poongsan Corp., Seoul
Eisuke Sakakibara, Professor, Keio University; former Japanese Vice Minister of Finance for
    International Affairs
SaKong Il, Chairman and Chief Executive Officer, Institute for Global Economics, Seoul; former Korean
    Minister of Finance
Yukio Satoh, President, The Japan Institute of International Affairs; former Japanese Ambassador to the
    United Nations
Sachio Semmoto, Chief Executive Officer, eAccess, Ltd.
Masahide Shibusawa, President, Shibusawa Ei'ichi Memorial Foundation
Seiichi Shimada, President and Chief Executive Officer, Nihon Unisys, Ltd.
Yasuhisa Shiozaki, Member, Japanese House of Representatives; former Parliamentary Vice Minister for
    Finance
Arifin Siregar, International Advisor, Goldman Sachs (Pacific Asia) LLC; former Ambassador of
    Indonesia to the United States; Jakarta
Noordin Sopiee, Chairman and Chief Executive Officer, Institute of Strategic and International Studies,
    Kuala Lumpur
Suh Kyung-Bae, President and Chief Executive Officer, Amore Pacific Corp., Seoul
Tsuyoshi Takagi, President, The Japanese Foundation of Textile, Chemical, Food, Commercial, Service
    and General Workers' Unions (UI ZENSEN)
Keizo Takemi, Member, Japanese House of Councillors; former State Secretary for Foreign Affairs

14

Akihiko Tanaka, Director, Institute of Oriental Culture, University of Tokyo
Naoki Tanaka, President, The 21st Century Public Policy Institute
Sunjoto Tanudjaja, President and Chief Executive Officer, PT Great River International, Jakarta
Teh Kok Peng, President, GIC Special Investments Private Ltd., Singapore
Shuji Tomita, Senior Executive Vice President, NTT Communications Corporation
Kiyoshi Tsugawa, Executive Advisor & Member of Japan Advisory Board, Lehman Brothers Japan, Inc.; Chairman, ARAMARK ASIA
Junichi Ujiie, Chairman and Chief Executive Officer, Nomura Holdings, Inc.
Sarasin Viraphol, Executive Vice President, Charoen Pokphand Co., Ltd., Bangkok; former Deputy Permanent Secretary of Foreign Affairs of Thailand
Cesar E. A. Virata, Corporate Vice Chairman and Acting Chief Executive Officer, Rizal Commercial Banking Corporation (RCBC), Manila; former Prime Minister of Philippines
*__Jusuf Wanandi__, Member, Board of Trustees, Centre for Strategic and International Studies, Jakarta
Etsuya Washio, President, National Federation of Workers and Consumers Insurance Cooperatives (ZENROSAI); former President, Japanese Trade Union Confederation (RENGO)
Koji Watanabe, Senior Fellow, Japan Center for International Exchange; former Japanese Ambassador to Russia
Osamu Watanabe, Chairman, Japan External Trade Organization (JETRO)
Taizo Yakushiji, Executive Member, Council for Science and Technology Policy of the Cabinet Office of Japan; Executive Research Director, Institute for International Policy Studies
Tadashi Yamamoto, President, Japan Center for International Exchange; Pacific Asia Director, Trilateral Commission
Noriyuki Yonemura, Consultant, Fuji Xerox Co., Ltd.

Note: Those without city names are Japanese Members.
Korean names are shown with surname first.

Former Members in Public Service

Hong Seok-Hyun, Korean Ambassador to the United States
Masaharu Ikuta, Director General, Postal Services Corporation.
Yoriko Kawaguchi, Special Advisor to the Prime Minister of Japan
Hisashi Owada, Judge, International Court of Justice
Takeshi Kondo, President, Japan Highway Public Corporation (Nihon Doro Kodan)

PARTICIPANTS FROM OTHER AREAS
"Triennium Participants"

Abdlatif Al-Hamad, Director General and Chairman, Arab Fund for Economic and Social Development; former Kuwait Minister of Finance and Planning
André Azoulay, Adviser to H.M. King Mohammed VI, Rabat
Morris Chang, Chairman and Chief Executive Officer, Taiwan Semiconductor Manufacturing Co., Ltd., Taipei
Omar Davies, Member of the Jamaican Parliament and Minister of Finance and Planning, Kingston; former Director General, Planning Institute of Jamaica
Hüsnü Dogan, General Coordinator, Nurol Holding, Ankara; former Chairman of the Board of Trustees, Development Foundation of Turkey; former Minister of Defence

15

Alejandro Foxley, Member of the Senate and former Chairman of the Finance Committee and the Joint Budget Committee, Chilean Congress, Valparaiso

Jacob A. Frenkel, Vice Chairman, American International Group, Inc. and Chairman, AIG's Global Economic Strategies Group, New York, NY; Chairman and Chief Executive Officer, G-30; former Chairman, Merrill Lynch International; former Governor, Bank of Israel; former Economic Counselor and Director of Research, IMF; former Chairman, Board of Governors of the Inter-American Development Bank; former David Rockefeller Professor of Economics, University of Chicago

Victor K. Fung, Chairman, Li & Fung; Chairman, Prudential Asia Ltd., Hong Kong

Frene Ginwala, Speaker of the National Assembly, Parliament of the Republic of South Africa, Cape Town

H.R.H. Prince El Hassan bin Talal, President, The Club of Rome; Moderator of the World Conference on Religion and Peace; Chairman, Arab Thought Forum, Amman

Ricardo Hausman, Professor of the Practice of Economic Development, Center for International Development, John F. Kennedy School of Government, Harvard University, Cambridge, MA; former Chief Economist, Inter-American Development Bank; former Venezuelan Minister of Planning and Member of the Board of the Central Bank of Venezuela

Serhiy Holovaty, Member of the Supreme Rada; President of the Ukrainian Legal Foundation; former Minister of Justice, Kiev

Sergei Karaganov, Deputy Director, Institute of Europe, Russian Academy of Sciences; Chairman of the Presidium of the Council on Defense and Foreign Policy, Moscow

Jeffrey L.S. Koo, Chairman and Chief Executive Officer, Chinatrust Investment, Bank, Taipei

Richard Li, Chairman and Chief Executive Officer, Pacific Century Group Holdings Ltd., Hong Kong

Ricardo Lopez Murphy, Visiting Research Fellow, Latin American Economic Research Foundation, Buenos Aires; former Argentinian Finance Minister and Defence Minister

Itamar Rabinovich, President, Tel Aviv University, Tel Aviv; former Ambassador to the United States

Rüsdü Saracoglu, President of the Finance Group, Koç Holding; Chairman, Makro Consulting, Istanbul; former State Minister and Member of the Turkish Parliament; former Governor of the Central Bank of Turkey

Roberto Egydio Setubal, President and Chief Executive Officer, Banco Itaú S.A. and Banco Itaú Holding Financiera S.A., Sao Paulo

Stan Shih, Chairman and Chief Executive Officer, The Acer Group, Taipei

Gordon Wu, Chairman and Managing Director, Hopewell Holdings Ltd., Hong Kong

Grigory A. Yavlinsky, former Member of the State Duma; Leader of the "Yabloko" Parliamentary Group; Chairman of the Center for Economic and Political Research, Moscow

Yu Xintian, President, Shanghai Institute for International Studies, Shanghai

Yuan Ming, Director, Institute of International Relations, Peking University, Beijing

Zhang Yunling, Director, Institute of Asia-Pacific Studies, Chinese Academy of Social Sciences (CASS), Beijing

Wang Jisi, Dean, School of International Studies, Peking University, Beijing

16

ENDNOTES

1. Will Hutton, *The Observer*, February 1, 1998
2. Pierre Beaudry, *The Mennevee Documents on the Synarchy*, Book 4, chapter 3, p. 97
3. Jean Lacouture, *De Gaulle: The Ruler 1945-1970*, Norton & Co. Inc., 1992
4. The following is a representative sample of some agenda items:
   1954 – Oosterbeek, the Netherlands
   > Attitudes towards dependent areas and peoples overseas
   > Attitudes towards European integration and the European Defense Community
   > Attitudes towards economic policies and problems
   1955 – Barbison, France
   > Survey of Western European-U.S.A. relations
   > Uncommitted peoples: Political, ideological, economic aspects
   1959 – Yesilkoy, Turkey
   > Unity and division in Western policy
   1960 – Burgenstock, Switzerland
   > New political and economic development in the West
   1961 – St. Castin, Canada
   > Changes in economic strength between the U.S. and Europe
   1968 – Mont Tremblant, Canada
   > Internationalization of business
   1971 – Woodstock, U.S.A.
   > Business and current problems of social instability
   1980 – Aachen, Federal Republic of Germany
   > America and Europe: Past, Present and Future
   1981 – Burgenstock, Switzerland
   > Obstacles to effective coordination of Western policies

5. Other regular Bilderberger attendees are/were Richard Holbrooke, Donald Rumsfeld, Donald Graham, Henry Kravis, Marie-Josée Kravis, Vernon Jordan, Richard Haass, Michael Ledeen, William Luti, Jessica Mathews, Kenneth Mehlman, Dennis Ross, Paul Wolfowitz. James Wolfensohn; George Soros. The Rothschild dynasty of Europe is the most powerful force within the Bilderberg Group. Some of the better known Europeans who have attended the secret conclave are Romano Prodi (Italian Prime Minister); Pascal Lamy (former Trade Commissioner); José Durao Barroso (President European

commission); Jean-Claude Trichet (Chairman of the European Central Bank); Prince Phillip of Great Britain; Denis Healey (former British Defence Minister); Manlio Brosio (Secretary of NATO); Wilfred S. Baumgartner (former Governor of the Banque de France and a former top executive of the big French multinational company, Rhone-Poulenc Banco de Francia); Guido Carli (Bank of Italy); Margaret Thatcher (Prime Minister of England); Valery Giscard D'Estang (President of France); Harold Wilson (Prime Minister of England); Edward Heath (Prime Minister of England); Lester Pearson (former Prime Minister of Canada); Pierre Trudeau (former Prime Minister of Canada); Jean Chretién (former Prime Minister of Canada); Dirk U. Stikker (Secretary-General of NATO); Helmut Schmidt (Chancellor of West Germany); Donald S. MacDonald (former Canadian Minister of National Defense); Prince Claus of the Netherlands; Marcus Wallenberg (Chairman of Stockholm's EnskiIda Bank); Hannes Androsch (Austrian Minister of Finance); Paul van Zeeland (Prime Minister of Belgium); Pierre Commin (Secretary of the French Socialist Party); Imbriani Longo (Director-General of the Banco Nationale del Lavoro in Italy); Vimcomte Davignon (Belgium Minister of Foreign Affairs); Baron Edmond de Rothschild; Pierce Paul Schweitzer (Managing Director of the UN's International Monetary Fund); Giovanni Agnelli (Chairman of Fiat in Italy); Otto Wolff (very important German industrialist); and Javier Solana (Secretary General of Council of European Community).

6. Richard Greaves, "Who Really Runs the World," *The Truth Seeker*, Feburary 2003, also available at http://www.truthseeker.com

7. Malcolm Macalister Hall interview with Will Hutton, *The Mail on Sunday*, June 14, 1998

8. Will Hutton, *The Observer*, February 1, 1998

9. *Guardian Unlimited*, Saturday, March 10, 2001

10. Jim McBeth, *Scotsman*, May 15, 1998

11. Reference: Hotel's main Web page http://www.borromees.it

12. Chatham House official rule book

13. Chatham House official rule book

14. John Williams, *Atlanticism: The Achilles' Heel of European Security, Self-Identity and Collective Will*, http://www.mtholyoke.edu/acad/intrel/nato.htm

15. Robert Eringer, *The Global Manipulators*, Pentacle Books, 1980

16. John Coleman, *Conspirators' Hierarchy: The Story of the Committee of 300*, America West Publishers, 1992

17. Pierre Beaudry, *The Mennevee Documents of the Synarchy*, ICLC Draft document, p.68

18. Working Class Movement Library, enquiries@wcml.org.uk

19. Carol White, *The New Dark Age Conspiracy*, New Benjamin Franklin House, 1980, p.5

20. William Shannon, "Plans to destroy America are exposed!" *American Almanac*, August 11, 2002

21. John Coleman, *Conspirators' Hierarchy: The Story of The Committee of 300*, America West Publishers, 1992

22. Ibid.

23. Ibid.

24. Ibid.

25. Ibid.

26. Cited inter alia by http://freedomlaw.com/coffee.html, which lists among its sponsors the Cato Institute, the Heritage Foundation, and the Mackinac Centre for Public Policy, all right wing, ultra-conservative, pro-Israel institutions.

27. John Coleman, *Conspirators' Hierarchy: The Story of The Committee of 300,* America West Publishers, 1992

28. Melvin Sickler, article: "Thirst for Justice, The Council on Foreign Relations and the Trilateral Commission — the two organizations that run the United States" at http://www.prolognet.qc.ca/clyde/cfr.html

29. Gary Allen, *The Rockefeller File*, '76 Press, 1976

30. *Our Global Neighbourhood,* Oxford University Press, 1995

31. James Perloff, *The Shadows of Power: the CFR and the American Decline*, Western Islands Publications, 1988

32. Companies listed as a current corporate member of the Council on Foreign Relations (July 28, 2007)

PRESIDENT'S CIRCLE

ALCOA, Inc.
American Express Company
American International Group, Inc.
Amgen Inc.
Archetype Discoveries Worldwide
Balyasny Asset Management, LP
Bennett Jones LLP
BP p.l.c.
Bridgewater Associates, Inc.
Chevron Corporation
Citi
Cognizant Technology Solutions Corporation
ConocoPhillips Company
Drake Management LLC
Exxon Mobil Corporation
Federal Express Corporation
Fortress Investment Group LLC
GlaxoSmithKline
Guardsmark LLC
H.J. Heinz Company
Hess Corporation
Investcorp International, Inc.
Kingdon Capital
Kohlberg Kravis Roberts & Co.
KPMG LLP
Landor Associates
Lehman Brothers
Lockheed Martin Corporation
McKinsey & Company, Inc.
Merrill Lynch & Co., Inc.
Moody's Investors Service
Morgan Stanley
Nike, Inc.
Pfizer, Inc.

Reliance Industries Limited
The Goldman Sachs Group, Inc.
The McGraw-Hill Companies
The Rohatyn Group
Toyota Motor North America, Inc.
U.S. Chamber of Commerce
Veritas Capital

PREMIUM
ABC News
ACE Limited
AEA Investors Inc.
Airbus North America
Alcatel-Lucent
Alleghany Corporation
Apax Partners, Inc.
Apollo Management, LP
ARAMARK Corporation
Aramco Services Company
Archer Daniels Midland Company
Arnhold and S. Bleichroeder
Holdings, Inc.
Avaya Inc.
Baker, Nye Advisers, Inc.
Banco Mercantil
Bank of America
Barclays Capital
BASF Corporation
Bloomberg
BNP Paribas
Booz Allen Hamilton Inc.
Boston Properties, Inc.
Bristol-Myers Squibb Company
Bunge Limited
CALYON Corporate and
Investment Bank
Canadian Imperial Bank of Commerce
Cantillon Capital Management LLC
Caxton Associates
CEMEX
CH2M HILL Companies, LTD

Cisneros Group of Companies
CIT Group Inc.
Continental Properties
Corsair Capital
Credit Suisse
DaimlerChrysler Corporation
De Beers
Deere & Company
Deloitte
Deutsche Bank AG
Devon Energy Corporation
DTAP/Duquesne Capital
Duke Energy Corpoation
DVS Group
DynCorp International
Electronic Data Systems Corp.
Eli Lilly and Company
Eni S.p.A.
Equinox Partners, L.P.
Estee Lauder Companies Inc.
Ford Motor Company
Freddie Mac
Future Pipe Industries, Inc.
Galt Industries Inc.
General Atlantic LLC
General Electric Company
Google, Inc.
Granite Associates LP
Greenberg Traurig, LLP
Grey Global Group Inc.
Hasbro, Inc.
Hitachi, Ltd.
Houlihan Lokey Howard & Zukin
IBM Corporation
Indus Capital Partners, LLC
InsCap Management, LLC
Interpipe Inc.
J.E. Robert Companies
Jacobs Asset Management, LLC
Jones Day
JPMorgan Chase & Co

KBR
Kleiner Perkins Caufield & Byers
Kometal GMBH Austria
Kuwait Petroleum Corporation
Lazard LLC
Lukoil Americas
Mannheim LLC
Marathon Oil Company
Marsh & McLennan Co. Inc.
Marubeni America Corporation
MasterCard Advisors
Masthead Management Partners
Mayer, Brown, Rowe & Maw LLP
MBIA Insurance Corporation
MeadWestvaco Corporation
Merck & Co., Inc.
Milbank, Tweed, Hadley & McCloy LLP
Mitsubishi International
Corporation
Moore Capital Management LLC
Motorola, Inc.
Natixis North America, Inc.
New York Life International, Inc.
Newlight Associates
NYSE Euronext
Occidental Petroleum Corporation
Paul, Hastings, Janofsky & Walker
Paul, Weiss, Rifkind, Wharton &
Garrison LLP
Pepsico, Inc.
Phelps Dodge Corporation
Phillips-Van Heusen Corporation
Pitney Bowes Inc.
PricewaterhouseCoopers LLP
Prudential Financial, Inc.
Rho Capital Partners
Rothschild North America, Inc.
Sandalwood Securities, Inc.
Shell Oil Company
Sidley Austin LLP
Sony Corporation of America

Soros Fund Management
Standard & Poor's
Standard Chartered Bank
Starwood Capital Group
Sullivan & Cromwell LLP
The Bank of New York Mellon Co.
The Blackstone Group
The Boeing Company
The CNA Corporation
The Coca-Cola Company
The Nasdaq Stock Market, Inc.
The News Corporation
The Olayan Group
The Tata Group
Time Warner Inc.
Tishman Speyer Properties, Inc.
TOTAL S.A.
Tribeca Enterprises
U.S. Trust Corporation
UBS
United Technologies Corporation
Verizon Communications Inc.
Veronis Suhler Stevenson
Vinson & Elkins LLP
Visa International
Volkswagen of America, Inc.
Vornado Realty Trust
Wyeth
Wyoming Investment Corporation
Wyper Capital
Xerox Corporation
Ziff Brothers Investments LLC

BASIC

AARP
Access Industries, Inc.
American Red Cross
Apple Core Hotels Inc.
Areva U.S.
Arnold & Porter LLP
Baker & Hostetler LLP

Baker Capital Corp.
Banca d'Italia
Banca di Roma
Barbour Griffith and Rogers
Bramwell Capital Management, Inc.
Brown Brothers Harriman & Co.
C & O Resources, Inc.
Claremont Capital Corporation
Cleary Gottlieb Steen & Hamilton LLP
Control Risks Group
Covington & Burling
Craig Drill Capital Corporation
Debevoise & Plimpton LLP
Ehrenkranz & Ehrenkranz LLP
Eisner LLP
Energy Intelligence Group, Inc.
First Atlantic Capital, Ltd.
French-Am. Chamber of Commerce
Hemispheric Partners
IC & A Inc.
Idemitus Apollo Corporation
Intellispace, Inc.
Interaudi Bank
Intesa Sanpaolo
Invus Group, LLC
Japan Bank for International Cooperation
JETRO New York

Joukowsky Family Foundation
KS Management Corporation
Linklaters
Mark Partners
Marvin & Palmer Associates, Inc.
McKinsey & Company, Inc.
Medley Global Advisors
Mine Safety Appliances Company
Morgan, Lewis & Bockius LLP
Munich Re America Corporation
Mutual of America
Nationwide Electrical Supply, Inc.
Oxford Analytica Inc.
Peter Kimmelman Asset Mngmnt LLC
Pillsbury Winthrop Shaw Pittman LLP
Rolls-Royce North America, Inc.
Saber Partners, LLC
Simpson Thacher & Bartlett LLP
The Baldwin-Gottschalk Group
The Consulate General of Japan
Tiedemann Investment Group
Turkish Indust. & Business. Assoc.
Warburg Pincus LLC
Weber Shandwick Worldwide
Wilpon Investors LLC
Zephyr Management, L.P

33. *American Free Press*, June 2002, Special Bilderberg issue
34. Quoted by Tony Gosling, Bilderberg critic, ex-journalist BBC
35. Pierre Beaudry, *Mennevee Document on the Synarchy,* June 2005
36. Pierre Beaudry, *Synarchy Movement of Empires*, Book IV, chapter 4, p. 112
37. All of the best known journalists belong to the Bilderberg Group, which is one of the reasons the general public isn't all too familiar with this secretive organization. Some of the other attendees are/were Jean de Belot of France, editor of *Le Figaro*; R. John Micklethwait of *The Economist*; Sharon Percy Rockefeller, WETA-TV president and CEO; John Bernder of Norway, director-general of Norwegian Broadcasting Corp.; Paul Gigot, editorial page editor of the "conservative" *Wall Street Journal*; Gianni Riotta, Deputy Editor, *La Stampa*; Anatole Kaletsky of *The Times* of London; Peter Job, *Reuters* CEO; Eric Le Boucher, chief editor of

Le Monde; Toger Seidenfaden of Denmark, editor-in-chief of *Politiken*; Kenneth Whyte of Canada, editor of *The National Post*; Conrad Black, owner of a string of newspapers around the world, attended as a regular; Mathias Nass, Deputy Editor, *Die Zeit*; Will Hutton, London *The Observer* editor; Albert J. Wohlstetter, *Wall Street Journal* correspondent and Council on Foreign Relations member; Osborn Eliot, Former *Newsweek* editor; Hedley Donovan, Henry Grunwald, and Ralph Davidson of *Time*; Joseph C. Harsch, former NBC commentator and Council on Foreign Relations member; Henry Anatole Grunwald, former editor-in-chief of *Time* and Council on Foreign Relations member; prominent political columnists Joseph Kraft, James Reston, Joseph Harsch, George Will, and Flora Lewis; Donald C. Cook, former European diplomatic correspondent for the *Los Angeles Times* and Council on Foreign Relations member; Gerald Piel, former chairman of *Scientific American* and Council on Foreign Relations member; Peter Robert Kann, Chairman and CEO of Dow Jones and Company, and member of the Council on Foreign Relations; Peter Jennings, anchor and senior editor of ABC's *World News Tonight*; William Kristol, editor and publisher of the *Weekly Standard* magazine.

38. Bernie Sanders, "Congress Can No Longer Ignore Corporate Control of the Media," *Sanders Scoop* newsletter, Summer 2002

39. Ibid. Sanders went on to serve as a U.S. Senator from Vermont.

40. Canada has already complied with its own law. In 1995, the Canadian federal government passed the Firearms Act requiring Canada's 7 million rifles to be registered by 2004. According to their 2003 report, 6,818,073 non-restricted firearms, restricted and prohibited firearms had been registered with the Canadian government. Failure to comply is seen as a serious criminal offense. Many Canadians and Americans see this as the prelude to later wholesale gun confiscation.

41. Roe v. Wade, 410 U.S. 113, 93 S.Ct. 705, 35 L.Ed.2d 147 (1973)

42. Headquarters Department of the Army, DA Pam 525-7-2, Pamphlet No. 725-7-1, The Art and Science of Psychological Operations: Case Studies of Military Application, Washington, DC 1 April 1976, prepared by the American Institutes for Research (AIR), 3301 New Mexico Avenue N.W., Washington, DC, 20016, under Department of the Army Contracts, Project Director Daniel C. Pollock. Vol. 1, p. 99

43. Ken Adachi, "New World Order — an Overview," *www.educate-yourself.org*

44. Ibid.

45. Dr. Byron T. Weeks, http://educate-yourself.org/nwonwotavistockbestkept secret.shtml, July 31, 2001

46. "Ways and Means of U.S. Ideological Expansion," A. Valyuzhenich, *International Affairs* (Moscow), February 1971, pp. 63-68

47. Pollock, Daniel C., Project Director & Editor; De Mclaurin, Ronald; Rosenthal, Carl F.; Skillings, Sarah A., *The Art and Science of Psychological Operations: Case Studies of Military Application,* Volume One, Pamphlet No. 725-7-2, DA Pam 525-7-2, Headquarters Department of the Army Washington, DC, 1 April 1976, Vol 2, p. 825

48. Thomas R. Dye, *Who's Running America? Institutional Leadership in the United States*, Prentice-Hall, 1976

49. According to Mary Scobey in *To Nuture Humaneness,* 1970, this statement was made by Professor Raymond Houghton.

50. As described by Berit Kjos in the book, *Finding Common Ground.*

51. The most important being the Ford Foundation, Lilly Foundation, Rockefeller Foundation, Duke Endowment, Kresge Foundation, Kellogg Foundation, Mott Foundation, Pew Memorial Trust, Hartford Foundation, Alfred P. Sloan Foundation, Carnegie Foundation.

52. Thomas R. Dye, *Who's Running America?*, Prentice-Hall, 1976, pps. 103-107

53. Rene Wormser, *Foundations: Their Power and Influence*, Covenant House Books, 1993 p. 65-66

54. Michio Kaku and Daniel Axelrod, *To Win the Nuclear War: The Pentagon's Secret War Plans*, South End Press, 1987, pp. 63-64

55. Mike Peters, "The Bilderberg Group and the European Unification project," *Lobster*, No. 32, December 1996

56. "Abolishing Our Nation — Step By Step," *The New American*, September 6, 2004

57. The 1992 CFR annual Report contains the following representative sample:

Page 21: "At all meetings, the Council's rule of non-attribution applies. This assures participants that they may speak openly without others later *attributing their statements* to them in public media or forums, or knowingly transmitting them to persons who will."

Page 122: "Like the Council, the Committees encourage candid discourse by holding their meetings on a *not-for-attribution basis."*

Page 169: Article II of the by-laws states: "It is an express condition of membership in the Council, to which condition every member accedes by virtue of his or her membership, that members will observe such rules, and regulations as may be prescribed from time to time by the Board of Directors concerning the conduct of Council meetings or the *attribution of statements made therein, and that any disclosure, public, or other action by a member in contravention thereof may be regarded by the Board of Directors in its sole discretion as grounds for termination or suspension of membership pursuant to Article I of the by-laws."*

Page 174: "Full freedom of expression is encouraged at Council meetings. Participants are assured that they may speak openly, as it is the tradition of the Council that others *will not attribute or characterize their statements* in public media or forums or knowingly transmit them to persons who will. All participants are expected to honor that commitment."

Page 175: "It would not be in compliance with the reformulated Rule, however, for any meeting participant (i) *to publish a speaker's statement in attributed form* in a newspaper; (ii) *to repeat it on television or radio, or on a speaker's platform, or in a classroom*; or (iii) to go beyond a memo of limited circulation, by distributing the *attributed statement* in a company or government agency newspaper. *The language of the Rule also goes out of its way to make it clear that a meeting participant is forbidden knowingly to transmit the attributed statement to a newspaper reporter or other such person who is likely to publish it in a public medium.* The essence of the Rule as reformulated is simple enough: *participants in Council meetings should not pass along an attributed statement* in circumstances where there is substantial risk that it will promptly be widely circulated or published...."

"In order to encourage to the fullest a free, frank, and open exchange of ideas in Council meetings, the Board of Directors has prescribed, in addition to the *Non-Attribution Rule*, the following guidelines. *All participants in Council meetings are expected to be familiar with, and adhere to these Guidelines.*"

Page 176: "Members bringing guests should complete a 'guest notice card,' and acquaint their guests with the Council's *Non-Attribution Rule governing what is said at meetings....*

"As a condition of use, the officers of the Council shall require each user of Council records to execute a prior written commitment that *he will not directly or indirectly attribute to any living person* any assertion of fact or opinion based upon any Council record without first obtaining from such person his written consent thereto."

Furthermore, in "A letter from the Chairman" in the 1994 Annual Report for the CFR, Peter G. Peterson states (page 7), "Members had occasion to meet in intensive *off-the-record sessions* with Secretary of State [Warren] Christopher, National Security Advisor [Anthony] Lake, Secretary [of State emeritus, George Pratt] Shultz, Ambassador [Mickey] Kantor, Under Secretary of the Treasury [Lawrence H.] Summers, the Joint Chiefs of Staff, and other ranking officials. Next on our agenda are plans for reaching out to congressional leaders as well, an opportunity we will fashion as one component of an enhanced Washington Program." [emphases added]

58. Arlene Johnson, "The Trilateral Commission: Effect on the Middle East," *True Democracy*, July 24, 1987

59. Sklar, Holly, ed., *Trilateralism: The Trilateral Commission and Elite Planning for World Management*, South End Press, 1980

60. Trilateral Commission annual meeting publications

61. Antony Sutton, *Trilaterals over America*, CPA Books, 1995, p. 3

62. Gary Allen, *The Rockefeller File*, '76 Press, 1976

63. Sklar, Holly, ed., *Trilateralism,* South End Press, 1980.

64. Michael Lloyd Chadwick, ed., *The Freeman Digest*, Provo, Utah, interview with Mr. Franklin

65. Sklar, Holly, ed. *Trilateralism*, South End Press, 1980

66. Henry Kissinger, "Toasts to the Trilateral Commission Founder," U.S. Group's 25th Anniversary, December 1, 1998, at www.trilateral.org

67. Will Banyon, "Rockefeller Internationalism," *Nexus*, Volume 11, Number 1 (December-January 2004)

68. Daniel Yergin and Joseph Stanislaw, *The Commanding Heights: The Battle for the World Economy*, Free Press, 1997, pp. 60-64

69. Joan Hoff, *Nixon Reconsidered,* Basic Books, 1994, pp. 168, 396n (including quotes)

70. Will Banyon, "Rockefeller Internationalism," *Nexus*, Volume 11, Number 1 (December-January 2004)

71. Senator Jesse Helms, December 15 1987, Congressional Record, p. S18146

72. John Rees, *The Review of the News*, February 27, 1980, Interview with Gary Allen

73. Michel Crozier, Samuel P. Huntington & Joji Watanuki, *The Crisis of Democracy: Report on the Governability of Democracies to the Trilateral Commission*, NY University Press, 1975

74. PBS web site

75. Arlene Johnson, "The Trilateral Commission: Effect on the Middle East," *True Democracy*, July 24, 1987

76. John Rees, *The Review of the News*, February 27, 1980, Interview with Gary Allen

77. Jeremiah Novak, *Atlantic Monthly*, July 1977

78. John Rees, *The Review of the News*, February 27, 1980, Interview with Gary Allen

79. Arlene Johnson, "The Trilateral Commission: Effect on the Middle East," *True Democracy*, July 24, 1987

80. List of CFR/TC members in the Carter administration: Sol Linowitz (Chief Negotiator on the Panama Canal Treaties/Mid-East Envoy); John C. Sawhill (Deputy Secretary of Energy/Head of the Synthetic Fuels Corp.);

Hedley Donovan (Special Assistant to the President); Lloyd N. Cutler (Counsel to the President); Gerald C. Smith (Ambassador at Large for Nuclear Power Negotiations); Richard N. Gardner (Ambassador to Italy); Elliot L. Richardson (Delegate to the UN Law of the Sea Conference); Henry Owen (Special Representative of the President for Economic Summits/Economic Advisor); Warren Christopher (Deputy Secretary of State); Paul C. Warnke (Director of the Arms Control and Disarmament Agency); Richard N. Cooper (Under Secretary of State for Economic Affairs); Lucy Wilson Benson (Under Secretary of State for Security Affairs); Anthony Solomon (Deputy Secretary of State for Monetary Affairs); Robert R. Bowie (Deputy Director of Intelligence for National Estimates); W. Anthony Lake (Under Secretary of State for Policy Planning); Richard Holbrooke (Assistant Secretary of State for East Asian and Pacific Affairs); C. Fred Bergsten (Assistant Secretary of Treasury for International Affairs); Leslie Gelb (Director of the Bureau of Politico-Military Affairs); Theordore C. Sorenson (Director of the Central Intelligence Agency); Richard Moose (Assistant Secretary of State for African Affairs); Brock Adams (Secretary of Transportation); Leonard Woodcock (U.S. Ambassador to Peking); Joseph Califano (Secretary of Health, Education and Welfare).

81. Antony Sutton, *Trilaterals Over America*, CPA Books, 1995

82. John Rees, *The Review of the News*, February 27, 1980, Interview with Gary Allen

83. Carter quotes: Laurence H. Shoup, *The Carter Presidency and Beyond: Power and Politics in the 1980s*, Ramparts Press, 1980, pp.50-51; and Jimmy Carter, *The Presidential Campaign, Volume One, Part One*, U.S. Government Printing Office, 1978, pp.268, 683.

84. Eustace Mullins, *Murder by Injection: The Medical Conspiracy Against America*, National Council for Medical Research, 1988, Chapter 10

85. In *Railroads and Regulation 1877-1916*, Gabriel Kolko's Ph.D. dissertation, he demonstrates how it was the railroad owners, not the farmers, who were squarely behind the effort to preserve state control of railroads through the Interstate Commerce Commission, which could protect their monopoly and abolish competition.

86. Gary Allen, *The Rockefeller File*, '76 Press, 1976

87. Antony Sutton, *Wall Street and the Bolshevik Revolution*, Arlington House, 1974, Chapter XI: The Alliance Of Bankers And Revolution

88. Jennings C. Wise, *Woodrow Wilson: Disciple of Revolution*, Paisley Press, 1938, pps. 45-46

89. Antony Sutton, *Wall Street and the Bolshevik Revolution*, Arlington House, 1974, Chapter XI: The Alliance Of Bankers And Revolution

90. Ibid.

91. Gary Allen, *The Rockefeller File*, '76 Press, 1976

92. Antony Sutton, *Wall Street and the Bolshevik Revolution*, Arlington House, 1974, Chapter XI: The Alliance Of Bankers And Revolution

93. Quoted in Eustace Mullins, *The World Order: A Study in the Hegemony of Parasitism*, Ezra Pound Institue of Civilization, 1985, Chapter 2, Soviet Russia

94. Antony Sutton, *Wall Street and the Bolshevik Revolution*, Arlington House, 1974

95. Z.A.B. Zeman, ed., *Germany and the Revolution in Russia 1915-1918: Documents from the Archives of the German Foreign Ministry*, Oxford University Press, 1958, Document 9

96. Ibid., Document 11

97. Ibid., Document 1

98. George Vernadsky, *Lenin: Red Dictator*, Yale University Press, 1932, p. 154

99. Most of the main events in the career of Helphand are available in any number of standard works on Lenin, Trotsky, Russia, and the Revolutionary period. For the finer details see Z.A.B. Zeman and W.B. Scharlau, *The Merchant of Revolution: The Life of Alexander Israel Helphand (Parvus)*, Oxford University Press, 1965.

100. Antony Sutton, *Wall Street and the Bolshevik Revolution*, Arlington House, 1974, p. 30

101. Granatstein & Hillmer, *Prime Ministers: Ranking Canada's Leaders*, Harper Collins.

102. Eustace Mullins, *The World Order: A Study in the Hegemony of Parasitism*, Ezra Pound Institue of Civilization, 1985, Chapter 2, Soviet Russia

103. Ibid.

104. Ibid.

105. George Racey Jordan, *Major Jordan's Diaries*, Harcourt, Brace & Company, 1952

106. Gary Allen, *The Rockefeller File*, '76 Press, 1976, Chapter 9, Building the Big Red Machine

107. *Testimony of Antony Sutton before Subcommittee VII of the Platform Committee of the Republican Party at Miami Beach, Florida, August 15, 1972*

108. Ibid.

109. John Hoefle, "Southern Strategy, Inc.: Where Wall Street Meets Tobacco Road," *American Almanac*, February 2001

110. "The Real Story Behind the TC," Special Report, *EIR*, March 1980

111. Ibid.

112. Ibid.

113. John Hoefle, "Southern Strategy, Inc.: Where Wall Street Meets Tobacco Road," *American Almanac,* February, 2001

114. Eustace Mullins, *Murder by Injection: The Story of the Medical Conspiracy Against America*, National Council for Medical Research 1988, Chapter 10

BILDERBERG REPORTS

BILDERBERG 2005
MAY 5-8
ROTTACH-EGERN, BAVARIA, GERMANY

While Bush, Blair, Chirac, Berlusconi and Company attended the G8 summits of the world's foremost democratically elected leaders, they were accompanied by the massed ranks of the world media. In stark contrast, the comings and goings at Bilderberg took place under cover of a virtual publicity blackout.

After three straight years of open hostilities and tension amongst the European, British and American Bilderbergers caused by the war in Iraq, the aura of complete congeniality amongst them had returned. Bilderbergers reaffirmed, and remain united in, their long-term goal to strengthen the role the UN plays in regulating global conflicts and relations.

Although George W. Bush didn't personally attend the meeting in Rottach-Egern, the U.S. Government was well represented by William Luti, Richard Perle, Dennis Ross and Allan Hubbard.

However, it is important to understand that Americans are no more the "Hawks" than the European Bilderbergers are the "Doves." Europeans joined in supporting the 1991 invasion of Iraq by President Bush's father, celebrating, in the words of one notable Bilderberg hunter the end of "America's Viet Nam syndrome." European Bilderbergers also supported former President Bill Clinton's invasion of Yugoslavia, bringing NATO into the operation.

UN GLOBAL OIL TAX AND PEACE-BUILDING PROPOSALS

A much discussed subject in 2005 at Rottach-Egern was the concept of imposing a UN tax on people worldwide through a direct tax on oil at the well-head. This, in fact, sets a precedent. If enacted, it would be the first time that a non-governmental agency (read the United Nations) directly benefited from a tax on citizens of free and enslaved nations. The Bilderberg proposal called for a tiny UN levy at the outset, which the consumer would hardly notice.

Bilderberg wants "tax harmonization" so that high-tax countries can compete with more tax-friendly nations – including the United States – for foreign investment. They would "harmonize" taxes by forcing the rate in the U.S. and other countries to rise so that socialist Sweden's 58-per-cent level would be "competitive."

According to sources, an unidentified guest at the conference asked how global taxation could be sold to the American public. One European Union commissioner suggested using as the battering ram the rhetoric of helping countries build peaceful, stable societies once conflict subsided. Someone asked for the timing of the appeal. A former commissioner mentioned that the best time to ask for cash is once a conflict subsides and the world is subjected to brutal images of destruction. A Norwegian Bilderberger disagreed. What looked to be Björn T. Grydeland, Norway's ambassador to the European Union, said that, on the contrary, it's much easier to get world attention and money for a region when a conflict rages.

This was confirmed a posteriori when Denmark's foreign minister Per Stig Moller, during a debate in the United Nations on May 26, stated on the record that "if the international community is not able to act swiftly, the fragile peace is at risk, with loss of more lives as a consequence." Denmark held the EU presidency until July 1, 2005, when it was replaced by the UK.

Bilderbergers were planning to use what they nominated as a UN Peacebuilding Commission, apparently to help win the peace in post-conflict countries, as one of the tools in secretly imposing the UN tax on an unsuspecting world population.

Mark R. Warner, governor of Virginia and a first-time Bilderberg invitee, expressed concern about how much additional financial responsibility the United States would take on as a result. At this point, José M. Durão Barroso, president of the European Commission, expressed a view held by many within Bilderberg that the United States did not provide a fair share of economic aid to poor countries. My sources confirm that "Kissinger and David Rockefeller, among other Americans, beamed and nodded approval."

Although the U.S. pays more into the foreign-aid piggy bank than any country in the world, the Bilderbergers and the United Nations were poised to demand much more funding from it to meet the peace-building proposal.

NEOCONSERVATIVE AGENDA

In full force was that faction known as the "neoconservatives" – those who have determined that Israel's security should come at the expense of the safety to the United States and be central to all U.S. foreign policy decisions.

Most notable among this group is Richard Perle. Perle played the critical role in pushing the United States into the war against Iraq. He was forced to resign from the Pentagon's Defense Policy Board, on March 27, 2003, after it was learned that he had been advising Goldman Sachs International, a habitual Bilderberg attendee, on how it might profit from the war in Iraq.

Another neoconservative figure on hand was Michael A. Ledeen, an "intellectual's intellectual." Ledeen serves at the American Enterprise Institute, a think tank founded in 1943, with which Richard Perle has long been associated. AEI and the Brookings Institution operate a Joint Center for Regulatory Studies (JCRS), with the purpose of holding lawmakers and regulators "accountable for their decisions by providing thoughtful, objective analyses of existing regulatory programs and new regulatory proposals." The JCRS pushes for cost-benefit analysis of regulations, which fits with AEI's (and Bilderberger) ultimate goal of deregulation.

These neoconservatives were also joined this year at Bilderberg by a handful of other top former Washington policy makers and publicists known for their sympathies for Israel, including former State

Department official Richard N. Haass, president of the CFR, former Assistant Secretary of State and "father" of the Dayton accord, Richard Holbrooke, and Dennis Ross of the pro-Israel Washington Institute for Near East Policy, effectively an offshoot of the America Israel Public Affairs Committee (AIPAC).

Declining Energy Reserves and Economic Downturn

Of course, discussion at Bilderberg 2005 turned to oil. An American Bilderberger expressed concern over the sky-rocketing price of oil. One oil industry insider at the meeting remarked that growth is not possible without energy and that according to all indicators the world's energy supply is coming to an end much faster than the world leaders have anticipated.

According to sources, Bilderbergers estimated the extractable world's oil supply to be at a maximum of 35 years under current economic development and population. However, one of the representatives of an oil cartel remarked that we must factor into the equation both the population explosion and economic growth and demand for oil in China and India. Under the revised conditions, there is apparently only enough oil to last for 20 years. No oil spells the end of the world's financial system. So much has already been acknowledged by the Wall Street Journal and the Financial Times, two periodicals who are regularly present at the annual Bilderberg conference.

During the afternoon cocktail, a European Bilderberger noted that there is no plausible alternative to hydrocarbon energy. One American insider stated that currently the world used between four and six barrels of oil for every new barrel it found, that the prospects for a short term break through were slim, at best.

Someone asked for an estimate of the world's accessible conventional oil supply. The amount was quoted at approximately one trillion barrels. As a side note of interest, the planet consumed a billion barrels of oil every 11.5 days.

Another Bilderberger asked about the hydrogen alternative to the oil supply. A U.S. government official stated gloomily that a hydrogen salvation for the world's imminent energy crisis is a fantasy.

This discussion confirmed a public statement made in 2003 by IHS Energy, the world's most respected consulting firm, cataloguing oil reserves and discoveries, that for the first time since the 1920s there was not a single discovery of an oil field in excess of 500 million barrels.

At the 2005 Bilderberg conference, the oil industry was represented by John Browne, chief executive officer of BP; Sir John Kerr, director of Royal Dutch Shell; Peter D. Sutherland, chairman of BP; and Jeroen van der Veer, chairman of the committee of managing directors at Royal Dutch Shell. (Queen Beatrix of The Netherlands, Royal Dutch Shell's principal shareholder, is a fully fledged member of the Bilderbergers. Her father, Prince Bernhard, was one of the founders of the group back in 1954.)

It should be noted that in late 2003, oil and gas giant Royal Dutch Shell announced it had overstated its reserves by as much as 20 per cent; in early 2004 it reduced its estimated oil and gas reserves by about 4.5 billion barrels, but in October had to apply an additional cut of 1.15 billion barrels in reserve estimates. In fact, Shell's three cuts in reserve estimates prompted the resignation of its co-chairman. The Los Angeles Times (January 18, 2005) reported: "For petroleum firms, reserves amount to nothing less than 'the value of the company.'"

At Rottach-Egern in May 2005, the industry's top executives tried to figure out how to keep the truth about diminishing oil reserves from reaching the public. Public knowledge of the diminishing reserves directly translate into lower share prices, which could destroy financial markets, leading to a collapse of the world economy.

An American Bilderberger wondered what it would take for the oil price to go back to $25 a barrel. Martin S. Feldstein, president of the National Bureau of Economic Research, added that $50 a barrel involves greater cash flow. Cheap oil slows economic growth because it depresses commodity prices and reduces world liquidity. Another American Bilderberger reported that if the price of oil were to go down to its previous low of $25 a barrel, the debt-driven asset bubble would explode. Yet another American Bilderberger, believed to be Allan Hubbard, confirmed that the general public does not realise that the price for cheap oil can be the bursting of the debt bubble. There was a strong indication that the U.S. Federal Reserve was extremely concerned about the debt bubble.

A British Bilderberger noted that oil at $120 a barrel would greatly benefit Britain and the United States, but Russia and China would be the biggest winners. An expert in international relations and policy studies noted that for the Chinese this would be a real bonanza. The Chinese imported energy not for domestic consumption but, instead, to fuel its growing cheap exports—a cost that would be duly passed on to foreign buyers. A European banker pointed out that Russia could effectively devalue the dollar by re-denominating its energy trade with Europe from dollars into euros, forcing Europe's central banks to rebalance their foreign exchange reserves in favour of the euro. Jean-Claude Trichet, Governor of the European Central Bank, was present during the debate.

Someone raised a question about the impact of a sharp rise of energy prices on asset values. A German Bilderberger responded that the net effect is a de facto depreciation of money, misidentified as growth.

EU REFERENDUM IN FRANCE

The first day was dominated by talk of EU referendum in France and whether Chirac could persuade France to vote Yes on May 29. A Yes vote, according to sources within Bilderberg would put a lot of pressure on Tony Blair to finally deliver Britain into the waiting arms of the New World Order through their own referendum on the treaty scheduled for 2006. Matthias Nass wondered out loud whether a No vote in France could cause political turmoil in Europe and overshadow Britain's six-month EU presidency starting on July 1. Bilderbergers hoped that Blair and Chirac, whose at times open animosity has spilled into a public arena on more than one occasion, could work together for mutual benefit and political survival. Another European Bilderberger added that both leaders must put behind them as quickly as possible all past disputes on such topics as Iraq, the liberalization of Europe's economy and the future of budget rebate Britain receives from the EU and work towards complete European integration, which could desintigrate if France's often "hard-headed and obstinate people," in the words of a British Bilderberger, did not do the right thing, meaning give up voluntarily their independence for the "greater good" of a Federal European super state!

A German Bilderberger insider said that France's "Yes" vote was in trouble because of the "outsourcing of jobs. Jobs in Germany and France are going to Asia and Poland" [to take advantage of cheap labor]. Poland was one of the former Communist republics that have been admitted to the European Union bringing the total membership to 25 nations. A German politician wondered out loud how Tony Blair should go about convincing Britons to embrace the European Constitution, when due to the outsourcing of jobs, both Germany and France were suffering a 10% unemployment while Britain was doing well economically. The French electorate handily rejected EU membership.

AUNA TELECOMUNICACIONES

At a Saturday night cocktail party at the luxurious Dorint Sofitel Seehotel Überfahrt in Rottach-Egern, Bavaria, Munich, several Bilderbergers sharing the standing bar with Queen Beatrix of Holland and Donald Graham, Washington Post's CEO were discussing the upcoming sale of Spanish telecommunications and cable giant Auna. Auna operates fixed line telephone services, a mobile-phone network, cable television system and is also an Internet provider. One of the Bilderbergers familiar with the matter [believed to be Henry Kravis, based on the physical description of the source at the meeting] stated that Auna's mobile operations could bring in some 10 billion euros including debt, while another Bilderberger, a tall man with a receding hairline added that its fixed-line assets could fetch some 2.6 billion euros. An abundance of cheap credit and low interest rates made Auna an appetising target for private-equity buyers.

Sources close to the Bilderbergers stated off-the-record that Kohlberg Kravis Roberts & Co, a private-equity firm, was interested in buying all of Auna. Kohlberg Kravis Roberts & Co is represented at Bilderberg meetings by its luminary billionaire Henry Kravis and his small town Quebec-born wife Marie Josée Kravis, a Senior Fellow at the neoconservative Hudson Institute.

CHINA

European and American Bilderbergers realizing the most urgent of needs to expand into developing markets in order to help sustain the illusion of endless growth agreed to name Pascal Lamy, a French Socialist and a fanatical supporter of a European super state as the next WTO President. It will be remembered that Washington gave conditional support to Lamy's nomination in exchange for European support of Paul Wolfowitz as head of the World Bank.

According to insider sources within the Bilderberger group, Lamy was chosen to help steer the global trading system through a time of rising protectionist sentiment in rich countries such as France and Germany, both reeling from high unemployment and reticent toward increasingly muscular demands for market access from emerging economies. Third World states, for example, were insisting on cuts to EU and U.S. farm subsidies. The WTO liberalization drive collapsed in acrimony in Seattle in 1999 and again in Cancun in 2003.

The Bilderbergers secretly agreed on the need to force the poor countries into a globalized market for cheap goods while simultaneously forcing the poor into becoming customers. The current rift with China is a good example, as the Chinese have flooded the Western countries with cheap goods, among them textiles, driving down prices. As a trade off, the Bilderbergers entered into an emerging market ripe and vulnerable to superior western know-how. Similar developing countries are slowly acquiring more purchasing power and the industrialized world is gaining a foothold in their domestic economies by targeting them for cheap exports.

Further discussion on China was led off with a series of rhetorical questions from the speaker. Was China really abusing its competitive advantage, or was it being victimized by the U.S. and the EU? Is a trade war imminent? Should China revalue the yuan (its currency), and, if so, how should it do this?

An American Bilderberger noted that China in 2005 was one of the leading world economic powers whose actions influence the world economy. Another American, believed to be but not positively identified as Michael Ledeen of the American Enterprise Institute, said that if China doesn't revalue the yuan it would cause the entire world trade system to go out of whack. Someone mentioned that the current situation could be dangerous for the Chinese economy due to the creation of excess liquidity. Elena Nemirovskaya, founder of the Moscow School of Political Studies, asked what would happen if the yuan were allowed to float freely. An economist responded that this could bring about serious consequences to the world's financial markets. China's foreign exchange reserves are to a large extent made up of U.S. Treasury bills. An appreciation of the yuan would cause its dollar reserves to depreciate.

A German Bilderberger pointed out that this could force the Federal Reserve to raise interest rates, thus causing the current housing boom in the U.S. to come to a screeching halt. An oversized Dutchman pointed out that the International Monetary Fund needs to play an active role in helping the yuan.

"Is there a real danger, then," asked an Italian Bilderberger, "of this dispute deteriorating into an all-out trade war?" "Not likely," according to an unidentified blond man from Scandinavia, believed to be a Swede, "because China has totally integrated itself into the market economy."

An American Bilderberger and a member of the U.S. Government noted that all the posturing is part of the act to keep the voters back home happy.

China's moves into the Mekong region did not go unnoticed at the conference. William J. Luti, U.S. Deputy Under-Secretary of Defense for Near Eastern and South Asian Affairs, explained that China's rapid expansion into the Mekong region, comprising Cambodia, Laos, Myanmar, Thailand and Viet Nam, could threaten U.S. interests in the area. Such moves by China would give it an enhanced role in South-East Asia.

Over the prior several years, China had invested heavily in transport infrastructure development linking China's southwestern Yunan province and the Mekong region. A European Bilderberger pointed out that China was heavily dependent on oil imports. Someone asked for a figure. A tall, lanky man with glasses, believed to be Jeroen van der Veer, Chairman of Royal Dutch Shell, responded that some 40 per cent of China's supply was imported. In fact, China's move into the Mekong region was the result of acute awareness that the country's energy supplies are vulnerable to interference. Overall, 32 per cent of its energy supplies, China's lifeblood, passed through the narrow and easily blocked Strait of Malacca.

U.S. Airlines and Pension Funds

An American Bilderberger inquired about the effect of $50 oil on the crisis in government pension insurance. High oil prices threaten the economic viability of airlines and motor vehicles sectors. The employees' pensions at U.S. Airways had been recently terminated by the bankruptcy court. United Airlines and others were on the list as well. An American Bilderberger noted that the U.S. Social Security System was going through its worst accounting crisis in years. The specter was raised of companies defaulting on their financial obligations to the workers. Someone commented that government-run pension funds would not be able to shoulder an industry-wide default on their obligations without a Federal bailout.

MEDIA ATTENDEES

The year's invitees included Nicolas Beytout, editor-in-chief, Figaro; Oscar Bronner, publisher and editor, Der Standard; Donald Graham, chairman of the Washington Post; Matthias Nass, deputy editor, Die Zeit; Norman Pearlstine, editor-in-chief, Time; Cuneyt Ulsevere, columnist for the Turkish Hürriyet; John Vinocur, senior correspondent, International Herald Tribune; Martin Wolf, associate editor, Financial Times; Fareed Zakaria, editor, Newsweek International; Klaus Zumwinkel, chairman, Deutsche Post; John Micklethwait, U.S. editor, The Economist and Adrian Wooldridge, foreign correspondent, The Economist. Micklethwait and Wooldridge acted as the meeting's rapport builders.

IRAN-RUSSIA-CHINA

According to reports, a French Bilderberger pointedly asked Henry Kissinger if the U.S Government's sabre-rattling against Iran meant the beginning of new hostilities. Richard Haass, CFR President, after asking for his turn to speak, dismissed the notion of an Iran invasion as unrealistic due to the sheer physical size of the country and its large population, not to mention the billions of dollars involved in getting the operation off the ground. Up to the eyeballs in the Iraq quagmire, the United States military was wary of any new adventures in hostile terrain against a much healthier enemy, both better prepared and organised.

A Swiss Bilderberger asked if a hypothetical attack on Iran would involve a pre-emptive strike against its nuclear sites. Richard Haass replied that such an attack would prove to be counterproductive because Tehran's counterattack options could range from "unleashing terrorism and promoting instability in Iraq, Afghanistan and Saudi Arabia, to triggering oil price increases that could trigger a global economic crisis." During dinner, according to several sources, Richard Perle criticised Haass' position and explained his opposition to his view.

A woman believed to be Heather Munroe-Blum, Vice-Chancellor of McGill University, Quebec, Canada, asked a rhetorical question about what would happen if Iran were to continue building its nuclear arsenal. Haass replied that in this scenario, the United States would have no choice but to grant Iran the same status as it did to Pakistan and India.

A U.S. General commented that the China–Iran–Russia alliance is changing the geopolitical situation in the area. Rapprochement between Russia and China was viewed by the Bilderbergers as a significant event not to be taken lightly, even though it had received little media attention in the West.

A secret U.S. Government report was cited wherein, according to sources, the Chinese had spent upwards of several billion dollars in acquiring Russia's latest and most sophisticated weapons technology. Someone pointed out that the Sino–Russian alliance was not limited to military trade and that the non-military exchange of goods had grown 100 per cent since the beginning of the Bush presidency.

A delegate at the conference, believed but not positively identified by Secret Service sources to be Anatoly Sharansky, a former Israeli Minister for Jerusalem and Diaspora Affairs, stated categorically during Friday night cocktails that the counterweight to the Moscow-Beijing-Tehran axis is the U.S.-Israel-Turkey alliance. A financial expert from a European nation intervened by stating that Russia was much better off financially than four years prior, before tax revenue generated by fuel and arms production and exports, as a result of heavy emphasis on military production, had financed strong growth of wages and pension incomes, boosting private consumption.

A German Bilderberger pointedly asked Richard Perle if the "war on terrorism" would intensify over the second term of the Bush presidency. Perle reportedly gave no reply but screwed up his face and looked away.

Bilderberg luminary Richard Haass pointedly told Richard Perle during Saturday night cocktails that the Bush Administration had overestimated its ability to change the world. Haass, according to several sources at the conference, is reported to have stated that regime change can be attractive because it is "less distasteful than diplomacy and less dangerous than living with new nuclear states." However, he noted, "There is only one problem: it is highly unlikely to have the desired effect soon enough."

IRAN

The presence of U.S. General James L. Jones, Supreme Allied Commander Europe, and Retired U.S. Army General John M. Keane at the Bilderberg meeting in Germany suggested that the next stage of the conquest was about to begin.

An American neocon at an afternoon drink-fest said he was convinced that the "Iranian opposition movement" would unseat the mullahs. Nicolas Beytout of Le Figaro exclaimed, "You don't really believe that!" A tall, bald, well-dressed Swiss gentleman, believed to be Pascal Couchepin, head of the powerful Department of Home Affairs, replied reflexively that it will only succeed in having the Iranians rally behind their government. He ended by saying, "You don't know Iranians."

Tempers boiled over momentarily when a French Bilderberger, raising his voice, told Kissinger that "an attack on Iran will escalate out of control." According to sources working for the CIA and the special unit of the U.S. Army charged with protecting the U.S. delegation at Rottach-Egern, both the CIA and the FBI were in open revolt against the Bush White House.

A member of the Greek Parliament asked Eival Gilady, strategic adviser to Israeli Prime Minister Ariel Sharon, "What would happen if Iran were to retaliate?" Someone pointed out that even if the United States or Israel were to show restraint in their use of tactical nuclear weapons, an attack on Iran's nuclear facilities would surely not only engulf neighbor states, raising the likelihood of a broader war, but also succeed in creating a nuclear disaster through radiation spilling over a wide area.

As a follow-up question, someone asked, "How much of this war has to do with America doing its utmost to prevent Iran from becoming a regional power?" A French Bilderberger wished to know if the impending attack on Iran would involve the United States and Israel working in tandem, or if it would be a NATO operation. The question was directed at NATO Secretary-General Jaap G. de Hoop Scheffer. Another European Bilderberger wanted to know how the U.S. was planning to cope with three wars simultaneously, referring to Iraq, Afghanistan and Iran.

The Israeli delegation was pressed to answer if Israel was prepared to use nuclear weapons against Iran. The answer was incoherent.

RUSSIAN VS AMERICAN FOREIGN POLICY

Policy discussion began with a European expert on international relations pointing out that over the next several years Russia was poised to assert itself and increasingly challenge Bush Government foreign policy goals.

Someone openly asked the committee if the world was safer than in 2001 and if it would be safer in four years' time. A Dutchman responded by saying there was little doubt that the hand of international terrorism has been substantially strengthened by the U.S. Government's policy in the Middle East. A Danish Bilderberger wondered about what had happened to the U.S. promise to take a lower-key approach in Iraq — referring to the heavy-handed tactics employed by American troops in the siege of Fallujah, which played an important role in alienating a large cross-section of moderate Arab states. Additionally, the Dutchman pointed out, terrorism hadn't been confined to the Iraq theater of operations but had escalated across Asia, Africa and most of the Middle East.

A blonde woman, believed to be Thérèse Delpech, Director of Strategic Affairs for the Atomic Energy Commission, said that unilateralist policy actions by the U.S. will only succeed in alienating friendly nations and emboldening enemy combatants. "The U.S. is the most powerful nation in the world, but it is not more powerful than the world. It must coordinate its policy with other great powers to achieve its ends."

An oil expert believed to be from Britain, possibly Sir John Kerr of Royal Dutch Shell, focused on the oil pipeline from Siberia to northern China. The Bilderbergers openly wondered at the medium-term repercussions of this deal. An American investment banker asked just how much oil was expected to flow through this pipeline. Another member of the oil cartel offered 65–80 million tons per year as a ballpark figure.

THE 2005 GERMAN ELECTIONS

The Bilderbergers also discussed how to dust off the "boring" image of Angela Merkel, Germany's "future leader," ahead of the German elections on September 18, 2005. A short, oversized male Bilderberger offered an opinion that in order for the widest cross-section of the German public to accept Merkel (leader of the Christian Democratic Union opposition) as Chancellor, it would be important to give a new definition to the term "family values." German Bilderbergers well-versed in the conservative Bavarian collective psyche believed that Merkel, a divorcee with a doctorate in physics, didn't have a "reliable" enough image to attract sufficient votes in that staunchly conservative area of the country. According to people within earshot of the discussion, the idea "in the upcoming campaign would be to stress the importance of families rather than marriage as an institution." Nevertheless, Merkel was elected.

Bilderbergers pushing Gerhard Schroeder aside in favour of a new candidate could very well signify that, after three years of strife between American and European Bilderbergers over the war in Iraq, the secret society was ready to move forward with a much-revised and more cohesive policy. It must be remembered that Schroeder, along with French President Chirac, was one of the most vociferous European critics of the U.S.-led Iraq intervention.

Both Schroeder, representing the left, and Merkel, representing the right, were owned by the Bilderbergers. It has been the group's policy since its inception in 1954 to own both horses in the race.

BILDERBERG 2006
JUNE 8-11
BROOKSTREET HOTEL, KANATA, OTTAWA, CANADA

The 54th Bilderberg meeting returned to Canada. The conference dealt with European-American relations, Energy, Russia, Iran, China, the Middle East, Terrorism and Immigration. Internationally renowned media groups were invited to participate, among them The Economist, Financial Times, Die Zeit and Der Standard from Germany, America On Line, International Herald Tribune, Le Figaro, The Times of London, Indigo Books, Grupo Prisa from Spain, Canada's The Globe and Mail and the Toronto Star, Time-Warner and Denmark's Politiken.

Technical problems prevented a more detailed description of the discussion at this meeting; the following summary will have to suffice.

ENERGY

E nergy problems continued to dominate Bilderberger discussions. Oil and natural gas are finite, non-renewable resources. From the beginning of the twentieth century mankind has used up massive quantities of hydrocarbons (oil, natural gas) created over millions of years on the planet. Do we, at least, have another one hundred years of oil reserves left, a good enough cushion, while we look for a feasible solution? Or do, we have about twenty years of proven petroleum supplies left, as the Bilderbergers themselves had confirmed at their 2005 Rottach-Egern meeting in Germany?

Oil wells are very difficult to find. The investments energy corporations like BP, Royal Dutch Shell, Exxon, Lukoil, Texaco, Unocal are required to make in order to find the oil can be counted by the hundreds of millions and billions of dollars. What's worse, in order to stay on par, they need to turn around and find another and then another and then another oil well that will guarantee them and their shareholders profit. Profit. That's the name of the game. And profit, which is achieved through growth, is not possible without energy.

As global demand for oil and natural gas continues growing much faster than new supplies are being found, these corporations, and their corporate profits and bottom lines, have a problem. As reservoirs dry up, the cost of exploration is skyrocketing and the rewards are diminishing. To stay competitive and be in a position to maintain a competitive advantage over their rivals, the energy corporations, whose board members and majority shareholders happen to be all of the most powerful individuals and corporations in the world, must maintain and expand their control over more and more oil fields in order to continue guaranteeing their shareholders profitable return on their investment. (This is the myth of infinite growth.)

As the world turns, and as oil and natural gas supplies dwindle while demand soars dramatically, especially with Indian and Chinese booming economies[1] who want all the trinkets and privileges of an American way of life, we, as the Planet, have entered a new phase of oil production and discovery. From now on, the only sure thing is that

---

1. The average American consumes 25 barrels of oil a year. Average Chinese: 1.3 barrels/year. Average Indian: less than one [The Christian Science Monitor, January 20, 2005].

supply will continue to diminish and prices will continue to increase. In these conditions world conflict is a certainty.

This sentiment was also expressed by French Prime Minister and Bilderberg member Dominique de Villepin, who was quoted by Reuters on September 1, 2005 saying, "We have entered the post-oil era. I want to draw all the consequences of this and give a real impulse to energy savings and to the use of renewable energies." Jeroen van der Veer, CEO of Royal Dutch Shell and a full-time member of the Bilderberg inner circle confirmed what the Bush administration and other energy experts have felt for quite some time. In an interview with the Bilderberg-influenced Financial Times on January 24, 2006, he stated, "My view is that 'easy' oil has probably passed its peak."

Rest assured, the Bilderbergers and their cohorts were well aware of the imminent oil crisis. Energy, in fact, over the past two decades has always been the first item on their annual agenda. In April 2001, four and a half months prior to 9-11, the Council on Foreign Relations and James A. Baker III (Bush I Secretary of State, CFR, Bilderberg and Trilateral Commission member) published a detailed study of world energy problems. The report, which appeared on the CFR's Web site, confirmed awareness of the catastrophic consequences: "Strong economic growth across the globe and new global demands for more energy has meant the end of sustainable surplus capacity in hydrocarbon fuels and the beginning of capacity limitations. In fact, the world is currently precariously close to utilizing all of its available global oil production capacity, raising the chances of an oil supply crisis with more substantial consequences than seen in three decades. These choices will affect other U.S. policy objectives: U.S. policy toward the Middle East; U.S. policy toward the former Soviet Union and China; and the fight against international terrorism. Meanwhile, across much of the developing world, energy infrastructure is being severely tested by the expanding material demands of a growing middle class, especially in the high growth, high population economies of Asia. As demand growth collided with supply and capacity limits at the end of the last century, prices rose across the energy spectrum, at home and abroad." (Strategic Energy Policy Challenges for the XXI century, CFR report).

James Woolsey, the former CIA director, is a member of a powerful circle responsible for promoting an extremist agenda known as the

"Project For The New American Century" (PNAC). This is an aggressive "defense" and foreign policy strategy developed since 1997 by a group backed by the neoconservatives around the Bush administration, and whose implementation in practice is led by Vice President Cheney. Anything Woolsey has to say is worth a quote in the press. Thus, in an interview by the Washington Post on June 7, 2000, Woolsey talked about the energy crisis, which, he said, "should have a severe impact, be global in scope, and be difficult to solve. Plainly, it will be unprecedented," and since "... the Mid East will increasingly become the source of the world's oil," he went on to say, "this is a strategic problem for us and for many other countries."

In fact, he admitted in an article titled, "The New Petroleum" for the journal Foreign Affairs, January/February 1999: "The underlying goal of the U.N. force in Gulf War I, which included 500,000 American troops, was to ensure continued and unfettered access to petroleum."

Energy for the Bilderberg cabal is clearly of utmost concern. One of the points discussed on the Bilderberger agenda in 2000 squarely dealt with oil and the Caspian Basin.

In our current world, energy is oil and natural gas. Bush is oil. Oil is Bush. Bush's administration is filled with ex-oil men and women: Bush, Cheney, Rumsfeld, and Rice (a former ExxonMobil board member). These people, before any of us even knew, were only too well aware of the situation and terrible consequences. Initially it was believed that the Caspian Basin held enough oil and natural gas reserves to supply the markets for the rest of the 21st century, but some time between the end of 1998 and the beginning of the year 2000, as top secret reports on drilling and exploration from the Caspian Basin came in, these people became aware of the pending calamity and the imminence of an international economic collapse. What would happen if the markets and subsequently, the shareholders and the politicians, and ultimately the people found out that the energy numbers were being inflated to hide the pending disaster?

The Caspian results could not be kept secret forever.

Some argue that oil price hikes are a speculative phenomenon. Others argue that production cuts are man-made, that they are artificial, and that this is a clear case of greed and price-gouging with the OPEC and capitalist west colluding to cut production in order to make more money. Assuredly the profits of the oil companies are at record highs and there are industry insiders that claim political and industry manipulation.

The pessimistic predictions have dripped continually, Britain's Foreign Secretary, Jack Straw, during his address to a group of more than 150 British diplomats on January 10, 2003, where the Guardian of London reported that Straw admitted future oil supply was a key motivator in Britain's decision to participate in the U.S.-led Iraq war. The Times of London, on December 11, 2004, also reported that with "the depletion of gas reserves in the North Sea and the Irish Sea ... it is expected that Britain will have to import 75 per cent of its gas by 2015."

According to the World Socialist Web site, "more than 92% of Europe's oil and 81% of its gas, will have to be imported from oversees within 30 years. The country, or countries, able to establish control over this vital resource will secure a major advantage over their international rivals. This is a prime factor motivating U.S. policy in the Middle East. By occupying Iraq and seizing its oil resources, the U.S. hopes to establish its undisputed hegemony over Europe and Japan."[2]

Oil energy expert Jan Lundberg's calculations say that the United States lost between 20% and 25% of its energy supply as a result of Hurricane Katrina. Oil prices rose to over US$70/barrel, yet the Saudis continued to not increase production. These are the same Saudis, who, for some time, have been bragging about the infinite quantities of oil to be found under their feet. Are they trying to gauge world markets? Or is the simple answer is that they just can't. That, they are flat out.[3] If the Saudis are out of spare oil, we are in deep trouble.

You can see this crisis of cataclysmic proportions happening all around you. Gasoline prices and natural gas prices are at, or near, their all-time highs. Fruit and vegetables are more expensive than ever, yet their quality has never been poorer. Transportation costs are expensive, so are your bananas. Mark Williams, writing for the Technology Review in February 2005 had this to say: "If the actions, rather than the words, of the oil business' major players provide the best gauge of how they see the future, then ponder the following. Crude oil prices have doubled since 2001, but oil companies have increased their budgets

---

2. "Britain: Foreign secretary admits oil central to war vs. Iraq," World Socialist Web Site, Julie Hyland, January 14, 2003.
3. "Paris Peak Oil conference reveals deepening crisis," From the Wilderness publication, May 30, 2003

for exploring new oil fields by only a small fraction. Likewise, U.S. refineries are working close to capacity, yet no new refinery has been constructed since 1976."

They are not drilling more because they are certain there are no more large oil pools out there to find. More drilling doesn't mean more oil. It means higher expense, which inadvertently cuts into their profit. It also means more holes in the ground. If these holes hold little or no oil, they are worthless. In fact, "oil companies are spending only 12% of their total capital expenditure on finding new oil fields, down from nearly a third in 1990," according to a report from investment bank Credit Suisse First Boston.

The bank's statement was picked up by the Dow Jones Newswire service on January 17, 2005. The implications of this should be self-evident. The reason that there is virtually no exploration or refinery construction is that the oil cartel, represented by the most powerful members within the Bilderberg group, such as the Rockefellers, Peter Sutherland [BP] and Queen Beatrix of the Netherlands, understand there is no more significant oil to find. Their investment will never pay off.

Does the end of oil mean the end of the world's financial system? This has already been acknowledged by the Wall Street Journal and the Financial Times, two fulltime confidants of the Bilderberger inner circle. An oil report from Goldman Sachs (another fulltime player of the Bilderberger elite), published on March 30, 2005 increased the predicted oil price-range for the year 2005-6 from $55-$80 per barrel to $55-$105. During the 2006 meeting, Bilderbergers confirmed that their short-range price estimate for oil for the 2006-07 period continued to hover around $150/barrel.

According to sources present at the meeting, the world's leading executives tried in vain to find a way to prevent the public from learning the truth about the alarming decrease of estimated oil reserves. Public awareness of the fall of the reserves could give way to a panic, causing an immediate price explosion, and forcing a collapse of the world economy, according to the same sources.

Besides, the Bilderbergers did not wish a drop in the price of oil because low oil prices might precipitate the implosion of the debt bubble.

The U.S. Federal Reserve System, which is heavily influenced by the Bilderberg Group is very concerned about the debt bubble.

Since the technology bubble burst in March 2000, many investors have sought the safety of the national debt and the housing markets as opposed to the inherent risks of the Stock Exchange, weary of the losses caused by the bubble and by the accounting scandals of the likes of Enron, Tyco, WorldCom, Global Crossing, as well as by the period of geopolitical uncertainties caused by 9-11 and the War in Iraq.

This and the deliberate policy of both the Federal Reserve Board of the United States and the European Central Bank of maintaining low interest rates, thus trying to assure that, in such a difficult period, liquidity would never be absent from the world's financial markets, bond prices increased to all-time maximums. The Federal Reserve thought that this trend would be modified as soon as they began raising interest rates, as it had been doing since 2004.

Nevertheless, bond prices, far from falling as was expected continued their upward climb to historical highs, giving way to the debt bubble. The problem is that, if now high oil prices unleash an inflationary process, this bubble could collapse, causing important losses amongst investors, especially the banking sector and the owners of the capital-risk hedge funds, unleashing along the way financial crises as devastating in scope and magnitude as the 1997 Asian crisis.

IRAN

Instead of knocking off Iraq then moving promptly to the next target — Iran — the Bush administration has now played the foil for Iran, and put within Iran's reach what it has sought for decades: the position of key political actor in the region and the world. But the going is tough. During Bilderberg meeting 2006, European delegates told the U.S. contingent in blunt terms that the Iran adventure was off the table, and that in case the Bush administration was still entertaining a notion of attack, it would have to do it alone.

The United States needs to control the region, not only to control its oil reserves but, most importantly, to help it sustain world economic hegemony. Under this strategic design, regional states will be turned to weak domains of sectarian sheikhs with little or no sovereignty, and, by implication, a pathetic agenda for their economic development. Regional chaos favors the spread of Islamic fundamentalism, which in turn reinforces the process of political and social disintegration supported by the Bilderbergers.

IMMINENT COLLAPSE OF THE U.S. HOUSING MARKET

The world found itself at the precipice of the most devastating financial collapse in modern history. There was no set date to this calamitous event, but it was expected to happen very, very soon. One of the principal reasons is the fact that today, the U.S. financial system is dependent for survival on the most important real-estate bubble in human history. A hyperinflationary spiral has forced housing price hikes of between 10 and 40 % per annum over the last several years in some areas, which have pushed the prices of millions of homes into the stratosphere.

Leading American banking institutions voiced their alarm at the precarious situation of the U.S. real estate market. Page one of the business section of the Washington Post on April 7, 2006 warned of the imminent collapse of the real estate bubble in some parts of the United States.

That year the cumulative value of all American homes was a chilling 12 trillion dollars. Millions of families have purchased $500,000 houses, making 40 to 60 % of annual earnings in mortgage payments, betting that if they could keep the house for a 2-5 year period, they would be able to resell it for a considerable profit in a bullish real estate market.

The bad news was that soon the pool of prospective buyers would have disappeared forever. Many families worked a combined three jobs per family to pay the mortgage. The next round of layoffs that eliminated one of those jobs would leave them without means to make their monthly payments, causing a major default en masse on mortgage payments throughout the country.

The percentage of foreclosures on mortgages insured by the Federal Housing Administration (used mainly as a barometer for low and mid income families) reached 10 % in urban areas of the United States — the highest percentage over the prior decade. When the accumulative wave of mortgage foreclosures spread, the real estate bubble would burst, annihilating trillions of dollars in housing value.

"We are sitting on top of the collapse of the real-estate bubble in the United States," said one Bilderberger delegate during the June 9 session at the luxurious Brookstreet Hotel. "The exact date of when it will explode, I do not know. But it will explode. People who have taken years to pay down their $500,000 homes will be lucky if they can get $100,000 for them."

WHERE TO INVEST THE MONEY?

The fundamental principles of gold and silver, in spite of their extreme volatility and recent price drop, were on a medium-term trend up; the American dollar and the Dow Jones, on a medium-term trend down. Although the manipulation (suppression) of the price of gold over the past several decades is very well documented, the prior two years had shown that the anti-gold cartel had lost its ability to keep gold prices down.

Furthermore, the central banks of both China and the Russian Federation had recently announced their intentions of buying large quantities of gold. The price of oil, as I mentioned, was expected to continue to rise.

BILDERBERG 2007
MAY 31 – JUNE 3,
ISTANBUL, TURKEY

After a sumptuous lunch on this warm and sunny 3rd of June, most Bilderbergers returned to their home countries, freshly armed with precise instructions from the Steering Committee regarding how to proceed in covertly expanding the powers of the One World Government.

As a rhetorical question, can someone please explain to me how it is that progressive liberals such as John Edwards and Hillary Clinton, as well as do-gooder humanitarians with multiple social projects ongoing such as the Rockefellers and every Royal House in Europe, can perennially attend Bilderberg meetings apparently knowing that the final objective of this despicable group of hoodlums is a fascist One World Empire? How can it be orchestrated?

The idea is to give to each country a political constitution and an appropriate national economic structure, organized for the following purposes: (1) to place political power into the hands of chosen people and eliminate all intermediaries; (2) to establish a maximum concentration of industries and suppress all unwarranted competition; (3) to establish absolute control of prices of all goods and raw materials (Bilderbergers make it possible through their iron-grip control of the World Bank, the International Monetary Fund and the World Trade Organization); and (4) to create judicial and social institutions that would prevent all extremes of action.

The following is a summary of some key points made, with additional commentary added. Other subjects discussed: climate change and global warming, Turkey's role in the new European Union, World Bank reforms, Middle East geopolitics, the conflict in Iraq, Iran's potential nuclear threat, and the future of democracy and populism.

ROBERT ZOELLICK AND THE WORLD BANK

The United States delegation was standing unanimously behind Robert Zoellick's candidacy as the next President of the World Bank. Zoellick is a 53-year-old Wall Street executive, a former official in two Bush administrations and a free-market fundamentalist. During the meeting, he pledged "to work to restore confidence in the bank."

"We need to put our differences aside and focus on the future together. I believe that the World Bank's best days are still to come," Zoellick said. The chances of Zoellick not being approved for the presidency were slim to none. The final decision was to be made in late June by the bank's 24-member board of directors.

The United States and Europe have a tacit agreement that the World Bank's President should always be a U.S. national, while its sister institution, the International Monetary Fund (IMF), should always be headed by a European. Nevertheless, according to our sources at the conference, European Bilderbergers were not at all pleased with continuing the status quo, in which the U.S. once again nominated a single candidate after informal consultations with World Bank members.

The Zoellick nomination also appears to short-circuit burgeoning calls for reform of this selection process at the World Bank, one of the cornerstones of the global financial architecture designed by the victors of World War II. One Belgian Bilderberger proposed "a merit-based selection process, without regard to nationality," something which will obviously be discarded by the inept Bush administration. What is quite remarkable is that on several occasions European Bilderbergers have openly rejected the current model, saying "the nomination reeks of double standards," especially because both the USA and the World Bank preach accountability and transparency to developing countries, the main clients of the bank.

But with the IMF under the control of a Spaniard, Rodrigo Rato, and the European Central Bank headed by a Frenchman, Jean-Claude Trichet, it was difficult to imagine that the U.S. would give up control of the World Bank. Only the U.S. Federal Reserve would then remain in the hands of the Americans.

"Replacing one Bush appointee with another will not resolve the fundamental governance problems of the World Bank," said one Scandinavian. "Member governments should reject a backdoor deal that leaves the bank's governance structure intact, and should press for an open, merit-based selection process," he said. Zoellick's name also raised eyebrows among development groups for his close ties to the U.S. establishment and corporate interests.

One of the attendees asked Zoellick how he was planning to patch up relationships with Third and Fourth World nations when he was best remembered during his tenure as U.S. Trade Representative for arm-twisting poor nations' governments to adhere to U.S.-imposed intellectual-property laws that make medicines, for example, unaffordable in the developing world. Zoellick has been a close friend to the brand-name pharmaceutical industry, and the bilateral trade agreements he has negotiated effectively block access to generic medications for millions of people.

However, what has really riled both the American and European delegates is the fact that the World Bank's dirty linen was being washed in public, thanks in great part to Paul Wolfowitz and his ineptness, which incidentally he blamed on the press.

On June 25, Robert Zoellick was unanimously elected President of the World Bank for a five-year term, taking over from Paul Wolfowitz on July 1. In a statement posted at http://www.worldbank.org, he said, "Once I start at the World Bank, I will be eager to meet the people who drive the agenda of overcoming poverty in all regions, with particular attention to Africa, advancing social and economic development, investing in growth, and encouraging hope, opportunity and dignity."

RELATIONS WITH RUSSIA

A nother issue of great concern to both American and European Bilderbergers was Russia's current muscle-flexing on the issue of energy. The controversy over the TNK-BP license, British Petroleum's Russian venture, was just one of many circumstances causing anger amongst the globalist elite.

One American Bilderberger said that after years of economic stagnation, "Russia is acting against unipolarity's accommodating ideologies and politics, against its recently resurgent manifestations and machinations, and against the instruments of its perpetuation, such as the North Atlantic Treaty Organization [NATO]."

Bilderberg 2007 served as a consensus-building exercise to decide on a common policy and strategy to deal with Russia's resurgence. In particular, Bilderberg was not at all happy with Russia's current strategy of actively dismantling what remains of "the atmosphere of acquiescence to America's will," in the words of one Bilderberger, which arose in the post-Soviet period and was absolutely crucial to the thriving of U.S.-led unipolarity.

That was in the beginning of the 1990s, the early stages of the Yeltsin reign. With the wholesale looting of Russia in the 1990s through shock therapy and the loans-for-shares scheme, engineered by the socialist theoreticians at Harvard such as Jeffrey Sachs, Andrei Schliefer, David Lipton and Jonathan Hay, the country was brought into the dawn of the 21st century capitalist economy. As a result, Russia eventually toppled into anarchy, its population rendered desperate; its ability to support a world-class military establishment was smashed, which then made it inevitable that colonial exploitation would occur. That is exactly what George Ball was proposing during the Bilderberg 1968 meeting in Canada.

Incidentally, the term "shock therapy" refers to the sudden release of price and currency controls combined with the withdrawal of state subsidies and immediate trade liberalization within a country — all the necessary ingredients for impoverishment of the society; in this case, Russia. Clearly, to the Bilderbergers, Russia was the beginning of the end game.

In Zbigniew Brzezinski's 1997 book The Grand Chessboard, "Russia" and "vital energy reserves," as it turns out, are mentioned more frequently than any other country or subject in the book. According to Brzezinski, global U.S. and thus Bilderberg hegemony depended on having complete control of Russia's vital energy reserves in Central Asia. As long as Russia remained strong, it remained a threat — a potential block to the complete imposition of Bilderberg-led economic and military will. Bilderberg energy imperatives and geopolitical control are once again coming to play a key role in the lives of hundreds of millions of unsuspecting people.

Brzezinski spelled out in The Grand Chessboard the compelling energy issue driving American policy: "A power that dominates Eurasia would control two of the world's three most advanced and economically productive regions. A mere glance at the map also suggests that control over Eurasia would almost automatically entail Africa's subordination, rendering the Western Hemisphere and Oceania geopolitically peripheral to the world's central continent. About 75 percent of the world's people live in Eurasia, and most of the world's physical wealth is there as well, both in its enterprise and underneath its soil. Eurasia accounts for 60 percent of the world's GNP and about three-fourth of the world's known energy resources."[4]

The history of mankind has always shown that controlling the heart of Eurasia is the key to controlling the entire known world. Azerbaijan, containing the riches of the Caspian Sea Basin and Central Asia, is a case in point. From the U.S. perspective, the independence of the Central Asian states will be rendered nearly meaningless if Azerbaijan becomes fully subordinated to Moscow's control. To the Bilderbergers, energy imperatives are the end game.

The energy theme appears again later in Brzezinski's book, written four years before 9/11: "The world's energy consumption is bound to vastly increase over the next two or three decades. Estimates by the U.S. Department of Energy anticipate that world demand will rise by more than 50 percent between 1993 and 2015, with the most significant increase in consumption occurring in the Far East. The momentum of Asia's economic development is already generating massive pressures for the exploration and exploitation of new sources of energy."

4. Brzezinski, Zbigniew, The Grand Chessboard: Americaan Primacy And Its Geostrategic Imperatives, Basic Books, 1997

Clearly, to the Bilderbergers, Russia was the beginning of the end game.

Could the eventual dismemberment and weakening of Russia – to the point that it could not oppose U.S. military operations that have now successfully secured control of the oil and gas reserves in Central Asia – been part of a multi-decade plan for global domination? Most credible senior analysts seem to believe so.

At a 1997 symposium held in Bonn, Germany, Dr. Sergei Glazyev, Chairman of the Economic Policy Committee of the State Duma of the Russian Federation, made a stark declaration: "This colonization, masked as reforms, destroyed the basic institutions of Russian society along the following basic lines: (1) destruction of the financial system of the state, by means of an endless buildup of the state debt pyramid, shrinking of the tax base, deepening of the non-payments crisis, and disorganization of the monetary system; (2) destruction of the scientific and technological potential of the country, achieved by means of a many-fold reduction in state financing of science, the collapse of technological cooperation and scientific production integration in the course of mass privatization, and the refusal of the government to have any scientific and technical, industrial or structural policy at all; (3) sale of controlling blocs of shares in the leading and most valuable Russian firms, in industry, electric power and telecommunications, to foreign companies; (4) Transfer of the right to exploit the most valuable Russian raw materials deposits to transnational corporations; (5) establishment of foreign control over the Russian stock exchange; (6) establishment of direct foreign control over the shaping of Russian domestic and foreign economic policy."[5]

But, one Finnish delegate's opinion that "no U.S.–Russia military confrontation is likely, no matter how tense things should get" is increasingly an unsafe one as a more desperate U.S. pushes back against a much more aggressive Russia.

Henry Kissinger added that "aggressive, unilateralist U.S. foreign policy has forced 'axis of evil' states to accelerate their pursuit of nuclear weapons to immunize themselves against U.S. military strikes."

Richard Perle pointed out that in response to aggressive U.S. tactics across the globe, Russia has undertaken asymmetric steps to undermine the ability of the U.S. to project its military power effectively into

---

5. Glazyev, Sergei, "From a Five-Year Plan of Destruction to a Five-Year Plan of Colonisation," EIR Bonn Symposium, 1997

their neighborhoods and into those of their partners and allies. When one American Bilderberger tried to object, European delegates brought up China's recent response to U.S. intentions to weaponize space: a simple and relatively inexpensive demonstration of a shoot-down of its satellite. The example produced snickering in the room, much to the chagrin of the Americans.

AFGHANISTAN

Another subject under discussion was Afghanistan. It was commonly agreed by the attendees that the U.S.-led NATO alliance/mission was in a state of quagmire, and that "the situation in the country is getting worse." The problem could be defined, in the words of one British Bilderberger, as "one of unreal expectations." He went on to explain that the dichotomy of clamoring for democratic reform while simultaneously propping up Pashtun warlords without delivering serious progress "has managed to discredit a lot of our basic notions in the eyes of the Afghans."

Bilderbergers, however, aren't the only ones left scratching their heads about how Western governments and their carefully chosen Afghan partners have managed to spend billions of dollars in development assistance with little to show for it. Catastrophe is good for business — always has been. Without suffering, there would be no humanitarian assistance. And without humanitarian assistance, there would be no room for undercover intelligence network operations as part of Western imperatives for geopolitical control.

The worse it looked, the better it sold. While the American people were getting their daily diet of ubiquitous images of repression, suffering and burka-clad Afghani women beamed into every living room, a propaganda campaign was surreptitiously launched in the pages of newspapers and glossy magazines. The New York Times and the New Yorker were greasing the gears of the misery machine by urging the U.S. government, the United Nations and anyone who would listen to "do something"—amid the jewelry advertisements. Terror and horror, like expensive jewelry, became commodities.

Afghanistan and its African cousins of Sudan, Ethiopia, Eritrea, Congo and Rwanda, and the rest of the nations blessed with Western humanitarian help, are now all basket cases. Bilderbergers seemed to be asking key questions: How is it possible that humanitarian missions of such scale and magnitude could have failed so miserably? Is it a case of good-intentioned exercises going bad due to corruption, greed and lack of oversight? Or it is the merciless dismemberment of yet more foreign lands and cultures exercised stealthily through humanitarian aid agencies tied to the larger apparatus of government?

Furthermore, the U.S. government's support for known Afghan drug warlords adds another vital clue to the puzzle. The amount of profit generated annually by the drug trade, according to the United Nations, is somewhere around $700 billion in tax-free cash-flow per year. Seven hundred billion dollars a year is too much money to hide in a sock. You need a lot of experience and expertise to move those kinds of funds stealthily. Does anyone doubt that Afghanistan is about drugs? Does anyone doubt that the CIA is involved?

For example, the CIA financed the Muslim Brotherhood in 1977 and trained the mujahedin in preparation for the campaign of collusion between Washington and right-wing Islam: the Afghan War. The roots of the Afghan conflict can be traced to Al-Azhar Mosque in Cairo, the center of the Muslim Brotherhood's activity. Shortly after the 9/11 attacks, alleged airline hijacker Mohammed Atta was identified as a Muslim Brother in several Western publications, such as the Washington Post (September 22, 2001), The Observer (September 23, 2001) and Newsweek (December 31, 2001). Other Muslim Brothers involved were Khalid Sheik Mohammed and Ramzi Yousef, who masterminded the 1993 bombing of the World Trade Center. Osama bin Laden's right-hand man, the Egyptian Ayman al-Zawahiri, is also a lifelong member of the Brotherhood.

Robert Dreyfuss, in his extremely important book Devil's Game,[4] explained it thus: "They returned to Afghanistan and formed a branch of the Brothers, the Islamic Society. Later, these same 'professors,' as they were known, would form the backbone of the Afghan mujahedin who waged a U.S.-backed, decade-long war against the Soviet occupation. The three leading 'professors' were Abdul Rasul Sayyaf, Burhanuddin Rabbani and Gulbuddin Hekmatyar." Sayyaf and Hekmatyar, two big-time Pashtun drug traffickers and CIA assets, were backed by Pakistani Intelligence, as well as Pakistan's own "branch" of the Brotherhood, and funded by Saudi money.[6]

---

6. Dreyfuss, Robert, Devil's Game: How the United States Helped Unleash Fundamentalist Islam, Henry Holt & Co., New York, 2005

There was yet another link between the Brotherhood and the Bilderberg Group. In the early 1980s, Bilderberger Michael Ledeen of the ultraconservative American Enterprise Institute and Bilderberger Richard Perle used Hekmatyar as a poster boy of anti-Soviet resistance at the time when Hekmatyar was actively working with Hezb-i-Islami terrorists to undermine America's influence in Afghanistan.

During an animated discussion, one Italian asked if the U.S.-led NATO forces had "the will to stay the course," perhaps recalling that, in the wake of the U.S. military siege of Tora Bora in December 2001, the commanding general, Tommy Franks, reportedly said it was not his intention to "get embroiled in a Soviet-style long-term engagement as in the 1980s."[7] In 2007, however, American Bilderbergers were pressuring NATO allies to provide larger troop contributions to the cause.

Henry Kissinger insisted that "the will" is lacking, and so "we must now begin to acknowledge our limits." One European Royal wholeheartedly agreed with Kissinger's assessment of the lack of commitment and will, adding, "The choices facing us are very difficult."

A NATO representative categorically stated that the West has neither the political intelligence nor the understanding to fight a protracted, decade-long counterinsurgency campaign in Afghanistan.

---

7. Smucker, Philip, "Missions impossible: NATO's Afghan dilemma", Asia Times Online, 1 June 2007, http://www.atimes.com/atimes/South_Asia/IF01Df01.html

INDEX

AUTHOR'S AFTERWORD

This conflict, between those who love freedom and those who wish to subjugate us, is far from over. Successes have been many, but so have disappointments. A group of very determined freedom-loving citizens from across the globe has forced the all-powerful Bilderbergers to take cover, to become more secretive, more paranoid, and henceforth less invisible. We have been joined in our fight by men and women from every Western and some Eastern European secret service agencies. Little happens in the corridors of power which is not almost immediately relayed to us through our trusted contacts. We operate within the law, triple checking our sources, references and leads. This effort is far from easy. But when I weaken and grow tired of the sacrifice this struggle has demanded from me, I think of millions of people from around the world who have fought and died so that one day, we, the generations who have come in their wake, can enjoy the privileges of liberty and the honest and decent pursuit of happiness their sacrifice has afforded us.

There was a time, when down on my luck, angry and frustrated because no one seemed to listen, to understand and to fathom the dark clouds gathering all around us, I felt betrayed by society and took it very personally and very hard. I wanted to run away, to be alone, to feel sorry for myself, and to blame the rest of the world for the misdeeds of a criminal few. Then, I grew up. I thought of the families of the Israelis and Palestinians killed in an ever spiralling violence of hatred whose lives have forever been destroyed by the unspeakable evil hatred represents. This hatred is not spontaneous.

It has been masterfully imposed and managed from behind the scenes by the Bilderberger/CFR/TC/Round Table/RIIA controllers, who are dragging the unwilling world to its utter decimation. I thought of millions of crack babies born in inner-city ghettos and tens of millions of opiate addicts whose future has been turned into drug addiction because a select few make a lot of money from the misfortunes of others.

I thought of the lies and deaths of hundreds of millions of innocent young soldiers who were sent by the slick propaganda campaigns to their demise at Verdun and every other engagement of WWI, WWII, Korea, Viet Nam, the Falklands, Panama, Afghanistan, Iraq, etc., etc., etc. I thought of Agent Orange and the Gulf War syndrome responsible for turning strong young, square-shouldered soldiers into frail old men at the age of 30. I thought of the hundreds of thousands dying in the firebombing of Dresden, unwitting "guinea pigs" in the Tavistock instigated psychological warfare experiments.

And I stand firm and determined with the ever-growing number of people worldwide who have lost all faith in their governments, who are sick to their stomachs of the lies and the greed and the duplicity, the pantomime, the facetiousness and the manipulation, by those who call themselves our "leaders."

Three hundred and seventy years ago, Galileo Galilei was persecuted for teaching that the earth was a round planet that revolved around the sun. The Catholic Church and much of the citizenry reviled the great man because they were terrified that this truth would upset the social order. As someone has said, "The problem is people's inherent unwillingness to face things of which they are afraid, thereby scapegoating and sacrificing their fellows to an evil they dare not confront themselves."

I live for the day and the hour in which men and women of honor will recognize that dignity, kindness, integrity, trust, love of thy fellow beings are as indispensable to the survival of the human race as Galileo's discoveries were. These principles of humanity should be enshrined on some document somewhere, so that should a future despot decide to betray Humanity once again, he will pay dearly for it.

On the surface, this book is about a secretive Group known simply as the Bilderbergers. On a much deeper level, however, it is about inner faith and conviction, which public opinion, bribery, lust for money and power cannot influence. This book is about the integrity and honor of many individuals. It is about helping people learn to think, and stand independent in their thoughts even from the so-called experts, masterfully represented by every major media group who would tell them which conspiracy theory not to believe.

This book is also about my life, about my refusing to live in fear. Until my dying breath, I shall live as a free man, walking the earth as a free man does, with my head held high. Only when we decide to let fear govern our actions will those whom we oppose and despise truly won.

Daniel Estulin
September 22, 2007

Dr. Mary's Monkey
How the Unsolved Murder of a Doctor, a Secret Laboratory in New Orleans and Cancer-Causing Monkey Viruses are Linked to Lee Harvey Oswald, the JFK Assassination and Emerging Global Epidemics
BY EDWARD T. HASLAM, FOREWORD BY JIM MARRS

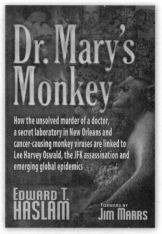

Evidence of top-secret medical experiments and cover-ups of clinical blunders
The 1964 murder of a nationally known cancer researcher sets the stage for this gripping exposé of medical professionals enmeshed in covert government operations over the course of three decades. Following a trail of police records, FBI files, cancer statistics, and medical journals, this revealing book presents evidence of a web of medical secret-keeping that began with the handling of evidence in the JFK assassination and continued apace, sweeping doctors into cover-ups of cancer outbreaks, contaminated polio vaccine, the genesis of the AIDS virus, and biological weapon research using infected monkeys.

Softcover: **$19.95** (ISBN: 0977795306) • 320 pages • Size: 5 1/2 x 8 1/2

Fighting For G.O.D.
(Gold, Oil, Drugs)
BY JEREMY BEGIN, ART BY LAUREEN SALK

This analysis delves into aspects of the larger framework into which 9/11 fits and scrutinizes the ancestry of the players who transcend commonly accepted liberal/conservative political ideologies. This comic-book format analysis examines the Neo Con agenda and its relationship to "The New World Order." From the privatized fund-raising system to which politicians are beholden to evidence contradicting the conventional wisdom that the 19 hijackers took our nation by surprise and the widespread suppression of human rights, this book discusses key issues confronting America's citizenry and steps the populace can take to not only halt but reverse the march towards totalitarianism.

Softcover: **$9.95**, (ISBN 0977795330) 64 Pages, 8.5 x 11

The Oil Card
Global Economic Warfare in the 21st Century
BY JAMES NORMAN

Challenging the conventional wisdom surrounding high oil prices, this compelling argument sheds an entirely new light on free-market industry fundamentals. By deciphering past, present, and future geopolitical events, it makes the case that oil pricing and availability have a long history of being employed as economic weapons by the United States. Despite ample world supplies and reserves, high prices are now being used to try to rein in China—a reverse of the low-price strategy used in the 1980s to deprive the Soviets of hard currency. Far from conspiracy theory, the debate notes how the U.S. has previously used the oil majors, the Saudis, and market intervention to move markets—and shows how this is happening again.

—Available in July 2008—

Softcover **$14.95** (ISBN 0977795390) • 240 Pages • Size: 5.5 x 8.5

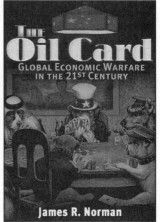

Expendable Elite
One Soldier's Journey into Covert Warfare
BY DANIEL MARVIN , FOREWORD BY MARTHA RAYE

A special operations perspective on the Viet Nam War and the truth about a White House concerned with popular opinion

This true story of a special forces officer in Viet Nam in the mid-1960s exposes the unique nature of the elite fighting force and how covert operations are developed and often masked to permit—and even sponsor—assassination, outright purposeful killing of innocents, illegal use of force, and bizarre methods in combat operations. *Expendable Elite* reveals the fear that these warriors share with no other military person: not fear of the enemy they have been trained to fight in battle, but fear of the wrath of the U.S. government should they find themselves classified as "expendable." This book centers on the CIA mission to assassinate Cambodian Crown Prince Nordum Sihanouk, the author's unilateral aborting of the mission, the CIA's dispatch of an ARVN regiment to attack and destroy the camp and kill every person in it as retribution for defying the agency, and the dramatic rescue of eight American Green Berets and hundreds of South Viet Namese.

—NEW SPECIAL VICTORY EDITION—   Commemorating our Free Speech Federal Court triumph that allows you to read this book exposing the true ways of of war!

—READ THE BOOK,"THEY" DON'T WANT YOU TO!—

DANIEL MARVIN is a retired Lieutenant Colonel in the U.S. Army Special Forces and former Green Beret.

Softcover: **$19.95** (ISBN 0977795314) • 420 pages • 150+ photos & maps

The Franklin Scandal
A Story of Powerbrokers, Child Abuse & Betrayal
BY NICK BRYANT

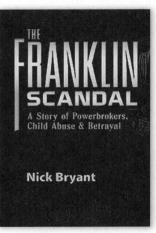

A chilling exposé of corporate corruption and government cover-ups, this account of a nationwide child-trafficking and pedophilia ring tells a sordid tale of corruption in high places. The scandal originally surfaced during an investigation into Omaha, Nebraska's failed Franklin Federal Credit Union and took the author beyond the Midwest and ultimately to Washington, DC. Implicating businessmen, senators, major media corporations, the CIA, and even the venerable Boys Town organization, this extensively researched report includes firsthand interviews with key witnesses and explores a controversy that has received scant media attention.

The Franklin Scandal is the story of a underground ring that pandered children to a cabal of the rich and powerful. The ring's pimps were a pair of Republican powerbrokers who used Boys Town as a pedophiliac reservoir, and had access to the highest levels of our government and connections to the CIA.

Hardcover: **$24.95** (ISBN: 0977795357) • 350 pages • Size: 6 x 9
—*Available 2008*—

Fixing America
Breaking the Stranglehold of Corporate Rule, Big Media, and the Religious Right
BY JOHN BUCHANAN, FOREWORD BY JOHN MCCONNELL

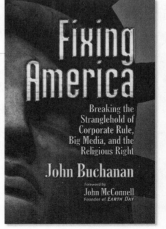

An explosive analysis of what ails the United States

An award-winning investigative reporter provides a clear, honest diagnosis of corporate rule, big media, and the religious right in this damning analysis. Exposing the darker side of capitalism, this critique raises alarms about the security of democracy in today's society, including the rise of the corporate state, the insidious role of professional lobbyists, the emergence of religion and theocracy as a right-wing political tactic, the failure of the mass media, and the sinister presence of an Orwellian neo-fascism.

Softcover: **$19.95**, (ISBN 0-975290681) 216 Pages, 5.5 x 8.5

America's Secret Establishment
An Introduction to the Order of Skull & Bones
BY ANTONY C. SUTTON

The book that first exposed the story behind America's most powerful secret society
For 170 years they have met in secret. From out of their initiates come presidents, senators, judges, cabinet secretaries, and plenty of spooks. They are the titans of finance and industry and have now installed a third member as United States President George W. Bush. This intriguing behind-the-scenes look documents Yale's secretive society, the Order of the Skull and Bones, and its prominent members, numbering among them Tafts, Rockefellers, Pillsburys, and Bushes. Far from being a campus fraternity, the society is more concerned with the success of its members in the post-collegiate world. Included are a verified membership list, rare reprints of original Order materials revealing the interlocking power centers dominated by Bonesmen, and a peek inside the Tomb, their 140-year-old private clubhouse.

ANTONY C. SUTTON was a research fellow at the Hoover Institution at Stanford University and an economics professor at California State University, Los Angeles and is author of 21 books, including *Wall Street and the Rise of Hitler*.

Softcover: **$19.95** (ISBN 0972020748) 335 pages • Size: 5 x 8

Fleshing Out Skull & Bones
Investigations into America's Most Powerful Secret Society
EDITED BY KRIS MILLEGAN

An expose of Yale's supersecretive and elite Order of Skull & Bones
This chronicle of espionage, drug smuggling, and elitism in Yale University's Skull & Bones society offers rare glimpses into this secret world with previously unpublished documents, photographs, and articles that delve into issues such as racism, financial ties to the Nazi party, and illegal corporate dealings. Contributors include Antony Sutton, author of *America's Secret Establishment*; Dr. Ralph Bunch, professor emeritus of political science at Portland State University; Webster Griffin Tarpley and Anton Chaitkin, authors and historians; and Howard Altman, editor of the *Philadelphia City Paper*. A complete list of known members, including George Bush and George W. Bush, and reprints of rare magazine articles on the Order of Skull and Bones are included.

Softcover: **$24.95** (ISBN 0975290606) 720 pages • Size: 6x9

The Octopus Conspiracy
and Other Vignettes of the Counterculture
from Hippies to High Times to Hip Hop and Beyond ...
BY STEVEN HAGER

Insightful essays on the genesis of subcultures from new wave and yuppies to graffiti and rap.
From the birth of hip-hop culture in the South Bronx to the influence of nightclubs in shaping the modern art world in New York, a generation of countercultural events and icons are brought to life in this personal account of the life and experiences of a former investigative reporter and editor of High Times. Evidence from cutting-edge conspiracy research including the real story behind the JFK assassination and the Franklin Savings and Loan cover-up is presented. Quirky personalities and compelling snapshots of life in the 1980s and 1990s emerge in this collection of vignettes from a landmark figure in journalism.

STEVEN HAGER is the author of *Adventures in Counterculture, Art After Midnight,* and *Hip Hop.* He is a former reporter for the New York Daily News and an editor of *High Times.*

Hardcover: **$19.95** (ISBN 0975290614) • 320 pages • Size: 6 x 9

Jaded Tasks
Brass Plates. Black Ops, & Big Oil - The Blood Politics of George Bush & Co.
BY WAYNE MADSEN

This investigative account details how America's economic and intelligence associations with Saudi Arabia and Pakistan led to the devastating September 11 attacks and illustrates the role that private military companies are playing in George W. Bush's "new world order." Based on personal interviews, never-before-published classified documents, and extensive research, this examination details the criminal forces thought to rule the world today—the Bush cartel, Russian-Ukranian-Israeli mafia, and Wahhabist Saudi terror financiers—revealing links between these groups and disastrous events such as 9/11.

Wayne scares the hell out of the Military-Industrial-Mendacity Complex — Greg Palast

Paperback: **$19.95**, 320 Pages, 5.5 x 8.5

Sinister Forces
A Grimoire of American Political Witchcraft
Book One: The Nine
BY PETER LEVENDA, FOREWORD BY JIM HOUGAN

A shocking alternative to the conventional views of American history.
The roots of coincidence and conspiracy in American politics, crime, and culture are examined in this book, exposing new connections between religion, political conspiracy, and occultism. Readers are taken from ancient American civilization and the mysterious mound builder culture to the Salem witch trials, the birth of Mormonism during a ritual of ceremonial magic by Joseph Smith, Jr., and Operations Paperclip and Bluebird. Not a work of speculative history, this exposé is founded on primary source material and historical documents. Fascinating details are revealed, including the bizarre world of "wandering bishops" who appear throughout the Kennedy assassinations; a CIA mind control program run amok in the United States and Canada; a famous American spiritual leader who had ties to Lee Harvey Oswald in the weeks and months leading up to the assassination of President Kennedy; and the "Manson secret."

Hardcover: **$29.95** (ISBN 0975290622) • 396 pages • Size: 6 x 9

Book Two: A Warm Gun
The roots of coincidence and conspiracy in American politics, crime, and culture are investigated in this analysis that exposes new connections between religion, political conspiracy, terrorism, and occultism. Readers are provided with strange parallels between supernatural forces such as shaminism, ritual magic, and cult practices, and contemporary interrogation techniques such as those used by the CIA under the general rubric of MK-ULTRA. Not a work of speculative history, this exposé is founded on primary source material and historical documents. Fascinating details on Nixon and the "Dark Tower," the Assassin cult and more recent Islamic terrorism, and the bizarre themes that run through American history from its discovery by Columbus to the political assassinations of the 1960s are revealed.

Hardcover: **$29.95** (ISBN 0975290630) • 392 pages • Size: 6 x 9

Book Three: The Manson Secret
The Stanislavski Method as mind control and initiation. Filmmaker Kenneth Anger and Aleister Crowley, Marianne Faithfull, Anita Pallenberg, and the Rolling Stones. Filmmaker Donald Cammell (Performance) and his father, CJ Cammell (the first biographer of Aleister Crowley), and his suicide. Jane Fonda and Bluebird. The assassination of Marilyn Monroe. Fidel Castro's Hollywood career. Jim Morrison and witchcraft. David Lynch and spiritual transformation. The technology of sociopaths. How to create an assassin. The CIA, MK-ULTRA and programmed killers.

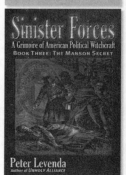

Hardcover: **$29.95** (ISBN 0975290649) • 422 pages • Size: 6 x 9